DIDN'T ANYONE EVER TELL YOU?
IT'S ALL A GAME!

Andrew J. Mullaney

DIDN'T ANYONE EVER TELL YOU? IT'S ALL A GAME!

Surviving and sometimes winning at life

Andrew J. Mullaney

Matador
9 Priory Business Park,
Wistow Road, Kibworth Beauchamp,
Leicestershire. LE8 0RX
Tel: 0116 279 2299
Email: books@troubador.co.uk
Web: www.troubador.co.uk/matador
Twitter: @matadorbooks

ISBN 978 180046 433 9

British Library Cataloguing in Publication Data.
A catalogue record for this book is available from the British Library.

Printed and bound in the UK by TJ Books LTD, Padstow, Cornwall
Typeset in 10pt Adobe Garamond Pro by Troubador Publishing Ltd, Leicester, UK

Matador is an imprint of Troubador Publishing Ltd

With lots of love for Catherine, Sarah and James.
I couldn't have survived for this long,
had some of the occasional victories,
or done any of this life without you.

andrewjmullaney.co.uk

Contents

Foreword

I started writing this book, my first, in August 2019. I had just ended a mentoring Skype call with Ellie, a highly intelligent young graduate, who was starting to find her way in life after university and was seeking employment. Ellie needed self-belief, and this call, in particular, had been extremely successful in helping to find more of her inner confidence. I felt that we had reached the point where she could go to an interview and give the very best account of herself that she could. Her best, I knew, would be good enough to get her the job that she was seeking… and it subsequently did.

That same night my sleep was disturbed and, as dawn was breaking, I woke suddenly at 4am. My brain instantly switched on and I realised, in that moment, that I had to write down everything that I knew about how I could help people to become the very best versions of themselves. It was a moment of genuine clarity, and one where I saw most of the chapter headings in front of me, and how to present this book to you, the reader. By the end of that day I had written a draft of the introduction and had the route map to completion clear in my mind. More importantly, it was typed up and in the memory of my iPad.

As I sat in my garden during the latter part of that summer and into autumn, at times baking under a hot sun, writing extracts, the world seemed to be in considerable turmoil as its political, social and economic tectonic plates were placed under considerable strain, but we all knew that it would surely sort itself out, wouldn't it? Well, it nearly always does, so why stress too much?

Brexit was dominating the news and seemed to be reaching a crystallisation point, where it would be concluded one way or another. The trade war between the USA and China was doing significant damage to the potential economic development of both countries, and that too, for the sake of world peace, must reach an amicable agreement; after all, it was in both countries' interests to do so. Hong Kong, now a part of China, seemed to be turning into something akin to civil war. North Korea was making overtures that it wanted more contact with the West, although it was still flexing its military muscles in very public displays. We were ever mindful of the fear that Russia wanted to continually bring to our lives after the dreadful poisonings in Salisbury, and constant cyber threats, testing our defences on many levels. The ever-prevalent issue of climate change was being taken more seriously by governments around the world, as pressure from the various groups lobbying for their cause grew louder and stronger. Rights for many people who felt themselves marginalised and without a platform, or a voice, such as the trans and Black communities, were gathering momentum. Business was starting to prosper as the economic shackles of austerity were beginning to loosen across many parts of the world, seeing some great benefits for developing countries too. Talk of a new mission to the moon and Mars from a collaboration across many nations was starting to fire the imagination, as interplanetary travel seemed to be a closer reality.

In the sporting world, a new football season was upon us, where new technology would begin to change the "beautiful game" forever. It was an incredible time for English cricket, with a dramatic "super over" World Cup win, and a wonderful Ashes test match series with Australia at its most crucial point.

The list goes on and there were so many other events and

activities taking place within our communities and across our United Kingdom that were truly bringing people together, despite the political divisions and an imminent general election that created so much toxicity and angst.

As we neared Christmas, even more words had appeared on my pages and a new brighter decade was dawning: a new roaring '20s, perhaps? Very few people had heard of Coronavirus and yet it was to become a word that would be known by billions of people across the globe, transcending all languages and cultures within weeks of January 2020. Because of those eleven letters, the world would never look the same again to us as a species and, within that, there surely must be a need for some help and rationalisation to enable people to better grasp the confusion, fear and challenges that life brings. Perhaps, through the medium of my book about how I view life as a game and how I believe we are all constantly playing, I could help to guide others in some way and also tell part of my story too, and in so doing stimulate some positive discussion and debate about how we live our lives. After all, in completing this and making it available to everyone, especially those who seek to be the very best version of themselves that they can be… what had I got to lose?

Some personal reflections before we begin

If you have the opportunity to play this game of life you need to appreciate every moment. A lot of people don't appreciate the moment until it's passed.

Kanye West

As a child growing up in the early 1970s, my winter Saturday evenings were dominated by television. There was precious little else for people to do as money was extremely tight, and families still mainly lived as a collective group, eating and spending most of their spare time together. It was a much simpler time, with fewer choices to make in life. You were lucky to have fish and chips once a month as a treat, and there were certainly no pizza takeaways. What was pizza anyway? The milkman delivered the milk, the bread man delivered the bread, the coal man delivered the coal, the pop man the fizzy pop, if you could afford it, and so on. There were always people coming to your house, and cash was handed over for the goods that were bought. Sometimes, when there was no money, the bill was carried over to the following week. This was known as "tick". Some people lived this way, and were forever in debt to one tradesman or another.

There were only three television channels (the internet was still to be invented) that you could watch in a black-and-white broadcast or, if you were "posh" and had one of the new sets, then you had colour. Family variety shows were seen as being a cornerstone of the British way of life. On cold, dark winters' evenings sat by the fire, the television became a massive source of escape and comfort for everyone.

The programme that no one seemed to want to miss was *The Generation Game*, hosted by Bruce Forsyth. He was then, and remained until his sad death in 2017, the consummate ever-present television family entertainer. Bruce was an all-rounder, in the true style of the old-fashioned English music hall. He sang, he danced, he played the piano and seemed to be capable of turning his hand to anything. The show was Bruce's own and, as the titles rolled and the music began, we all settled down in expectation, knowing a great hour was ahead of us. His instantly recognisable voice carried the lyrics which told us that "Life is the name of the game and I want to play the game with you".

The Generation Game featured teams of families with two representatives from different eras. Often it was a father and a daughter, a mother and a son, or any other combination, but it was always an older male and a younger female, or vice versa. Before anyone complains, the age of discrimination and gender awareness was still to have public awareness.

The show was fun, and placed people in unusual situations where they had to work together, or individually, to quickly learn a new task. These were often demonstrated by a skilled professional, or professionals, and usually in a very short time period of two or three minutes. From cake making and pottery to dancing and dressmaking, there was an endless list of inventive ways to create entertainment from fairly normal jobs. Bruce encouraged the contestants, the audience cheered them and they supported one another. Sometimes you could see that one person had a natural skill, or talent, but overall they were raw, untrained and occasional figures of fun, making lots of mistakes along the way. Bruce was unafraid to laugh at them too, to laugh with them and also to laugh at himself. He held it all together, despite it seeming to be out of control at times.

The families were given scores by the professionals and, after several rounds of madness, the winners progressed to the final. This was where they then had to use their memories to recall a number of objects that had passed before their eyes, in one minute, on a speedy conveyor belt. They won what they remembered before the buzzer told them that their time was up, and the crowd applauded no matter what, always shouting out, like we did at home, the prizes to help them win more. There was the ever-present cuddly toy, for some strange reason, and Bruce's catchphrase "Didn't they do well?" became part of our daily language and culture.

In creating and writing this book, I have reflected long and hard on *The Generation Game* and the lessons that it unconsciously planted into my pre-teenage brain, some of which actually stuck. Many, though, were just lost in the desire to be entertained.

So, consider this. Have you ever played a game where beforehand: you didn't know the rules; you didn't necessarily have the skills to play; you didn't know how to win, as you were oblivious as to what success looked like; you didn't know what your reward would be at the end; you didn't know who your opponent or opponents were; you certainly didn't know how many people would be watching in judgement (often fifteen million people and more); and, no matter what, you would likely fade into obscurity afterwards? That was *The Generation Game* and its players and, yet, it is also true of so much of our daily lives. The purpose of this book is to try to help you, the reader, to consciously play the game of life better, so that you can understand more of what is happening to you, why it is happening to you and how you can influence the game, especially your learning and working environments, to be a better all-round experience.

Before I begin, though, it's only right that I tell you a little about me and, to some degree, why I am writing this, my first book, designed to inspire, help, guide and teach people about life, and how to get the best that you possibly can from it.

The only child of an insurance agent and a housewife, I grew up as, what is known today, a baby boomer in the 1960s and 1970s in a suburb of Birmingham, in the Midlands. I was small for my age, and regularly bullied, and went through school, on reflection, constantly frightened. I was reasonably bright, although not exceptional, excelling at music. Looking back, I think that I chose music ahead of sport, which I love watching to this day, to avoid the physicality.

My parents had been born around the war years and really knew poverty. They had scrimped and saved to get away from their inner-city backstreet terraced house two years or so after I was born. It took every penny that they had to move into a more suburban area and get their semi-detached house, which had been built not long after the war. They were desperate to create a better life for us as a family, wanting safety and security, and did the very best that they could with their limited knowledge and experience, and very limited resources, to help me through life. For that, I will be forever grateful, and feel extremely lucky to have had parents, like them, who cared so much. They wanted me to be the best version of their unrealised ambitions, though, and, with the bar set that high from the beginning, my best was never going to be good enough. What they failed to teach me was what that standard exactly was and how to be the very best version that I could be of me. I was often paraded around by them like some performing animal at times, always pushed to the front, and there was no margin for error. Failure was never an option. Achievement and success were everything.

At the age of eleven I cracked. I remember it clearly – the pressure to achieve at school, coping with over two hours of homework every day (we were streamed according to ability and I was in the "super class", but in the relegation zone), and the need to pass my Grade 5 piano exam, learn the clarinet and take a lead in the school play all became too much. The tears wouldn't stop, and for a while the pressure was reduced as the expectation was scaled back.

However, the disappointment from my parents was evident and, like all issues surrounding mental health at that time, was dismissed and never spoken of again. It was a dirty secret and one that was dripping in shame. Looking back, I know that I had a form of a breakdown caused by this style of "hot housing" and I simply couldn't cope. More importantly, though, I didn't know how to cope, and neither did they. This event has haunted me all of my life, meaning I always felt that I was a source of some disappointment to my parents, no matter what I achieved. Don't get me wrong, I had a very loving home. Mom and Dad spent their last few pence on giving me a chance in life and I will never forget their sacrifices. My mother in particular, though, had grand ambitions for "Andrew", and the fact that I never went to university and became a doctor who saved the world was something she resented all of her life. We are all, I am convinced, products of our upbringings.

My dad, I think, realised my limitations and psychologically drilled into me the need to get a secure and safe job. "Become a solicitor, an accountant or a bank manager, son. Jobs for life that mean you get to wear a suit, get a good income, a lot of respect and a great pension." So when I said, after going into the bank with my dad one day during the school summer holidays when I was fourteen, that I liked the idea of working in a bank, my mother immediately latched onto this and told everyone who she could score some social points with that "Andrew was going to work in a bank." And guess what? Andrew worked in a bank! The tramlines were set, and it was virtually impossible to break out of them. If I suggested anything else, then the negatives were presented for that idea versus their more acceptable one. I remember recounting a discussion that I had with my music teacher one day, when he suggested that I could join the forces and get paid to play music. This was immediately dismissed with, "Yes, but you would still be a soldier" and there then followed some graphic descriptions of war, death and "horrific sights that your Grandad rarely spoke about after the war finished when he left the Army. That's not you, is it?" The emphasis was placed heavily on the final words. As I said, I was in the tramlines and would struggle to ever break out.

My parents sadly died relatively young by modern standards. My dad was sixty when he passed suddenly on Christmas Day 1995, and had only been taking his much-longed-for pension for some eighteen months. My mom gave up after he died and she didn't last much longer. Her heart was broken. They were very close and she desperately wanted to be with him. Her cancer, which she had beaten over a decade earlier, returned and she left us at aged fifty-six. They both lived to see me become a bank manager and marry, and Mom had a little over a year with our then newly born daughter, Sarah. They had lived for their retirement once I moved out to get married, but, like so much of their lives and so many others from their generation, their ambitions were never realised. I still miss them to this day, and I know how lucky I have been to have parents in my life who cared so much for me. You will find that I make reference to them again in future chapters. Considering the start that they had in life, and the impact of the war on their early years, they achieved so much. The game they played, though, was badly flawed because of the way they played it: their lack of knowledge of how to play it; to know especially what they wanted; their inflexible expectations of themselves, and of me in particular, all meant that they were never consciously in control. I played their game fully for so long, and it nearly cost me mine.

Twenty-two years later and, as I write this introduction, I have now reached my mid-fifties and have decided to formally retire as a contracted employee. I know and truly appreciate just how lucky I am to be able to do this. In my spare time I currently volunteer within education as a way of giving something back to the communities and assisting with the development of our younger people close to where I live. I will always help anyone who asks. I am still married to the amazingly patient and supportive woman who I met on my first day in the bank in the summer of 1982, and we now have two grown-up children who are forging wonderful careers for themselves in fields of their choosing. I have had a nearly thirty-five-year career working in retail, corporate, private and international banking and attained positions of "middle" and "senior management", working alongside some phenomenally talented colleagues and leaders, some of whom I will also discuss later in this book. These are people who inspire you, believe in you and selflessly stretch your potential, whilst creating environments that mean the near-impossible heights of achievement are always within your grasp. I have also worked alongside and for some people, too, whom I personally would never want to meet or converse with again. These are the blockers, the energy sappers, and negative naysayers. Those who want you to play the game of life for them, for their benefit and for their glory. They don't care about the consequences for you, your health, your family, your values, etc. They just want to own you so that they can win, and win at all costs. Their kind are also referenced here. Your management of them, and the maelstrom that they can bring to your world, is critical to playing your game in your way for your longer-term success and survival. I cannot stress this point enough.

So why did I decide to write this book? I have always enjoyed mentoring, whether acting as a mentor or being mentored, and have been fascinated by people and their stories. My questions for them, no matter what their age or experience, have always centred around what drives them on, what their motivations are, and what has made them the people that they are.

One thing has struck me throughout, and that is I believe that life is a game and a series of games within that, and we are all in play whether we like it or not. There is no set rule book laid down on how to play. We make it up as we go along. There are many excellent supportive texts, websites, apps, programmes, people, coaches and practitioners, who all give some great guidance. I would also include here the religious stories from around the globe that are open to a variety of interpretation: ancient works such as *The Art of War* by Sun Tzu, and the many writings and teachings of the various "gurus" both old and new. I have yet to find one, though, that describes the "game of life" in the detail as I see it, and that is also applicable to the rapidly changing modern world of the twenty-first century. Many simply want to give you a winning formula or recipe for what they deem to be success. They tell you what you should aim for and, in that, they want you to play their game in their way by their rules. Few, if any, seem to view your entire life as a game, and your success in that game as being your survival, which I personally believe is the greatest achievement that we have within our grasp. Anything else above survival is a bonus and the celebration of survival, for us as individuals through the maze that life is, should be more widely acknowledged.

Like *The Generation Game*, we take our own chances on a daily basis with many alien situations that come at us, and we have to try to make the very best of them. We apply what we learn along the way, often from making our own mistakes, as we try to create a series of reactive plans. This often involves manipulation, persuasion and negotiation, whilst trying to maintain an air that we are fully in control. Look around you the next time you are in a shopping centre, in the office, at a train station... almost anywhere, in fact. You will see people all at various stages of the game they are playing, with many often struggling to cope as they do not know what is coming at them next, or how to handle the unexpected. Many are wired and on guard, and sometimes revert to aggressive behaviour. Fight or flight can often kick in and, with a sense of inevitability, we fail to understand why.

We, as humans, are all born as individuals; no two people are exactly alike and none of us comes with an instruction manual.

We are not robots or like computers. Yet, we are expected to work to set programmes and to conform to so many rules and regulations, none of which are really written down for us in plain language that we can easily translate or understand. It is little wonder, therefore, that we react with such variance, and our reactions often surprise, infuriate and sometimes disappoint us. Think as a child how many times you were (or are, if you are still a younger person) chastised for not doing something that you were expected to know automatically. Even in adolescence and adulthood, there are situations that we face that create significant instant challenge and, again, we often fail to reflect and learn from them.

No matter what age you are, the chapters within this book will provide considerable help to you as a mentor, or as an individual, to better understand the game and games that we all are playing, whether willingly or not. Some chapters will be quite lengthy and will require more time to read and absorb. Others will be short and very much to the point. There are relevant quotations that set the scene for you at the start of each one and these are designed to get you thinking about what is to follow. I compare the game of life that we all play to the board game of snakes and ladders and you will find at the end of each chapter a series of quick bullet point summary sentences. Think of these as helpful tips whereby you can capture "the quick wins and the ladders", as well as avoiding some of "the traps and the snakes".

Please also note that I do bare my soul on occasions, but hopefully this helps you with your game and game plans. That is my intention, and not to be overly introspective, self-absorbed or biographical.

What this book is not is a definitive list, a set programme or a solution with the answers to life. If that is what you seek and you have any concerns about your own, or anyone else's mental health, you should always refer to an appropriately qualified health professional.

What this book is, though, is a series of tips, advice, support, counsel, suggestions and help that you can read, grab, absorb, adapt and apply to many of the challenges that life throws at you as you play the game. There are some familiar repeating themes throughout, which will mean you get consistency in the messages that I am seeking to convey. Read the last chapter first, if you wish, or take a highlighter to sections of the book and to key phrases that work for you. Make notes across the pages, dog ear the corners, but do whatever makes it work best for you, and please use it practically. It will help you with your game plans and you will see that I give some relevant examples, not only from my life and career but from others' too. They may just make a difference, and assist you with your development and understanding in how you can be the very best version of you. You may not agree with some of the points that I make, and that is ok as it leads to awareness. This means that you will be playing the game, and games, of life much more consciously, and so much more effectively for you and for those that you love and care for. Perhaps look on it as another means of support to help you survive and sometimes win. And, like the words from Bruce in *The Generation Game* theme tune, "life is the name of the game and I want to play the game with you." Good luck!

The game itself. You are playing several all at the same time

Part of playing the game of life
is you're going to have some losses.

Joe Gibbs

If you want a practical example of what I see the game and games of life are like, beyond a TV show from many years ago, then look no further than the old board game of snakes and ladders. Most of us have played it at some point in our lives, usually as children. Just in case you are unaware of the game, or need a refresher, here is how it works. You play against at least one other person rolling a die and moving your counter along consecutively numbered squares on a board, by the number of dots that are shown when the die settles. If the square that you then land on is at the bottom of a ladder, you move up to the square where the ladder ends, and then continue your progress onwards from there. If you land at the top of a snake, in a similar fashion, you "slither" down and again you carry on. Some of the snakes and ladders are short, so the penalty or gain is minimal; others are very long, having the opposite effect. Finally, you keep progressing through the board, moving up the ladders and down the snakes, taking turns until, when you land on the last square, the game is then over and someone wins. Or, as can often happen, you end up becoming disillusioned with the time that it is taking to get to the end, eventually declaring the one that has made the most progress towards the finish as the winner.

Unlike this game, though, your progress through the game of life does not rely on the throw of a dice, or is entirely left to chance. You can be in control much more than you realise, and from a very early age too. It is critical that you understand, though, that you are constantly in play. You must remain consciously aware of this fact all of the time. That way you will play the game, and the games that you become embroiled in, so much more effectively and productively, finding more of your own ladders to ascend, whilst avoiding many of the snakes that will take you and your progress backwards. You will not avoid all of the snakes, and you will miss some of the ladders, but you will find that you see so much further ahead of you than you otherwise would have with this new-found level of consciousness.

Snakes and ladders, as a game by itself, would be just one very small part of your day. Imagine if you were playing thirty or more of these games all at the same time, and every one of them at different stages of play. Some will have possibly lasted days, weeks, months and years. Some will be over in a few moments. That is life, and these are the games of life that we play. Welcome, my friends.

So here is where it starts. Two adults perform an act of reproduction that is common across all species on this planet and, nine months later, if all goes well, a child is born. New life is created and a new player enters the game, whether they like it or not. They have absolutely no say in their creation. Where we differ from the animals, though, is that this new life may also be unplanned, and the parents may actually be unable to support it. Therefore, the child can enter the game at an apparent disadvantage. And here is something else. Even if you, as a child, are desperately wanted, loved, supported and needed, you may also have your life already planned ahead for you by your family, so you can only really play the game in their way and in one direction. Or can you?

No matter what your start in life may be, you will be playing several games at once from the off, and the sooner that you can grasp this concept, the more in control of them and the rules you will be.

If you have ever watched a film called *The Truman Show* you may get a sense of what I am alluding to here. If you haven't, then find a way to watch it, as it covers the life of a character called Truman, played by Jim Carrey, whose every breathing move, unbeknownst to him, is streamed live to a worldwide television audience. Every aspect, no matter how small, is controlled by the team of directors and producers, surrounded by hundreds of monitors, all while he is completely unaware that every situation, scene and event that he encounters is manufactured for him. He is forced to play the way that the show and the script takes him. Everything about his life is false, from the time that he wakes up to the time that he falls asleep. He has no influence whatsoever over the direction that he can take. I won't spoil the plot of the film here, or reveal its ending, but I am sure that you can guess that Truman does eventually fight back, using many techniques to gain control, realising that honesty, integrity and truth must always prevail.

Our lives aren't exactly like *The Truman Show*, but there are times when we feel as though we have no option but to go down a certain path or route. Like Truman's awakening, if you question why things are happening to you, then you can better determine how you can take more control over your destiny. It is in your hands, and that is the essence of the way you play the game.

As a child you will learn quickly that you can either fight or take flight from threatening or challenging situations. It is inbuilt into all of us and, as well as playing the game of survival, which many find particularly difficult at this age, you then have to work out who is the strongest. You will not have developed all of the skills to establish yourself through means of a negotiated resolution and so, very often at young ages, the strongest and biggest seem to rule.

Is this fair? No, it isn't, and remember that there is inevitably someone bigger and stronger than them further down the line. Therefore, as soon as you can consciously be aware of how to fight fairly, and in a less aggressive, physical and more intelligent way, the smoother it will be for you.

Ask yourself this question? Why do *most* adults choose not to settle every argument or debate physically? The answer is because they know how to play for a better outcome without compromising themselves and who they really are. The emphasis here is on the word "most", as this does not apply to some who will never graduate from the playground.

Only the truly brave walk away from a fight, and to do so at a young age takes genuine courage. Often it is out of fear, but it takes more strength of character to not physically stand in combat than it does to accept the physical battle. There are more chapters that cover this later, and I will keep reiterating that your integrity is never a negotiable item, or for sale, as integrity will always be the enemy of those who seek to bully and terrorise. I am not saying that you should fade into the background either, or concede defeat and seek obscurity, but observe closely the behaviours of others, know who is around you, what their motivations are and, of even more relevance and importance, know specifically who your real friends are.

A great way to learn new skills to develop your abilities and mental agility in another form is via a sport, or any other similar environment, such as drama groups, Scouts, Guides, etc., where you are often part of a team. Anything can work that requires participation from you at any age. Many of the daily challenges that you face, which I call games, are replicated in these situations, and you can use these to your advantage for practice and rehearsal, no matter how old you are. You will observe how people behave, react and adapt to what happens when things go well, or sometimes go wrong, how people move, how they think, and how they react to pressure. You will understand more of yourself too, and get to know your strengths and areas for development. Never say no to an opportunity to take part in some way when it is offered to you, even if you think you may not like it, as it is a chance to develop and see the games being played out. Always, and especially afterwards, take a period of reflection for yourself and come up with one or two things that you have learned about you, and about others. You may find that there are good traits that you find, and you will also come to understand what could have been done better, and never just focus on the good either, as you will learn just as much, if not more, from the less positive areas.

One thing that I would recommend to all younger people is the chance to complete at least one level of the Duke of Edinburgh Award Scheme, or some other activity that involves a number of different disciplines. You will learn so much about life from schemes like this, and also from anything else that actively promotes "citizenship". By completing at least one of these types of activities, you will have had the chance to expand your horizons in most aspects of life, including serving your community in some way. Your all-round awareness of the world will develop and you will better understand the transition that you make into adulthood and into responsibility. You will also get the chance to put your own skills into practice in a non-threatening environment, and play some games along the way. It is also very good to have these types of scheme on your resumé as it demonstrates a strong commitment to your own personal growth.

Some disciplines in life do require you to be more of an individual than a team player and, again, if you get the chance, then always have a go. What is the worst that can happen? You will have learned a little more about yourself, even if afterwards you realise that it is an area that may not be for you in the future.

With knowledge and skill also comes great power. One question to consider is whether you use these skills for your benefit, for the benefit of others, for your community and to do the right thing by your fellow man, or whether you use them to cheat, steal and oppress others. You will see daily those who choose the latter options, and this will be very apparent to you from a very early age. It then comes down to a clear choice for you between playing the games that are in front of you selfishly or playing them selflessly.

By choosing selfishly, you then ensure others play in your way, and you make sure that they do so by harsh enforcement of your own self-made rules. You create their games for them and operate on a series of short-term wins. There is no longer-term plan here, with the winners and losers clearly defined. The losers are often the weak, and they are then forced to make your position stronger, never fulfilling their potential. And so the cycle continues through each successive generation.

The harsh truth here is that life expectancy becomes lower, communities poorer, learning is repressed, and fear reigns. It is a brutal environment that lacks fairness and balance. The fault for this is often laid at other people's doors, with personal accountability and responsibility apparently absent. Study any totalitarian regime throughout history and you will see this very clearly.

Yet, these strengths and skills, if used selflessly, could be so much more by setting some achievable goals, targets and ambitions at the very earliest stages of awareness. Never set these, though, so that they are way out of your reach. This all requires bravery and collaboration with many others including teachers, professionals, community leaders, coaches, mentors and those who wear a uniform, to name but a few. Not to draw off these people for improvement and development would be a waste of their talents, skill and knowledge. No one should ever say no to helping someone who asks with genuine humility. The hardest parts of this process are the acts of asking, trusting and seeking out the support. The people who do that, for me, are amongst the most courageous of them all.

The fundamental questions to ask yourself, and as early in your life as you can, are: what do you want from life? What do you want from life for those around you, including those you love? And what do you want your legacy to be, or for you to be remembered for, long after you are gone? Continue to keep asking these questions and challenging yourself from the earliest of times, as the answers will vary as you grow older, but the theme and basis of your answers will shape your true values and game plans.

The quick wins and the ladders

- Considering that the game is like snakes and ladders. There are multiple games in play for you at any one time.
- Playing each game consciously.
- Questioning everything that comes at you, and everything that you do.
- Learning to fight using your intelligence, conscious knowledge and awareness of others' behaviours.
- Being aware that integrity will always be the enemy of those who bully and terrorise.
- Never missing a chance for self-development.
- Being one hundred per cent committed team player.
- Reflecting at every opportunity on what you have learned.
- Knowing what you want from life, for yourself and others, and keeping those goals in sight.
- Playing your game selflessly, never suppressing others, particularly the weak in order to give you an advantage.
- Knowing what you want to leave as a legacy, or to be remembered for after you have gone.

The traps and the snakes

- Being unconscious in everything that you do.
- Blindly following the instructions of others without questioning their motivations or reasons.
- Allowing physicality and outward strength to dominate your world, and those around you.
- Missing out on opportunities to participate in activities for your self-development that would lead to you making a positive contribution to society.
- Being selfish, not selfless, with your approach to life.
- Failing to ask for help and support.

What are your definitions
of success in the game?

Life's full of tricky snakes and ladders.

Morrissey

Overall success in the game of life, as I see it, is very simple in concept and here is my definition, which you could also call a mission statement:

> *From the moment that you are conceived to the time when you expire, it is about your survival: making the very most of the time that you are on this earth to be the very best version of you that you can possibly be, whilst positively influencing the world around you and the people that you encounter, thereby leaving a legacy, so that the world is a better place for you having been in it, and the victories that you have along the way will be a just reward for your gameplay and strategy.*

There is much in those words to absorb, and I would encourage you to read the paragraph above several times before progressing further to check whether this agrees with your own views. If it does, then please read on and take in all of the chapters that follow, as they are aimed specifically at you. If you read this definition and feel that you do not agree with some or all of it, then please still read on selecting the appropriate headings, taking away what you feel will help you and those around you with their games, as there will be some advice that you will still find helpful and of use.

At the start of any game, plan or journey, it is important to always know what your end result is, or the destination that you are aiming for. This can be flexible, and very often does change, but it is important to have an idea of what you define as success and what your end point will be. Otherwise you are just heading off blindly without any clear direction. Your mission statement, or objective definition, should give you some foundations, but you may choose alternative words and phrases that work better for you. Having something written down is a great discipline to keep referring to and, after all, it is what all organisations across the globe do regularly as a "business as usual" activity.

If you say that your aim is to win, well, what does winning mean in the game of life to you? You need to quantify and break it down, so that you can not only understand your desired outcomes, which may also change over time, but also what you need to do to get there.

Consider the following as potential destinations, or stop-off points, along the way for your game to succeed, no matter what that definition may be: health, wealth, happiness, family and friendship, truth and honesty, honour, and loyalty.

I'll break these down to give you some further food for thought:

Health (including your mind and body)

Without good health your game is at a disadvantage. By taking good care of your body, and also your mind, you are giving yourself a chance to make all of your definitions of success a reality.

Much is written and said about good health. Most of us use a car, or a form of transport in some way. To run effectively and efficiently, these have to be correctly fuelled and serviced regularly. Our bodies are the physical vehicle that we have to take us to our life destinations, and we have to make the best of what we have. As with transport, we come in a variety of shapes and sizes, and we do not always work as we would like. With a good diet, though, avoiding comfort eating and snacking, and some regular exercise, we can make the vehicle that we have work so much better.

The same is true of the mind, and later in this book you will find some chapters that will help with your own positivity and mental well-being. All I will say at this point is that you must seek out as much help and support as you can to keep your mind as strong as it possibly can be. This is not easy, and seeking help here is nothing to be ashamed of: seeking out a coach, a counsellor and any other means of support is a positive thing. It is never a sign of weakness, as some would have you believe (not least that inner voice that can talk you down at times), and must be viewed by you as important as the way you look after your own physical well-being. Celebrate the successes every day, and find one reason, no matter how small, to shine a light on something that you have done. For some, that may be just getting out of bed on that particular day, but it is an achievement and one that can be built on.

Throughout all of the success factors that you choose to adopt, as your life develops, positive self-talk at every opportunity will be a way of keeping going and motivating yourself. This is why everything that you seek to achieve is dependent on the strong foundation of your mental well-being and overall mental health. Be ruthless in looking after it, because if you do then it will look after you.

Wealth

When is enough enough? As you progress through the game, you will find that what you want and what you need, with both measurable and immeasurable wealth, changes. For some people, the need to accumulate assets and physical wealth becomes addictive. There is never an end point when they want to stop, and that is ok if you are staying true to your own values and playing the game fairly for others as well.

For many people, material wealth is a key measure of success, with the importance being to have enough to live, both now and in the future. Leaving the responsibility to others will always put pressure on everyone else's game, as this leads to a drag on them, and also on the state machinery and system. A draw on resources means that everything that is provided (health, education, law, etc.) for your game to be effective becomes more stretched, and those with an established game plan find they are taxed even more to support the state. This leads to negative game changers and a breakdown of society if not handled correctly. There is no shame in receiving state support, and it is important that when you need to you do. What I am advocating is the taking of ownership, as much as you can, of your own destiny. This will see you identify what your needs are and what wealth you initially feel that you need. I use "initially" here, as this may well change over time. However, knowing your first stop-off point without leaving it to others, whilst having a flexible plan, means that you will have more control over your game. Also always leaving something in reserve for when the "rain" or financial hard times come will ensure that you maintain autonomy.

Immeasurable wealth is a concept that I would also encourage you to always keep within your field of view. This is the wealth that you have in your life that is borne out of love, friendship, kindness and compassion. You will never know its material value as it does not have a price and, like your integrity, it cannot be ever bought or sold. It is very easy to lose sight of as you grow older, and also to take for granted once it is there. You can have all of the gold that there is in the world, but, without any of this kind of wealth in your life that is genuine, honest and pure, you will always be a pauper, in my opinion.

I recently walked the beautiful rolling Clent Hills, near to where I live, with a friend of mine, on a beautiful sunny day. As we looked out onto the amazing vista, that saw the horizon stretch for over forty miles, he was awestruck and said, "You'll always be a rich man with views like that." His words really impacted me as I thought that no amount of money could bring the same sense of inner peace and happiness that we both had in that moment.

Happiness

Like a Holy Grail quest, we seek happiness throughout our lives, occasionally finding it, but most of us seem wired to be forever searching for more. There is a school of thought that, as we increase our knowledge of our world and our universe we become more unhappy and even more dissatisfied. Once we have acquired one thing, we then invariably seek out the next, and the next, and so on.

Take a step back and think about what actually makes you feel happy. Write a list, take a photograph, keep it to hand or easily accessible and reflect on what that moment, or those things, mean to you. They will make you smile for sure and, in that act alone, you will have found happiness.

Never try to piggyback on someone else's happiness either, as what makes them happy may not work for you. It will affect your game and take you to a place where you enter the world of the envious and jealous. This then leads to bitterness and negativity. Before you know it you have lost all trace of what makes you happy and you forget your own goals. You lose your own game and there is a threat to your own mental well-being. Know your own happy places, the happy triggers that are uniquely yours and be happy for others when they have theirs.

There is a song by the late Ian Dury, and his band the Blockheads, from the late 1970s called "Reasons to Be

Cheerful, Part 3". It is more a list of things that are, in their eyes, reasons to be cheerful. Listen to it and take in the lyrics. It always makes me smile and reflect as well on why I should count my blessings.

Family and friendship

There is a saying that you can choose your friends but you cannot choose your family. Coming from a viewpoint that not everyone has a family, and not everyone has a close circle of friends, means that sometimes you are in a no-win situation here. For your game to be successful, you will need to pick someone, or a small group of people, to support you. No matter what your goals, you will always need others in your life, if only to give you an opposing view and genuine honesty. Therefore, pick the person, or people, who you choose to have alongside you very carefully, viewing friends and family as one entity. Do not differentiate between them, or let the "bloodline" adjust your thinking. The best advisors and counsellors are usually the ones who tell you the truth, regardless of the outcome. They speak without fear as they know what they say to you will be taken as advice, and not as a direct challenge. These people are part of your team in your game, and must be seen that way assisting, supporting and cheering you on, as you will do for them. They are that important. Call them partners, mentors, role models, counsellors, advisors, consigliere or any other suitable name. The best title that they will have, though, is as your friend, and a true friend that you can talk to at that.

I would also say, as one word of advice from massive personal experience, never go to sleep on an argument with one of the people mentioned above. Ideally you should do this with no one in your life, but I recognise that is not always possible. However, your closest circle and the most important people are in your life for a reason. Sometimes you, and/or they, may say things that you do not like, or that you do not want to hear. If you are right, then keep to that opinion, but find some common ground and a good reason to keep talking. Walking away with any form of angst, or anger, always means that at some stage you may well have to walk back and communicate with them. If you choose not to, then think of what you have lost, although there will be times when you feel that act is too much of a personal compromise. However, walking back, making the situation right and moving on is essential. Sorry really is the hardest word to say and, by making the first move in this instance, you may find that you get back even more and your relationship is that much stronger for the test. Not to make a move, or to attempt to build a bridge with the person, would be a mistake for you and your game. Good counsel is equally hard to find, and in a professional capacity becomes very expensive too. Honest, unconditional advice is a form of love, and an act of kindness, and that alone makes it priceless no matter how hard it is to hear.

Truth and honesty

I have added this as a reference point for your game as I would like you to consider the impact of not being truthful. An act of dishonesty, and the telling of a lie, compromises everything, and most of all yourself. There is a very fine line between diplomacy and being economical with the truth (i.e. not telling all of the relevant and salient facts). To create an outright lie damages everyone, and most of all you, as this is your integrity and your life and it can create many casualties too.

Look no further than the high-profile and notorious case of John Profumo in the 1960s, where a lie told by him, as a senior government minister as he was at that time, to protect himself ultimately led to the collapse of the government. The consequences saw a destabilisation of the country and its economy, together with a fundamental change in society that is still talked about today as the "Profumo Affair". Profumo was a talented, ambitious politician, a decorated soldier, a husband, a father and also in many ways a flawed man who conducted an affair with a young lady that he later went on to deny. This was at a time when moral standards for society were set very high, particularly for public figures, and the world was still operating to a semi-puritanical code. When the truth of what actually happened emerged, his life was almost ruined. He spent the rest of his days trying to make amends with charity work and good deeds, but his reputation, and his name, will be forever sullied. His game was ruined, as was that of his wife, who was a well-known actress at that time, and he tumbled down one of the biggest snakes of them all. To be a good liar, and to be dishonest, you have to have a very good memory, and also know that someone somewhere will always remember or know something, or prove incorrect a fact that you have stated as being true.

Being truthful and honest will mean that your game is never flawed. It is never compromised and your memory will be faultless as you are recounting events that actually happened. Your energy levels will never be diminished either and your sleep will be good. You may find that truth and honesty do not always sit comfortably with some people. If it does not, then question yourself as to whether these people should be a part of your inner circle. This is the view from a very pious position, and the reality of life is often very different. If, however, you can make truth and honesty a realistic and achievable ambition for you, then you have nothing to fear.

Honour

Every now and then you have an opportunity to act in an honourable way. This is what previous generations may have called chivalrous, but I prefer to badge it as simply doing the right thing. Helping others with your unconditional good deeds and actions benefits everyone in society and can also make others reflect on themselves and on their own approach to situations. You will change your game, and that of the beneficiary or beneficiaries, for the better, and may even set in train a pattern of thinking that has long reaching positive effects, even life-changing, for all. The time that you have the opportunity to stop and assist someone else who is struggling, when you do not really have that available time, and you actually make a difference, is when honour is a massively important marker towards your success at playing the game of life. You are helping another with their own play and chance of survival.

Loyalty

The game of life does not require any form of loyalty, and you are not beholden to any one person or organisation for any reason. Loyalty can be destructive, as it can align you to one path or course that you can never change from. Others will lay heavy "guilt trips" on you to retain your loyalty, and may even try to blackmail you or use some form of coercion and mind control with you. Be loyal, yes, but only to those who deserve it by their examples and actions, and encourage loyalty to yourself from others in a similar vein. Do not be taken in by blind loyalty to act in a lawless way, or to the detriment of others. The world has enough people who wish to follow organisations and leaders who would harm others in pursuit of their ambitions. If you wish to follow your heart, then always let your head be the rational voice of reason, and make your decision using rationality and reason. In other words, your head will invariably always be right and the correct arbiter for your loyalty.

Some acts of loyalty are driven by a need to protect and preserve. Always remember that the game you play must be for the long run, and not in the short term, so make your decisions and nail your colours to a specific mast only when you are completely sure that you can live with yourself and the consequential outcomes that decision can bring. Otherwise, give yourself an escape route and, in nailing your colours and your loyalty, perhaps make sure that the nail has some flexibility in it.

The quick wins and the ladders

- Defining what success means to you as early as you can, knowing that it will always be flexible and truly representative of you.
- Considering, and keeping in view, the following as you strive for your version of success: Health, wealth, happiness, family and friendship, truth and honesty, honour and, finally, loyalty.
- Health. Always seeking help for your physical and mental well-being.
- Wealth. Knowing what you need, and when enough is enough.
- Wealth. Keeping in view the need for immeasurable wealth in your life, i.e. love, friendship, kindness and compassion.
- Happiness. Knowing what makes you happy and enjoying it.
- Family and friendship. Treating family and close friends as one, and choose those who you trust from that pack very carefully.
- Truth and honesty. Keeping to the truth.
- Honour. Doing the right thing when you are presented with a dilemma.
- Loyalty. Giving loyalty only to those who deserve it from you.

The traps and the snakes

- Not setting off on any journey in life without a plan.
- Health. Not looking after yourself physically and mentally.

- Wealth. Not leaving it to others to support you and being greedy.
- Wealth. Not considering love, friendship, compassion and kindness in your life as important assets.
- Happiness. Avoiding finding your happiness, and also using others' ideas of happiness for you.
- Family and friendship. Having "fair weather friends" who are only there in the good times and also listening to relatives who play on the "bloodline" trope.
- Truth and honesty. Not telling the truth means that you will be caught out at some stage. Your game and integrity will be lost.
- Honour. Missing, or passing up, the chance to do the right thing, no matter who you could help.
- Loyalty. Following or supporting people without a valid reason.

3

Who are you? What is your brand? Oh, and the power of the media

A brand for a company is like a reputation for a person. You earn reputation by trying to do hard things well.

Jeff Bezos

As the chapters of this book develop, there are many common themes that you will see begin to form. I constantly refer to your own self-awareness and, at the very outset, before you can play your own game in the best possible way, you need to fully understand just who you are. You must also get to develop and form your own brand.

The first stage of brand building is to create a strapline, or a headline, that tells people who you are. It will also say what you do and how you do it. Like your mission statement, this will evolve over time, regularly reforming and reshaping. Every person is unique, and so too should be the messages that you are conveying. The very best are the ones that help to say something about you as a human being, not just about what you do. It is not as easy to compose as you might think and, again, make this a habit early on in life and you will come to understand more of who you are as a person. Look at others and then take the best of what is out there, making sure that your messaging reflects you and that you can also be true to your headline when you are with others. Personally, I am always drawn to the people who use the words "with a passion for…", as this tells me how strongly they feel about, and are committed to, something that they do.

Some people will use their specific job or status titles and will leave it at that, for example, "I am a manager". This is all well and good, but what exactly does "manage" mean and, if that is their job title then what specifically do they do? Others will give indications of the work they carry out with an array of buzzwords and machine-like technical jargon. There are some people who put a phrase, or phrases, that arouse your curiosity like "I solve problems". It will likely make you want to know more about them. This is something that is very personal, but getting your branding right is essential to raising the awareness of others of your presence and existence in the world. Keep it relevant and true to you and you will not go far wrong. The following chapters, which cover beliefs and values, will help you significantly here too, but at this early point I want you to begin to formulate and understand the way that you present yourself to the world.

As you progress through this thought process you should naturally collaborate with others who are within your trusted and chosen circle. They may also be your advocates and, by having them on board, it is a great way to influence your brand further: people who will recommend you and outline just why you are the right "go to" person. They will say exactly what you represent and why they turn to you. They will tell their story of their experiences with you, and these are ways in which other people then become influenced to look more closely at what you are offering. These can be verbal or formal by way of references, advocacy/testimonial statements or just complimentary letters. You should ideally choose to put them on appropriate available sites that you use and certainly include them when you need to market yourself, but please get them out there.

This is no different to what any company or organisation does when trying to recruit customers and advocates. Look at their websites and social media feeds. The answers are all there.

Consider some brands that you associate and identify with, whether they be national, international, local, charities, anything that resonates with you as this will help you to realise as well some of what is required. We are surrounded by them, and they dominate our lives, so there are plenty out there to choose from, whether it be fast food, sports and leisure, retail, charitable, etc. It is a very crowded space.

Two great recent examples for me, that show just how companies try to develop a wave and capture mood with branding, are Nike's "Just do it" and Coca Cola's "share a Coke". In my opinion, Nike, when they launched this, were saying directly to you that you can do it with them and go for whatever you want in life. They will be there with you, supporting you along the way and you will be wearing their products as you go. They want you to feel that nothing is unattainable.

Coca Cola tried building on their branding by making it more personal to you. They put names on the side of the bottles so that you could find one with your name, or buy one for someone else. It represented personal empowerment and ownership: a differentiator and very unique. It was designed to make you feel like it was yours and no one else's. It was like they were almost gifting it to you.

Both brands are long established so they constantly keep looking to make their market position even stronger with an evolving series of messages, reinventing themselves periodically. And if you think about these brands, and so many others, and the effect they have on you and your life, well, think on this: they are getting you to play their game for them. By supporting them, and buying into them and their messaging, you are making them powerful, strong, successful and with tangible increased stock value. You will likely act as an advocate or ambassador for them too, as we love to tell other people about good experiences. Just holding their logos in your hand, or displaying them on your body, tells everyone just how important they are to you. You will be a regular, returning consumer. We are also even more likely to shout out when someone gets it wrong so, for them, retaining you, your support and your loyalty is vital for their survival and progress within the game.

If you can grasp the concept that you are being played countless times every day by the adverts that you are exposed to, in so many different ways, then you will begin to understand why creating your own brand is essential to get others to buy into you in exactly the same way.

And, as important as it is to develop your own brand, as I am suggesting, it is also important that you understand too the threat that branding can present to you as an individual, and also to your game. If you then go further into total awareness and consciousness, you can see how this, coupled with an advertising theme, can also represent a clear and present danger to what you are trying to achieve.

A good example to use to illustrate my point here is Christmas. Every year, as we approach the festive season, the one-hundred-day countdown begins somewhere in late September. "There are X number of shopping days left to Christmas" is regularly announced by retailer after retailer as some rallying cry for you to spend, spend, spend with them. And the fever builds up almost daily from then on. "Are you ready for Christmas?" and "How we can help you to make your Christmas the best ever" will be blasted at us from every angle. Finally, on Christmas Eve, and at around 5pm, the pronouncement is made that the shops have closed and you are likely to be too late if you have not done all of your Christmas shopping. The messages will then change in tone almost immediately from a sorrowful "You've missed out" to a joyous "and on Christmas Day the online sales will start". The next bugle call to max out your credit cards and drain your bank account dry has sounded and off we all go again like sheep, heading in the same direction, thinking that we have bagged a bargain in the January sales. Summer holidays also start to take over the airwaves at this time, and the feel-good factor about how we should live our lives kicks in again. The days and nights are dark and cold, so the thought of a sun-kissed beach means that the adrenaline rushes like an express train through our collective systems and before we know it we are suddenly justifying spending all over again.

Then, somewhere in the newspapers, online and in magazines, early into the New Year too, among the sales adverts and pictures of exotic climes, come the health warnings, the diets and the oh-so-caring and considerate money advice, just in case you may have overindulged and overspent. And here is the next message that they give: it was actually all of your own fault that you ate too much, spent too much and are now in debt. Then, with sage-like advice, they patronisingly tell you to beware for the next festive period.

What they fail to say is that, as the year progresses, their temptations continue. Getting beach ready starts in the spring with what to wear and feel great no matter what. Easter arrives, with all of its unhealthy offerings, and then it is those all-important last-minute summer bargains. If you have kids, then there is the prom to consider for those leaving school, followed by a rush to not miss out on Halloween. Before you know it, you are under pressure 365 days of the year. We all seem to fall for it, too, as though we have never heard any of the messages before. You are playing the game by the advertisers' rules, at their pace, and you personally career out of control if you remain vulnerable and without consciousness.

And this is true for so many of us. We love the spontaneity of it, and there is some merit in actually living in that moment and taking their suggestions on board. However, beware as unconscious spontaneity can result in things spiralling out of control. The bargain that suddenly appears, and that you buy, believing you have saved some money, can sit as hard debt on your credit card for several months. It is no longer a bargain in real terms but a financial millstone. The result means that you are playing your game for the finance company too, as well as the advertisers, and now you are haemorrhaging not only money but considerable energy.

With advancements in technology, including things like facial recognition increasing at a seemingly hypersonic speed, we are even less in control of how we are directed. If you have ever watched the film *Minority Report*, you will be familiar with the scene where the main character, played by Tom Cruise, walks through a futuristic shopping centre and has multiple personalised adverts instantly directed at him as he progresses past an array of virtual billboards and shops. This is the way we are heading. In fact, we are almost there now so, to keep control of your game, you have to be awake and aware of the tactics that are used on you to get you to submit to the will of the advertisers' games and strategies.

It has actually been around for longer than most realise. Subliminal advertising was outlawed in cinemas many years ago, but it is so hard to police. You have to be wise to the semi-hypnotic tactics that are used to get you to give up your hard-earned cash to companies who seek to influence you without you realising. This form of advertising is where one frame of, say, a hot dog, is inserted into a film reel. One frame would account for less than half of one second of the film and, whilst your eyes would see it, the conscious part of your brain would be unable to tell you that you had seen it. The hot dog had failed to register in your immediate consciousness. However, your senses would know that it had been seen: your mouth would water, the hunger pangs kick in and you would crave a hot dog. The sale of hot dogs would rocket when there was a break, or at the end of the movie and, consequently, so too would the profits. Only when slowed down to such a point that the reel was shown very slowly, one frame at a time, would you know that you had been exposed to the image.

Many subtle techniques are used and product placement is

rife within the film and television industry. You will see many brand names pushed in most forms of entertainment, with sport leading the way, hence why you will feel compelled to buy. And, again, in so doing you play the game that the companies want in the way they want you to. This may be ok with you, but be very aware of what is happening and how you are being "played". The current move towards gambling advertisement within sport, for example, has replaced other known vices like alcohol and tobacco, which were prevented from advertising in this way many years ago. And what then happens? Gambling companies' profits soar and it becomes the new must-do activity, never mind the underlying health costs that are a direct consequence.

Before concluding this chapter, I would like you to also consider a further aspect that the media present. Most aspects of the mainstream media (also known as the MSM) have an agenda of one sort or another now. They actively and subtly control your thinking, unless you question and seek to question the rhetoric and narrative that they promote. It becomes like a series of puzzles where you see only one part of an image that they choose to reveal and you have to guess what it is, based on what they show you. They want you to guess, but in such a way that what you believe you see is what they want you to see.

Please take some time to develop an independent train of thought and forensically examine all sides of the issue or challenge that you are reading about, hearing or watching. Is the argument one-sided and heavily biased, or is it well balanced? You will read in a later chapter about adopting a holistic thought process, and this is exactly what I am advocating here. Being consciously aware of what you are being told, and then following up with a deep examination of the subject will lead you to the answers that you seek. Blindly accepting the news feeds or commentary, from whichever source, places you at their mercy and vulnerable to unconscious indoctrination. Question, challenge, and only when you are satisfied that you can see all sides of the argument can you then decide which way you will go with your judgement, or even whether you will abstain, which is often the hardest decision of them all.

I have gone into great detail here to help you to now be fully aware of just what is being presented to you, and also to show how branding and advertising go hand in hand. Learning from this, and applying it to your own situation, will mean that you can not only develop an amazing branding for you as an individual over time, but you can be even more conscious as to how to get your messages across to influence other people to your way of thinking. If companies can be so successful at pushing their agenda towards you that you buy from them, then why can't you with promoting yours?

The quick wins and the ladders

- Differentiating yourself by creating your own branding, as a company would for itself.
- Letting people know exactly what you do, what your passions are, and what arouses your curiosity.
- Recruiting as many advocates as possible, including written testimonials.
- Being "brand aware" by knowing exactly what advertisers are promoting and trying to get you to buy and do.
- Knowing your own individual limits and not exceeding them.
- Questioning everything that comes at you from the media and forming your own thoughts once you have all sides of the argument.

The traps and the snakes

- Not knowing or understanding who you are, and what you represent.
- Using jargon, or non-specific headlines, to describe what you do and stand for.

- Having no advocates that would otherwise give people confidence to buy into you.
- Living in the moment and being overtaken by your own spontaneity.
- Blindly accepting the messages that are being pushed towards you by advertisers and by the media as a whole.

4

What do you truly believe in and stand for? What are your non-negotiables?

If you don't stand for something, how can
anyone respect what you do?

Miranda Lambert

As you develop your brand, you will begin to discover what you actually believe to be true and what you truly believe in. You will come to know exactly what you stand for, what is acceptable to you, what is unacceptable and what you consider to be a non-negotiable. A non-negotiable, in modern terminology, is referred to as a "red line". This for me means that it is a moral line that you lay down and, no matter what, you will never concede ground on or negotiate away. It is a fixed marker that is never crossed or diluted. Sound familiar, parents and kids, when setting or agreeing boundaries?

As your techniques for playing your game begin and form, these "red lines" become very important standpoints. As children we start to understand the negotiation process for completing a task that adults set. Sometimes this is when it is an acceptable bedtime for good behaviour, say, or any one of a number of scenarios, but from the earliest age most of us understand that a completed task invariably earns a reward. Where this falls down now, though, is that adults are under such pressure in so many other aspects of their lives that their starting point is rarely the end point for the negotiation. Many will concede ground almost immediately, so that the child does not have to do all of the task, if indeed any of it, to get the reward.

For me as a youngster, it was always "Wait till your father gets home and hears about this!" It was a major threat and one that instantly got my attention and willingness to conform. This thought of incurring my father's wrath was something that I, and many others of my generation who have an inbuilt fear of authoritarian figures, couldn't stomach. It is interesting to note that I still feel nervous when I pass a policeman in the street, even though I have done nothing wrong.

Times have changed and so has the discipline. I do not, and never would, advocate a threat as a way of gaining conformity for a task to be done, as it only ever gets short-term results. It destroys trust and invariably gets circumnavigated in some way. It creates a "need to know" culture, where only what is necessary to be disclosed actually is. We then go back to economies of truth.

However, justice, democracy and the rule of law are for most people the standards that they will run their lives by and are largely non-negotiable. Even here, though, the desire at times to challenge these can help to shape the world to be a better place, as not all forms of justice and law, for example, in any society are fair and equitable. Playing the game with absolute "non-negotiables", therefore, can be extremely restrictive for you. At the same time, they can also help you to form your beliefs as well.

By way of an example of the power of beliefs, consider this. There have been, and still are, a number of high-profile sportsmen and women who have strong religious beliefs that prevent them from competing on a day sacred to their religion. They may be the very best at their sport but they believe so strongly that they will not break the covenant with their faith that they hold so dear. This can result in them missing out on big events, sponsorship, prize money, and many of the trappings that go with sporting success and fame. These are their red lines and non-negotiables and, no matter what, it is a line that cannot ever be crossed.

Establishing your non-negotiables is essential as you begin to put together your plan for playing your game of life. Belief in a god is just one of thousands of "belief" dilemmas that we all face, and conspiracy theorists can really play with your mind as they seek to impose their ideas over what you hold dear and true. You may consider that you do not have any specific beliefs, and that you would negotiate on everything in life for a fair outcome for yourself within your game. Reflect, though, and as you think hard you will find that you do have some of these hardwired into you. It is because of what you believe in that you develop a framework and foundation for your game and what defines you as a human being, unique and different from everyone else. Your own individual beliefs may change in time but they are, in essence, what you stand for as the difference between what you believe to be right and what you believe to be wrong.

I have adopted a very simplistic approach to this incredibly complex subject, but, as you develop your game, your beliefs will constantly be challenged. I would also encourage you to regularly question and sense-check yourself too regarding your own thoughts here, as only in this way will you retain true independent thinking.

The quick wins and the ladders

- Knowing what you believe in and what your own "red lines" or non-negotiables are.
- Being prepared to challenge yourself about your beliefs.
- Being prepared to challenge whether all aspects of your beliefs (e.g. the rule of law) fit with your own standards.

- Regularly checking that none of these are becoming blurred in any way to you.
- Respecting others' beliefs and right to believe.

The traps and the snakes

- Not having an awareness of your beliefs, taking each moment in time as it comes at you.
- Negotiating on your own "red lines" and "non-negotiables".
- Failing to create a strong foundation of beliefs and therefore failing to differentiate between what you know as right and wrong.

5

What are your values?

I have learned that as long as I hold fast to
my beliefs and values - and follow my own
moral compass - then the only expectations
I need to live up to are my own.

Michelle Obama

Building on the theme of non-negotiables and your beliefs,
the bedrock of your game of life strategy is bound together
by your values. These are the standards that you work to
that shape the way that you operate on a day-by-day basis.
Get them right and you will follow your own path, playing
the game exactly how you want. Compromise on them and
your whole strategy is flawed and you will never be true to
yourself. They are like a mortar or a glue that holds everything
together.

Most large businesses and organisations have values and
try to create a values-based environment and culture. This
only works, though, if everyone buys into them and practises
them all day, every day. They are owned as much at the bottom
of the organisation as at the very top. By keeping the values
simple alongside your branding, with one-line or two-word

definitions, you have a clear outline of what you represent, your own rules, and a stable framework for life.

With these (what you believe in at your very core) you can have a one-page, clear outline of who you really are and what your proposition is. You can do this as a square, a circle, a Venn diagram, whatever works for you. All games have rules and, whilst I am determined not to set exact specific rules for you, this can be a way that you form some guidelines for playing the game in your own way.

Here are just some of the values, or words that can be considered to help you form your own list. There are many others and add as you see fit, or just change the words to suit yourself. Some naturally run into each other but this is a start:

Accountability
Bravery
Character-forming
Citizenship
Clarity
Commitment
Common sense
Compassionate
Consistency
Courage
Courtesy
Dependability
Determination
Empathy
Ethical
Excellence (in search of)
Fairness
Family
Fortitude
Freedom
Generosity

Gratitude
Growth
Happiness
Honesty
Honour
Humility
Improvement (continuous in all aspects)
Integrity
Justice
Kindness
Leadership
Loyalty
Sincerity
Team commitment
Thoroughness
Transparency
Trust
Truth

Some of these words crossover with the list of adjectives that is provided as Appendix 2. The important thing is to select those words that you aspire to hold, whilst knowing the ones that you already own and that are locked away safely within your personal armoury.

As I was preparing the background work for this book, I discussed the concept of values with several of my contacts. All agreed that in their interactions the value that is lacking from society today is empathy. One went a stage further to talk about the absence in the world of compassionate empathy. We were talking specifically about the recent upturn in knife crime, and how difficult it is to relate to another person who can consciously plunge a knife into the body of someone else. Empathy, in simple terms, is the ability to stand in someone else's shoes and relate to their circumstances at that moment in time. It is another differentiator for us as a species. It was the use of the phrase "compassionate empathy" that struck me the most, and by this they meant taking empathy one stage further, to actually feel the pain of the other person with an overwhelming desire to help them, and never to cause them harm.

The virtual world carries some responsibility here, too, as it has taken away some of our ability as people and human beings to relate specifically to each other. We have become desensitised to the world around us, and to how we react and respond to situations. Can we differentiate between the games we play as humans every day and the games that we play in virtual worlds online? Our values as humans, where we have boundaries with responsibilities and consequences for our actions, are clearly different from the characters that we can become when assuming avatar identities. If you can commit a murder without consequence in an artificial environment, somewhere, someone will be unable to differentiate between that persona and their real-world existence, with the lines becoming extremely blurred.

This is why, for your game of life to be played as true to yourself as is possible within your own values and moral compass, you will naturally develop a sense of empathy, and within that develop your own form of compassionate empathy too. Add full consciousness to this, never losing sight of that or taking it for granted, and you will have a strong framework to play your game with positive outcomes for all.

Being aware of the values you hold dear means that you derive greater pleasure from the game, giving you a much stronger position to control the way that it is played, including when you play and how you play.

The quick wins and the ladders

- Treating your values like a glue that holds your structure of standards together.
- Knowing your own values and being able to define them.
- Understanding and displaying empathy in all that you do.

- Being able to differentiate between the real and virtual worlds.

The traps and the snakes

- Not knowing or setting your own values.
- Compromising on your values.
- Agreeing to values that are not owned by you.
- Not displaying empathy when you have the opportunity.
- Not being able to define where the real world ends and the virtual world begins.

6

Failure to prepare means preparing to fail. Conscious gameplay

*If we did all the things we are capable of,
we would literally astound ourselves.*

Thomas Edison

The importance of understanding exactly what you want from the game, and your own definitions of success, should now begin to become really apparent. These will naturally change and develop, as you too change and develop, but always keep in mind what *you* want to achieve, without ever compromising your values and beliefs.

What we have discussed to this point, therefore, are the foundations for your game. This is very similar to the building of a house. The plans have been drawn and, as we all know, without solid foundations being laid, the property becomes unstable, being reduced to rubble at any time by any movements or forces. The same applies to your game, as without foundations you will always lack strength, consistency and stability. A house with solid foundations will support its walls and a roof and, for you, these then give you a basis for your survival and success. You will never be found saying "If only I had…"

So, with this base firmly in place, you can consciously embark on playing the game to give you what you want and, as you play the game, you realise that you will have a combination of definitions of your successes running together at any one time. These may be daily, weekly, yearly and beyond. Being consciously aware of these and having them visible in some way can make them come to life even more. I'll explain more.

Several years ago, I had the privilege of listening to a number of elite athletes talk about how they won gold medals at Olympic and Paralympic Games. They all gave a consistent message about how they prepared. They reached a point in training where they ran their races in their head so many times, knowing exact stride patterns and/or key marker points that they had to hit, and exactly when. They said how they controlled their training, their diet, their sleep and who would be part of the process to help them. A relay team told how at one point they had reached a standard whereby they could run the race in a sealed and darkened room, silently standing still with no available visuals or sounds besides the boom of the starter's pistol. They would then pass the baton at the right time with split-second timing in the right way, counting in and out to each handover again and again, so that they got it absolutely right. They then transposed this to the track, building up the movement and choreography of the whole race, section by section. It then all became second nature to them and nothing was left to chance. If they were beaten, then it was by athletes who were simply better than they were, but they would view defeat as failure. They had done all that they could to gain even one hundredth of a second advantage. The margins at that level can be that close. We can learn so much from sport about this, but sadly, all too often, we leave things to chance, forgetting those very tight millisecond calls that can make all of the difference in the end.

The phrase "failure to prepare means preparing to fail" has stuck with me ever since I heard one of these gold medallists say these words as he proudly showed everyone his medal that evening. He made it crystal clear that the medal was his goal and he would do everything within his power to get it, apart from compromising his personal and moral standards. Anything less than his very best was his failure, and to fail meant that he would have missed something along the way in preparation.

It is the same in many professions: actors, musicians and most who seek to entertain will rehearse and rehearse until they reach a peak, when they perform their part to the very best of their ability, knowing success is all but guaranteed when the curtain finally draws back and the audience awaits.

This type of intense planning and execution can be applied to every goal that you are striving for, whether it be short, medium or longer term. The more that you plan, the more the odds will fall in your favour. Leave absolutely nothing to chance. As Sam Goldwyn, a famous film producer, once said, "The harder I work, the luckier I get."

Sometimes it merely takes what some would call a "kick up the backside" to make yourself focussed and tuned into your objective. I once worked with someone who always had pictures visible of far-off places on her desk. She was working to fund holidays to these exotic destinations, and the constant visualisation of a white sandy beach with palm trees, clear turquoise sea, and a bright orange sun in a blue sky was enough of a daily kick to spur her performance on.

All of our lives, whoever we are, and whatever background we come from, we need to deliver a performance of sorts, and the more that we can prepare for that, the better that performance will be. The challenges will vary and, for some, just getting out of bed can be as challenging as performing in front of thousands of people can be for others. But visualisation, game planning and having something to aim for is essential.

Everyone's goals and definitions will be different and you must ensure that yours are too. Be yourself and do not try to take on someone else's life or dreams. They are their dreams for a reason and do not belong to you. Imitation is a great form of flattery, but you will never be totally satisfied or at peace with yourself if you try to attain something just for the mere fact that it was originally someone else's, and you perhaps beat them to it. It is a hollow and a pyrrhic victory that will take more from you than it gives back.

Changes will also happen in your life and some that you cannot control: accidents, illness, death, loss of a job – again, it's a long list of variables. These will affect your definitions of success and change the way you play. Therefore, it is essential that you make sure that you have flexibility built within.

Know who will be there with you; counting with you; supporting you; encouraging and cheering you on. Who do you trust and turn to whilst ensuring that your goals and ultimate success become realistic? Going back to athletes and actors, they will all have coaches and people around them. There is always someone to help, and having the humility to seek help and support is part of the way that you can build the foundations to be stronger for you to play the game in the way that you wish.

When you work for any company, or offer any input, no matter what size the organisation is, they will have their definitions of success and mould you so that your output, when combined with that of your colleagues, produces enough to make the corporate entity greater. This is when you have to compromise and adapt your own successes and definitions to work alongside and within theirs. This can be very challenging, particularly for those of a free spirit. This is why knowing yourself and being fully conscious as you embark on any journey, and at the start of any venture, is essential.

In this kind of scenario, my advice is to play the game as they want you to, though never compromising on your all-important integrity. You play their game to the very best of your ability. If you are remunerated in any way for this, keep in mind that you owe them, and never take that for granted. But also be aware that you can take so much from this situation and develop the skills that you want to within their framework. The additional rewards will also be that you can create independence for yourself too. Having a strong performance, commitment and dedication to your name means that you can shape any environment to work for you. This also results in their game being your game, and not vice versa.

Being conscious throughout, no matter what you are doing, whether it be studying, working, volunteering, etc. means that you never take things for granted and you remain fully in control of your life. It's like driving a car just after you have passed your test, when every situation, from entering the vehicle through to stopping and turning off the ignition, is done with magnified self-awareness. Every movement that you make and decision is taken, assessing all of the facts and information that you are seeing, hearing and feeling. You never go through the motions and every situation is taken on its merits, assessed and played in the way that you want. This is called being consciously competent and, coupled with intense forward planning, is a skill that I see as essential to survival and playing your game in your own unique way.

The quick wins and the ladders

- Consciously playing the game. Being aware as much as you can of your thoughts, actions and impact on every situation that you face.
- Thinking like athletes and actors do, by visualising, rehearsing, learning and leaving nothing to chance in preparation.
- Using coaches and teachers at every possible turn to help you.
- Always being prepared for the unexpected.

The traps and the snakes

- Being unprepared and taking everything as it comes at that moment in time.

- Not taking advantage of, or listening to, good advice from others with experience.
- Being unconscious as to how your actions can impact on you and others.

7

What is your unique selling point?

What is your Unique Selling Proposition?
What makes you different than your
competitors? Wrap your advertising
message around that USP and communicate
it in a clear and concise manner.

Lynda Resnick

At this early stage in learning how to play the game, I want you to be able to say in one or two short sentences just what makes you so very different from everyone else. What skills, qualities, talents, characteristics, achievements, personality traits do you possess that make you different from everyone else? This is usually the point in a classroom situation where people make eye contact with their shoes, shuffle uncomfortably in their seats, sigh, shrug their shoulders, look confused, and there usually follows a prolonged silence that feels like an eternity. There is no room for false modesty here, or for being shy, as someone else will always be willing and able to stand up and outline their unique selling point (aka USP) in detail. The frustrating thing for you could well be that theirs is not as good as yours. So let's make it clear that finding your USP and establishing yourself as a player in the game means that you have something very different to offer from everyone else.

For some people, your USP will change as time goes by, and for others it will remain constant. It may even be seen as a talent or a gift. Some will treasure and nurture it with further coaching, training and support. Whatever it is, as soon as you become aware of it, then don't hesitate to develop it. The act of embracing and nurturing your USP will then, in itself, give you the discipline of added learning, and your all-round game will take on a new momentum. You may even find that it changes your destiny and how you play the game of life.

My advice here, though, is also to not overwork it, especially for younger people. You can end up with massive burnout, and the shining light of the USP can easily be dimmed, or extinguished, by an intense "hot housing" style of development. This was evident in the 1960s and 1970s with the Eastern Bloc of countries developing exceptional sportsmen and women. Children were subjected to military-style discipline and forced to train for many hours each day. They were given performance-enhancing drugs, with a further cocktail of hormones and stimulants. Their talents won glory and medals for their countries, but the price was the lost lives and personalities of many of these exceptional young people. They became robot-like and their USP, as they grew older, was suddenly anything other than unique.

It is a fine balance but, in a child, if you find any form of talent, skill or quality, then nurture it like you would a flower. Overwatering and overfeeding can cause irreparable damage. Find the balance, but make sure that there is sufficient air and sunlight to allow it to grow and grow well, so that it has sustainability, strength and longevity to be itself. The time for any intensive development must come as it reaches maturity, not as a seedling. Know that it can cope with what is being asked of it. If you are in a position where you have a young person who is developing a task or discipline, just be aware as to how you can make or break their USP and positively influence their game by keeping your own ambitions for them realistic and aligned to what theirs are. There will always be some need to "push", but push too hard and you can push them away. Their game can change, as can your relationship with them. By pushing positively, and less forcefully, you can make everyone's games stronger and more enjoyable. Sometimes less can be more.

When looking for a USP, if you aren't already aware of what yours is, then look at who inspires you and what it is about them that makes them so special. It may be someone famous and in the public eye, or just someone that you know and admire, but try to find what your USP is. Schemes such as the Duke of Edinburgh Award, as I have previously mentioned, can help here, as can joining groups like Scouts and Guides. They enable you to develop a variety of skills and disciplines designed to help you to become better versions of yourself, whilst finding and developing overall talent. Sporting clubs, theatre, etc. – no matter what age you are, try anything as there is so much out there and there are so many people, often unpaid volunteers, willing to help. These volunteers can themselves be awakening to their own USP, whether it be as a coach, teacher or helper.

For some, a USP can be a blessing as well as a curse. How often have you heard of a young person with immense talent struggling with their own mental health because other people have decided to try to bring them down with acts, in various forms, of jealousy and critique. It is hard to know how to counter this, as every situation is different. However, I would say to those who may be subjected to this form of behaviour to always talk about it with someone who is trustworthy and responsible. Share the problem and find the solution. Suffering in silence will mean that the level of your USP will dip and the haters will have won. It is easy for me to offer this advice, but your game can be so much better and fulfilling for you now, and in the future, with a USP that you exploit to the absolute maximum. Letting your talent do your talking is the greatest way of all to pay back those who try to close you down.

Oh, and if you are one of the haters and jealous people, this book really isn't for you, unless you want to change and contribute positively to the world, to society and to your fellow man by making you and it a better place. Stop the hating and jealousy as it just takes energy from everyone, and your game is badly, badly flawed. You may not see it now, but you will regret it in years to come, that I can guarantee, and you will have missed out on so much happiness.

For those who are later developers, sometimes your USP is less apparent and may not reveal itself for many years. Please do not view it as a treasure that must be instantly found. You must seek and try to find it if you can, being aware that everyone does have one. Often it can be seen in your ability to help the generations that follow, to learn from you and your knowledge. Too many people play this down and feel they have missed their time or their chance as they get older. It is never too late, and your game of life, if played for your and everyone else's benefit to the end, will be enhanced considerably as a result.

As an example of how you can find your USP later in life, I'll briefly mention my friend John, who, at the age of seventy, took it upon himself to begin to visit old people's homes, prisons and other community organisations with the simple aim of encouraging people to talk.

John has worked all of his life, mainly in sales. He has a vibrant personality and a generous nature and would be the first to get everyone dancing at a party. He'll talk to anyone and is someone who, I have no doubt, would be your favourite uncle. The conversations that he creates when he embarks on his visits are often linked to music – he plays songs, sings a little himself, getting others to join in as well, and tells stories about the era, time or theme that he has selected. "I'll go anywhere where people congregate," he said to me recently.

John has no formal background in entertainment, and this

"calling" is completely new to him. It came as a result of his own very personal experience witnessing his mother sadly pass away very lonely in an old people's care home. He felt, after seeing this, that he needed to make a difference. He wanted to better understand how communities develop, and why people who live in close community groups could still be desperately lonely, like his mom. He attended several community meetings, focussing specifically on social enterprises and not-for-profit businesses. His desire was inner-driven, and from this energy alone it has taken him to places, and to meet people, he never knew existed. They now regard him as a lifeline, a friend and a source of happiness. He is someone they look forward to seeing.

John's game of life isn't driven by money. He just wants to make people happy and change their world, their games, and possibly their chances of a better outcome, even if it is only for the hour or so that he is with them. "It's never too late, and you're never too old to do something," he said.

Colonel Sir Tom Moore is another prime example of someone at the grand old age of one hundred who suddenly found his own USP by raising millions for the NHS during the first lockdown of the Covid-19 pandemic.

Your USP is something that can define who you are and what your legacy will be, very much like John and Colonel Tom. It is the chance for you to showcase your talents and individuality, and that can be anonymous or as outrageously overt as you want. Just never lose sight that your USP, when used positively as a force for good and allowed to grow, can benefit and bring pleasure to so many people, not just you. This makes your game, their game and society as a whole more united and all the stronger for it.

The quick wins and the ladders

- Getting to know and understand your USP.
- Never giving up seeking it out.

- Using it as a force for good for you and for others.
- Not listening to those who seek to put you down.
- Supporting others who are seeking their USP.

The traps and the snakes

- Using a "hot housing" style of development, particularly in the young, to bring forward a USP.
- Being jealous of someone else's USP.
- Not seeking out or using your USP to its fullest extent.
- Allowing those who seek to prevent you using your USP to do so.

8

It's ok to be different

I think being different, going against the grain of society is the greatest thing in the world.

Elijah Wood

The world has changed considerably since my birth in the 1960s, with new waves of industrial and social revolutions taking place. The set ideals and ways of doing things from the "war generations" have been replaced with quicker, slicker work practices and flows of information many times faster than the speed of light, together with a more accepting and inclusive society for all. We have come so far, and still have so much further to go. Human evolution, and our inbuilt curiosity, will always drive us forward to new levels. We will always ask ourselves how we can make things even better.

It is wonderful that people now are able to be proud of their gender, ethnicity, background and sexuality, and not be judged for it. People with disabilities are embraced and celebrated for their potential, and mental health is talked about openly. This has not always been the case, I know, but the limit of our capabilities is now more in our control than ever. People can play their games of life by being as true to themselves as possible without the fears of prejudice, knowing that society, and often the law, will protect them. This still takes immense courage and bravery and leaves me awestruck when I see people placing themselves in the public eye embracing their own uniqueness.

Schools, colleges and workplaces can still be brutal proving grounds though and, whilst times have moved on, there is a perceived need for many to feel that they must conform and "fit in". If this is you or someone you care about, then here is some great news for anyone struggling with being themselves. It's ok to be different, and many of the people now setting the pattern for the world are different to what others wanted them to be when they were younger. You may not agree with them all of the time, but they are setting out to make change happen and, we hope, to facilitate a better form of mankind.

Bill Gates, one of the most influential and philanthropic leaders of our time and the founder of Microsoft, once said, "Be nice to the nerd. The chances are you'll end up working for one." Never has a truer phrase been said, and his game, as a self-confessed "nerd", is arguably one of the most successful on all levels of human assessment.

Part of the purpose for me to write this book, as you now know, is to encourage everyone to be unique and to be the very best version of themselves that they can be. It is a mantra that I will keep chanting throughout, without apology. It is crucial for your game that you do this too, and, within that, you will find your own happiness and contentment along the way.

I once did a presentation on finance to the sixth form students at a school for the blind. It was one of the most nerve-wracking moments of my career. I was clearly very different to everyone else as I was the only sighted person there, and in that sense I stood out from the crowd. I was also the main speaker at the event. The students were the norm in their environment. We were in their common room and this was definitely their world. There was no stage, and I had to adapt and change my style, being consciously aware all of the time that I had to make an impact whilst holding their attention. I had prepared beforehand and knew what I would say. I had decided to take myself into their world at first and closed my eyes as I spoke. Yes, I did drop the typical faux pas of saying, "... so you see..." to which someone said, "You know we can't, don't you?" And they all laughed at my expense. I laughed too, as I knew that this comment was a form of compliment from them. I was reaching a type of acceptance from them with my rather clumsy choice of words, although I was still not being true to myself. I was trying to conform and to fit in with them. My strengths were, and still are, my delivery and passion for my subject, and I can never do that by just sitting down, or standing still, especially with closed eyes. I then chose to walk around and among them. The armchair style seats, typical of an area of relaxation, were randomly arranged and in no set order, yet everyone knew where I was. It was fascinating to see how their heads moved as I roamed around the room. I adapted my style and still retained who I was. At the end, as I sought out a strong coffee to quell my nerves, one of the students asked me how much training I had gone through to present to groups with disabilities such as theirs. I said none, which was true, as it was still the early days of companies reaching out to embrace and provide specific services for organisations with additional needs. The student said that what I had done had impacted all of them as they didn't feel patronised (which they had with some other presenters) but felt respected and valued. This, from a standpoint of me being very different.

I use this example not to boast about my capabilities but to show as an example of how you can be different and adapt at the same time, so that others still feel good around you. You have to be you, true to your own values and true to that continually developing contract that you have with yourself about who you really are.

If people seek to influence you to become someone that

you are uncomfortable with, then ask for help and get support and advice from those independent of your situation. People you can trust, people with a few years of life experience under their belt who know what you are going through. As I keep repeating, there is always someone to turn to and I do list some organisations that may be of help at the end of this book.

I appreciate that for many this is a big challenge and, if you are faced with adversity you may ask, "What right does anyone have to tell me what to do?" My plea is that everyone has so much to offer the world, no matter where they are, and you will pick up this message loud and clear from the people who I profile in a later chapter. And even when you feel that you are in complete darkness, you can always find some light if you really want to.

It is ok to be different from what you perhaps perceive as being the norm. The real caution here is to find out who you really are, who you really can be and not what you think you are or what others say you should be. The game of life is a long one and you will develop, learn and grow as you play each situation that comes towards you. The decisions that you make can have lifelong consequences, though, so, before making a life-changing decision, make sure that you have the counsel to help you to make the right judgement call for you. Retain your values and retain your individuality. Be different and love the unique you that you become as you roll the dice for your next move.

The quick wins and the ladders

- Being yourself, embracing your uniqueness and being positive about what it offers to you and to the world.
- "Be nice to the nerd. The chances are you'll end up working for one." Bill Gates.
- Seeking counsel and support from those you trust with conversations about embracing the different you that you seek.

The traps and the snakes

- Conforming or blending in so that you do not appear different.
- Not showing appreciation of others who may seem different to you.
- Not seeking out support and help.

9

The faceless minority called "they", and the dangers that "they" present to you, including social media

> Particularly Instagram, people look like they
> have a much better life than they really do.
> People basically seem like they are way
> better-looking than they really are, and they
> are way happier seeming than they really
> are.
>
> Elon Musk

Reading to this point, you will have begun to understand how you can consciously be in control of your game, and to some degree of other people's too. What I will cover now is where that group of other people, who you may sometimes refer to as "They", begin to play dirty with you and with your mind.

"They" are often an anonymous, faceless minority who you sometimes allow to hold sway, and have so much power and influence over your game. "They" are the collective group you will regularly refer to with generalities, assumptions and occasional observations. You will use "they" as a principal reason not to do things, to underperform, and to underachieve. "They" can be a very convenient excuse and a very inconvenient distraction. "They" can wreck your game and end your dreams if you let them.

Do "they" exist? Do "they" regularly meet up and form a united strategy to plot and sabotage your game? The reality is usually no as "they" do not ever physically meet. But fitting in is important to so many of us, despite our need to be different, so "they" and their opinions really can matter to you if you let them.

Consciously we create "they" in our own minds, giving energy and life to their potentially destructive forces. Not everyone does this and I applaud anyone who can stand on the sidelines without caring too much about what other people think. However, most of us will know of their presence in our psyche. You will become very aware, after reading this, when you next catch yourself asking someone, "What do you think people will think?"

There is a dilemma, though, and the dilemma is this. You need people to collaborate with you and, in so doing, you occasionally need to get them around to your way of thinking. To do this you have to accept feedback, occasional criticism and observations from those you seek to engage with. "They" are unlikely to be a part of this process at the start, but "they" may well feature for you as your uncertainties and insecurities kick in. I will be honest and say that there have been many times when these feelings have come into my mind in writing this book. It is my first, as you know, and therefore the waves of uncertainty do often bubble to the surface. However, it is more important for me to get my messages to you, so that you can be the very best versions of you that you can be, rather than give airtime in my head to what "they" might think. Your true friends and supporters will always tell you the truth, and that is really what matters and where a real strength in your life lies.

If, by chance, you come across anyone who sits in the camp

of "they", then this is the time to think of your game strategy with them using a form of reverse psychology. Give them some credit for helping you with their commentary, as they may actually provide a trigger for you with some good ideas. Stay true to yourself, though, to your principles, your values and beliefs. Time will tell you that you are right in doing this, but, by taking an independent stance now, you are playing the game your way. Your foundations, if built with strong values and beliefs, will be strong enough to take the weight, The other thing here is that you sow seeds of doubt into their minds too about the effect that their game is having on you (if subterfuge is their aim) and by doing so you create an advantage for yourself.

We have seen a communications revolution over the last decade that has enabled so many people to make contact with each other, to find partners, friends, missing people, markets for goods and outlets for everything, right the way through to instant opinions. I would argue that social media is now as essential to the working of our world as the invention of the wheel was to the ancient empires. We just cannot survive without it, and on so many levels it is a force for good, although the negative side seems to be in providing anonymous safe houses for "they" to live in. My desire here, and for your personal game, will always be to help you to avoid the "snakes" and this area, in particular, presents a real threat if it is not correctly managed by you. You and your game are as susceptible to these potentially negative influences as to anything else that you face in life, as they are there on your screen, invited into your life courtesy of a fibre optic cable or an invisible signal through the air. There is no polite knock on the door and the chance for a refusal by you. Once you switch the on button and sign into the various sites then you are actively participating, until you switch off or choose to block.

Whatever personal platform you use, whether it be Twitter, Facebook, Instagram, etc., there is a need for you to be seen. It can feel like you are attending a mass gathering or a party, and you are trying to be heard, or to raise awareness of your presence. No one wants to miss out and may have the fear of missing out, commonly known by its initials as FOMO. This is not always the case but by posting, in any way, you are placing yourself out there and, as a consequence, making yourself available for immediate judgement. Unless you are in a private mode and liaising with only those you trust or want to be involved with, your words, pictures and actions are being assessed by the many, most of whom you do not know, you never will know and yet who seem to be in control at times over how you view yourself. One bad comment, phrase or emoji can suddenly turn the spotlight onto you, and, before you know it, there is a "pile on" of people dispensing instant justice. This, in its extreme forms, is out and out bullying and by its very nature is brutal and gladiatorial. Unless you have a massive inner strength and a very thick skin, it is likely that you will fold at some point. It is also very difficult to resist the trend, and not to become an active keyboard warrior yourself, fighting back in these arenas when everyone else seems to be too. But your game must be played for you in the first instance, and the power of the crowd and the mob must be turned to work for your advantage.

The same is true for private messages, emails and any other means of communication. If you feel threatened, or negativity is being thrown at you, as well as switching off, muting, blocking or closing down, then always seek help and support from a trusted person, or an organisation that is independent and there for these circumstances. Again, there are so many people you can reach out to.

Before we had social media, what did we do to communicate? We physically met people and interacted verbally, visually and in a written form. We shared our innermost thoughts only with those whom we knew and, whilst there has always been playground and workplace bullying, it rarely got out of hand or went unpunished.

I accept that, for many young people in particular, social media is the only way that communication now takes place. The truly brave and independent thinkers throughout history who have pushed mankind's boundaries, though, never had a herd mentality like this. They followed their beliefs, passions, intellect and instincts, without fearing what would follow. They were so single-minded and, whilst the path was never easy for them, they never let the doubters bring them down or stop them. What they all did extremely well was to take themselves away from their environments, bringing space, time and creativity, whilst giving positivity to their thought process. For your game, I am going to recommend the same, in that you take regular enforced breaks or sabbaticals from all social media for a while at various points in your life. Make it a date on a calendar and also allow it to be an instant release too, if necessary. Think of it like a "get away from it all" holiday. Break your addiction as, if you read this and feel it is impossible to switch off, then an addiction is what you have. Phone people, talk to people, write a letter and use the time to focus on you. Be like the people from the past. Use the tools that you have to their greatest effect and power. I know that it is easier said than done, but nothing that is worthwhile is easy. You will find that you come back refreshed and with a much broader and better outlook to your game. You never know, you may now have the free brain space to be the next great pioneer.

The quick wins and the ladders

- Seeing "they" as a faceless minority who you will not allow to negatively influence your game.
- Using reverse psychology if you have to engage with "they", seeking out their opinions and alternative views.
- Being strong enough to mute, block and switch off.
- Using social media as a force for good for you and others.
- Taking enforced pre-planned breaks from social media.

The traps and the snakes

- Listening, paying attention to and acting in a way to please "they", rather than to please yourself.
- Trying to influence someone else's game by becoming part of "they" yourself.
- Not discussing your concerns with others.
- Not taking breaks from social media.

There is always someone who knows better

Those who always know what's best are a
universal pest.

Piet Hein

Building further on the theme of "they" and of "other people",
consider this next sentence. Many of us do secretly enjoy control
of, and controlling, other people's games. The phrase "If I were
you I would…" is one that we regularly trip out without any
thought or feeling. We happily deliver it, feeling self-satisfied as
we have gifted some of our own wisdom and worldly advice to
another person. Their game must surely be better as a result if
they take our advice, shouldn't it? And, after all, it is their loss if
they choose not to implement it.

Yet, when we say these phrases, have we truly taken into
account every single factor? Do we know all of the relevant
circumstances that the person we are imparting our suggestions
to is facing? Have they told you everything that is relevant? Have
you thought through the full consequences for them, and for
their game, of them taking your seemingly well-intentioned
advice? Keep in mind, too, that the risk of taking any advice in

this form is totally on the receiver and never on the giver. There is absolutely no accountability here so, yes, we can gladly trip out our words of enlightenment free from any future prosecution.

And if you, the receiver, regret acting on the advice, and then challenge it retrospectively, the response will nearly always be, "What I meant to say was...", "I didn't actually say that..." or any other one of a thousand combinations of words that deny culpability.

The people I am referring to here have often been called "barrack-room lawyers" or the anonymous "bloke down the pub", and they are many in number. Beware of taking their advice too seriously and acting on it without seeking a more qualified professional opinion. They may be cheaper, but invariably will send you down the wrong path, creating more stress and tension. You will often face an added cost to your problem for reparation and wish you had taken the professional advice in the first instance.

Here is a story that I heard of where an elderly lady had seen a solicitor, after talking to her family, and finally made her will. This was a big step for her as she was more aware of her mortality than ever and was therefore concerned about the future and her legacy. What would happen to her assets after she had gone was a question featuring more prominently in her mind. Like so many of her generation, she did not like to talk about it to anyone as she felt that it was a very private matter and something that, she thought, might actually bring on her demise. It is also a very common train of thought for people of her age to believe that, if you formalise your wishes in this way, you may actually die. She added certain important codicils and bequests that she felt were necessary, and the documents were signed and locked away for safe keeping until a time when they would be needed. Needless to say, the advice was expensive, but no more so than she should have paid for correct advice in this way, and a professional job too.

And here the story should end. Sadly, though, it does not.

A few days later, in a moment of weakness, she was speaking to her neighbour and mentioned what she had done. She positioned the discussion with her children in such a way that it came across as though her son and daughter had pushed a conversation forward to the point where she felt compelled to complete the documentation and pay the invoice. The neighbour, a lady of a similar age, was very critical of the advice given by the professional to the family. With no legal training, qualifications or professional indemnity to her name, she was not in a position to give the commentary that she did, and had no in-depth knowledge of the relevant circumstances. She was very happy to impart the "If I were you..." and "You should have talked to my advisor as he would have been so much cheaper". These words not only sowed massive seeds of doubt in the lady's mind but also started to drive a wedge into the family, who were only trying to do the right thing for everyone. She made several phone calls, and went and saw the solicitor on her own to reconfirm what she had done. She came very close to cancelling everything. She even spoke to her neighbour's advisor, who, it turned out, was a retired solicitor who hadn't practised for over twenty-five years and was no longer registered to advise.

Fortunately, in this instance, the correct action had been taken before this conversation over the garden fence happened. The neighbour's game, she thought, was to be a good friend, and I have no doubt in that. However, her well-intentioned words created consequences that mean that the trust within the family is soured, at a time when it should be at its strongest. They cannot now discuss the wishes of their mother without further creating an air of tension and suspicion. There is always doubt on the part of this lady that her family failed to do the right thing by her, cost her money and possibly even had a hidden agenda.

This tale is repeated day in and day out across all parts of society, whether it be something as complex as estate planning, through to a leaky tap. There is always someone who seems to know of someone else who they feel could do the job for you, giving in their opinion, better and cheaper service and advice. Within the game of life they can also be called "back seat drivers", who seek to control your game taking no responsibility for the accidents and casualties that they can cause.

Accept all of the advice that you can, always going with the person, or company, who you feel the most comfortable with. Get several opinions, as you will gain considerable knowledge from talking to the people who you look to employ or engage with. The big question to ask yourself, though, is "Who can give me the best possible outcome for me?" Sometimes, that means paying more in the short term, by having the professional job from the outset, but in the longer term it can work out cheaper. You will have something that lasts, that has sustainability and also carries a guarantee.

If something is too good to be true, then it usually is. Walk away. Use recommendations by all means, but make sure that they are from more than one source and you are aware of the professionalism and quality of the work. Bad advice and bad workmanship will cost you so much from your game and your wallet, diverting your energy and attention, usually at a time when you need it the most.

There is always someone who knows better. Make sure that person, when it comes to what is right for you, is you. This will ultimately mean that with great conscious gameplay your worst will therefore always be better than everyone else's best.

The quick wins and the ladders

- Seeking out professional and competent advice if you need help, or at least a very strong recommendation from a trusted source.
- Not listening to those who are unqualified or lacking competence.
- Getting several opinions and drawing off the knowledge that you subsequently gain.

- Using the people or companies who will give you the best outcome for you.
- Knowing that, if something is too good to be true, then it usually is, so walk away.

The traps and the snakes

- Listening to and taking advice from the "bloke down the pub".
- Always being cost-driven.

There is always someone who knows better

Do what you love and love what you do – just don't "do a Ratner"

> Do what you love; you'll be better at it. It sounds pretty simple, but you'd be surprised how many people don't get this one right away.
>
> LL Cool J

As I have already mentioned, we are sometimes driven to do things that we think will either look good, or appear to be good, in the eyes of "other people". We will tweak and sacrifice some of our own happiness and talents on occasions, to conform, to fit in, or just to give our personal profile added kudos. This can prove to be a short-term gain and may even be the course alteration in your own game, as you may have lacked satisfaction from what you were previously doing. This inner curiosity may lead you towards something better. Keep in mind, as you progress, that, if you genuinely love doing something, it is legal and is not causing harm to anyone else, then do it. What have you got to lose?

Recently, on a long drive I was listening to a local radio station and heard about a choir that is open to anyone of any age, whether they can sing or not. The programme was a magazine-style show and gave the singers a feature for about twenty minutes. They sang and sounded, well, frankly dreadful, totally murdering several famous anthems and arias in the process. The presenter was very dismissive and disparaging of them at first, but this was purely a judgement call by him based on their singing. He then proceeded to interview several of the founding members. What came through from the discussion that they had was not only their clear love of singing but the fact that they loved singing together in public. They valued each other's company and it gave them a reason to sing, a purpose and a sense of belonging. They all showed massive courage in doing what they did and had strength in numbers. They had a bond, even though their ages were extremely diverse, ranging from some in their early twenties through to a ninety-year-old. They were also a good mixture of men and women. They all agreed that their confidence levels had risen and they had discovered and, for some, had rediscovered a love of life. I found that, in listening to them, I could not help but smile to myself. They lifted my mood and also my energy levels.

Those minutes were memorable and truly enjoyable for me, and the interactions that I subsequently had with other people afterwards were probably better as a result. I stopped for a coffee and I know that, because I felt in good spirits, I bought a couple of other things that I did not intend to. I also made the effort to make conversation with the shop assistant, and asked her how her day was. It might just have helped her for a moment having someone engage with her; I will never know. The domino effect here, though, could have been that, in helping to raise her mood, she did the same with others, and so on. The singing and discussion had had a direct and positive impact on me.

For some, a form of utopia is reached where everything that they want from life is suddenly there wrapped within a profession, a pastime, a form of study, however you are pursuing your dream. Within this can be found a purpose, together with a career, a lifestyle and all-round satisfaction. If you reach this point you will know you are there, as everything suddenly feels easy and within the game of life you feel invincible.

People at this juncture exude confidence, give off so much positive energy, never watch the clock and are like magnets for other people, who just crave their company. Their knowledge and expertise about their specialism are usually encyclopaedic, and their network of contacts is inexhaustible. They play the game simply because they love it, and whatever they do is like a hobby to them. Some of them would say they would do it regardless, even if they weren't paid, and you can actually believe them. Please also be very wary of these people, though, as they can be like religious fanatics at times and can recruit and indoctrinate you if you aren't careful. I know, as I was there at least once in my life and took people along with me who all felt the same on a wave of positivity, feeding off my energy, giving life to their own games and consequently improving mine. The innovation and creativity were infectious. It is like being at the start of a roller coaster when you keep ascending, pushed on up by a force that is never-ending and you have people with you, all of whom are excited for what lies ahead.

Giving people a freedom like this, without restricting their boundaries is essential. Yes, observe the law and regulations, but push the edges out as far as you can. Count nothing out, as people's imagination and potential for achievement have no limitations. You will find that you wake up in a morning and cannot wait to be in that head space and environment. You long to be with the people who collaborate with you, and you talk constantly about just how great it is and how much you are enjoying it. You laugh and feel free. The money can roll in too, if you want, and your lifestyle improves, although, as I have cautioned, beware of this being your definition of success. It is true to say that many people who are in this zone do see their intrinsic wealth increase. As I type this section, I can remember those times clearly and the speed of my typing has become quicker as my own serotonin levels have gone into overdrive; my breathing has become more rapid as I relive some of those moments. It is a high like no other, for sure.

"So what is the downside, Andrew? Surely this is it, the game is cracked? Make your job or your passion in life your hobby and that is it. End of the story and end of the game. Why read on? The job is done and the ladders have been found and ascended!" I hear you cry.

I am sorry to disappoint you, but, unless you have an unlimited well of resources, including financial, then like all highs there have to be some lows to give you balance. There are significant dangers to living in this world all of the time. You can survive and make it possible, but you have to impose some very strict rules and regimes on yourself, otherwise everything can be lost. It is a natural part of our existence as humans that, like our need for sleep, we need also to consciously rest and switch off. We cannot be flat out 24/7 forever.

When you do something really well, and you crave it more and more, it can become drug like and addictive. If you have that sort of personality (I do to some extent), then you want to hold on, keep the party going and hope that it never ends. What may start off as very good noble intentions can sometimes end up becoming a huge uncontrollable beast. Some find that they then do things that compromise everything they have worked for. They talk and behave differently to keep firing the embers of the addiction back to life, and eventually their game dies, they lose everything, including that most precious of all commodities, their integrity. Then, they are back to where they started, if not worse.

The impact is also not only on you but others around you: loved ones, friends, colleagues and their families too. Remember, too, that, for every employee that an employer has in their care (I believe that word is the most appropriate, but often forgotten by organisations, employers and line managers), there are often at least a further four people who depend on that person for their lifestyle and standard of living. So, when we hear of a thousand jobs being lost, the true figure is closer to 5,000 people who are directly impacted. That could be the ultimate cost of one person's addiction.

One well-publicised incident that demonstrates this clearly and sticks in my mind from the early 1990s involves the businessman and entrepreneur Gerald Ratner, who owned a national chain of jewellers named after himself, "Ratners". Ratner was a self-made man who was in the prime of his life, highly driven, incredibly wealthy and outwardly the model of success. A genuine entrepreneur with style and a great outgoing personality. He owned properties, expensive cars and was seen at many high-profile parties and events. He led a jewellery empire with prime high street sites and was hailed as an example of how to make it and make it big in the world from humble beginnings. He was held up as a retail genius, a modern-day success story, and was addicted to the job that he loved.

At the height of his powers Ratner made a speech in 1991 at an Institute of Directors dinner in which he referred to two of his products as "crap". This was seized on by the media, was publicised worldwide and saw the collapse of the business, almost overnight. The public and investors refused to support anyone with this level of arrogance. Would you want to purchase something that the store owner calls "crap"? The effects on Ratner are well documented, with a loss of status, lifestyle, respect and position. I have seen very little reporting of the effects on the thousands of workers, families, suppliers and communities that were reliant on him, though. Ratner will forever be rebuilding and, to a large degree, has recovered his losses, but his story is a great case study for everyone's game, in my view. Business suicide of this nature is now known to all as "doing a Ratner".

Another warning sign to be aware of, which can creep up on you, is burnout and I am not ashamed to admit that I had a breakdown in my late thirties, caused, in no small part, by my playing the game too hard and trying to feed my addiction to my job. I failed to recognise the warning signs until it was too late. Someone else had absolute control over me and my game, and I refused to let go. I failed to accept that the high I was on was over, that someone else's strategy was to ruin me and that their game was more important to them than mine. I carried on, without stopping. In fact, I pushed even harder and, on reflection, failed to accept the loss, which I later found included the death of my parents a few years earlier. I had complete and absolute burnout. I was mentally and physically exhausted. Fortunately, I didn't lose everything, like some do. The reality was that my loss, in hindsight, was around five years' position in the game, plus a considerable amount of pride, confidence and reputation. Looking back on that time now, I didn't lose what those who are more exposed than me could have and my wonderful wife, family and close circle of true friends stood by me. Many people did drift away from me, and it is at times like these that you do find out who counts with you. I am also sorry that the people who worked with me in the two years that followed during my lowest points who I hadn't known before, never got the very best from me. Some only ever knew me as a shell of the person I was and that, for me, will always be a source of regret.

My game changers were:

Admitting that I had a problem and needed help, which was diagnosed as very bad stress and depression. Being depressed is ok, by the way, although it does need correctly diagnosing and treating. What is not ok is being told in condescending tones by others, who are supposedly older and wiser than you, "What have you got to be depressed about?" "Pull yourself together" and "Go for a long walk; that'll get rid of it".

Having a new line manager take over whilst I was off ill and who, for want of a better phrase, "saved" me. He reached out, listened and accepted his responsibility as a leader and a human being.

Having an amazing doctor and counsellor who I opened up

to and helped me realise that underpinning everything was my failing to deal with the loss of my father.

I still struggled for many years with a sense of bitterness and injustice at the way that I had been treated at work, but that gradually subsided with time. My closure happened when I found out a few years ago that my "bully", as that was what he was, had died. It meant that I would never see him again with a chance encounter in the street or some other unexpected interaction. That part was over and I could finally properly move on.

I have told this personal story, under what is a very positive heading, as I want you, the reader, to recognise that, no matter how in control we feel we are of our own game, there are others manoeuvring in the background to possibly sabotage your position. The higher in status and responsibility you get, the more exposed you are to these forces. That is why it is so important for you to consistently check and review yourself, taking soundings from those you trust.

Love what you do and do what you love. Make your job, or whatever it is that you do and have a passion for, as close to being as enjoyable as it can be. Feel the rush and enthusiasm it brings, but be aware of the fire that you are lighting within, and how quickly it can burn out of control if you let it.

If it helps your game and gives you positive energy, a sense of well-being, belonging and purpose, then do what you love doing, no matter what level of attainment you are at. What have you got to lose? And, if all else fails, then sing as you roll the dice for your next move.

The quick wins and the ladders

- Doing what you love means that you will take others with you.
- Making your job, or your cause your hobby.
- Being passionate about what you love doing.

- Helping others to find their passion.
- Being aware that your passion may not inspire and enthuse others in the same way as it does you.
- Remembering your responsibilities as an employer to those who work for you.
- Counting nothing out by having a go at anything that is presented to you.
- Seeking good advice and counsel from your trusted circle.

The traps and the snakes

- Advising others that they should not attempt to try out new things.
- Not knowing or being aware of the drivers and needs of those around you.
- Not trying or attempting anything yourself.
- Using illegal activities to create your own "high".
- Not knowing when you are taking your passion too far, particularly when you have an "addiction" to it.
- Failing to listen to any advice given by those you trust.
- Allowing arrogance and pride to rule your world.
- Ignoring the difficulties that you have faced without talking them through and dealing with them at the time.

Dare to dream, and never say never

> Dare to visualise a world in which your most
> treasured dreams have become true.
>
> Ralph Marston

Rudyard Kipling, in his iconic poem "If", said, "If you can dream—and not make dreams your master." In those ten words he created for me, as an impressionable young teenager when I first read them, a call to action about how we should view dreams. We can dream, but our lives should not be ruled by them to such an extent that they take over and dominate our reality.

In the 1960s, Dr Martin Luther King delivered his world-changing speech "I have a dream", in which he listed his dreams for a better society, and a better world, starting each sentence with the four words, "I have a dream". He made people believe that his dream, where everyone is judged by who they are and not by the colour of their skin, could be possible. In this speech alone, he accelerated a process of social change for America and, subsequently, for much of the world too. Over fifty years later, society still has some way to go to realise his dream, but we are so much closer because of it.

Dreaming for improvement, for a better life, and a better world, is healthy and creates an energy and ambition all of its own. It is good to share with others and helps to form and shape game plans. If we never dreamed, then it is unlikely that the seemingly impossible would ever be realised.

Dreaming must be tempered, though, with a form of reality, or at least a specific plan to make your dream come to fruition. Collaborate with others and share when you are ready, but beware of the unhealthy side of dreaming, as Kipling warns, about making dreams your master.

I do believe that dreaming about what we can be, what we can attain, and what we can achieve from our own talents and efforts, is a vitally important part of our own personal development. It creates a massive flow of positive energy. This is something that you need a lot of if you play the game for you in your own autonomous way. Dreams should be nurtured, treasured and coveted, and, in the game of life, form another one of those possible destinations for you in the future. What right does anyone have to say to a child "You cannot do this because…" or "There he goes, dreaming again," as was said to me in disparaging tones many times as a child. The crushing weight of those words is incalculable, and the cost to the world, and society as a whole, can be huge. Imagine if someone had said that to the great inventors, explorers, pioneers and leaders who have created so many things to make our world a better place. So much of what we have become as human beings could have been missed.

Please dare to dream, write them down, set your plans, make them flexible and changeable, but please dream. Add to them, adjust, alter, overhaul, rip them up and start again, but dream, for God's sake, dream. You can be anything that you want to be; you just have to want it badly enough to work so hard that it comes true. Never say never if you believe that something is within your grasp and attainable. And never let anyone with influence or sway say no to your dreams without them hearing all possible sides of your argument first. Even then, they have no right to say an unqualified no.

There are many techniques that we can use to make our dreams a reality, and the setting of an action plan is a good way to begin. Use my DREAMS acronym and the Dreamcatcher Worksheet (Appendix 1) as a starting point, with the heading being what your dream is:

- **D – Date** when you set this dream.
- **R – Reason(s)** why you have set this dream. This is to remind you as you progress what your motivation(s) was.
- **E – Environment and Energy.** What resources do you need, and what do you have to do differently, commit to and change in you, and the world around you, to make this dream possible?
- **A – Activities and Actions.** These link into the above, but be very specific around exactly what you will do to make this dream come true.
- **M – Marker points along the road.** Where do you wish to be at with your dream at key points? What will you hope to have accomplished along the way, and by when? For example, I will need to attain X by this year to be on track for the dream to continue for it to come true. Also, keep the marker points very flexible if you can. This can further reduce some of the pressure that you may place on you.
- **S – Success.** Know what it will feel like when you achieve your dream. Visualise and write down your thoughts now, at the very start, as to how you will feel once you have achieved it. Document your progress as you edge ever closer to realising the dream.

Is this process risky for your game? Yes, it can be as you may find that you become disappointed if you do not achieve it first time around. If you want it badly enough, though, and have enough belief and commitment, then it will happen, or you will reassess things, make changes, or another dream will become possible.

Be careful with the visualisation part here as well, and the effects that it can have on you. Keep your dreams very flexible, remembering that they are yours and yours alone. Trying to visualise something that is not yours, or that you are not totally committed to, can lead to inner confusion. And, as we know, this will lead to a loss of position in the game for you.

If you hit a negative, or a place of doubt, then follow this train of thought through to its own natural conclusion in your mind. Get ahead of this and then go back to the last positive place you were at, reworking it forward from there. In other words, adjust your route to accomplishment, ironing out the bumps in the road ahead.

I followed this type of format in writing this book, sharing the concept with some people that I trust, some of whom are listed in the acknowledgements. They were and are among those I call my cheerleaders and closest friends, who I can quite comfortably and safely turn to for advice, support and help. This gave me a form of commitment to myself, and also to them, to complete it. I have never written like this before and dreams, with a visualisation of what could be, have proved to be one of my sources of inspiration, strength and direction over many years.

I read in the newspaper some time ago about a father who had lost the use of his legs in an accident and dreamed he would be able one day to walk his daughter down the aisle at her wedding. He made this ambition a reality by being persistent, relentless and challenging, including recruiting other people into his world as collaborators. They became co-owners of his dream, opted in to make it a reality. Anything is possible if you set your mind to it and you want it badly enough.

Dreams can be materialistic, tangible, intangible, ambitious, and anything that you want. Dr King's dream was not for him alone. It was for everyone, which is why he shared it so publicly.

The Dream Catcher Worksheet is available in Appendix 1 and will help you to capture your dreams, making them come more to life and real as, after all, they are yours and yours alone.

The quick wins and the ladders

- Being a dreamer; with a concise and structured plan, you can make them come true.
- Collaborating with your trusted circle.
- Never saying never if you believe that something is within your grasp and possible.
- Visualising your dream as a reality.
- Redrafting, varying and altering your dream if you have to.
- Using the DREAM acronym and the Dream Catcher sheet to capture your dreams.

The traps and the snakes

- Not dreaming about what is possible for you.
- Crushing the dreams of others without thought for the impact on them.
- Not trying, or planning to make your dreams a possibility.
- Using other people's dreams as your own.

13

Managing those who "manage" you

Manage yourself first and others will take
your orders.

David Seabury

From the moment that we emerge into the world, our game is totally dependent on other people and, as a result, we have to become very manipulative, without realising it. As children, we will try all sorts of different techniques, which can range from the stamping of our feet with open defiance and aggression, through to using our puppy-like eyes with displays of passive body language at the same time. This can also see the heartstring-pulling effect of head tilting, whilst looking very sad, and almost tearful. Some can even cry on demand. These are the very first stages of learning about managing those around us to get our own way. As we get older, these techniques become more subtle and honed. We experiment and begin to understand how being emotionally intelligent, and emotionally aware, can help us to play the game to our advantage.

But do we really learn as we get older? Do we just revert to a childlike state when things fail to go our way? Is someone else controlling our playbook?

The easiest and most direct route is to ask the person "managing you" how you can get the very best out of them and, to tell them how they can get the best from you. You can do this at any point in your relationship, but ideally at the very beginning. This approach will certainly confuse some, but the really good ones, at any point when you ask them, will give you straight answers. Some may see it as confrontational, but if you frame it correctly when you ask, then I believe you will get a better response. It is brave and requires a leap of faith, but it will give you a faster track to controlling your own game, developing your relationships and managing more of the outcomes. The greatest leaders, and most open-minded ones at that, will get it straight away and, like I advise in so many chapters, the younger that you start the better the potential outcome is for you.

(Top tip for any kids reading this. Note that this is a great tip to totally confuse your parents, guardians or teachers, taking them way out of their own comfort zones. Try it and see the shock that you create in them. You must also see through the answers you get, though, knowing what you want from them otherwise you will lose your advantage.)

The first type of authoritative figure that I will cover are those are a parent/guardian/teacher/coach/supervisor/boss and who are fully in tune with you and themselves. They are so good at collaborating with you that you almost feel as though you are managing them, even though you both know that you are not. These are the greatest people of all to be around, and I had the privilege of working for at least five of these types of people in my career.

What they do incredibly well is to give you autonomy and freedom, as much as they possibly can. They allow you to be creative, expressive and innovative and will never make decisions that affect you negatively just because a higher authority above them says so. They allow you to create your own plans, give you the freedom to implement them, never fencing you in and allowing you to take ownership and credit for your own outcomes. They never take the glory for your success, or boast that it is down to them.

What they do to manage you (and they actually prefer to use the phrase "work with you") is to create an atmosphere of reflection, and a chance for you to constantly challenge yourself as to whether the paths that you are choosing are the right ones. They have the ability to take you outside of yourself and to allow you to look safely inwards at the movie that is figuratively playing, seeing the actions and results well before they happen. This skill of creating conscious holistic thinking is what, for me, makes them brilliant life leaders, not just limited to their role in supporting you. They care, and look at the whole picture of your life too, not just what part is important to them. They also have phenomenal memories, remembering so many of the names of people, places, and events that you may mention in passing to them that form part of your very foundation.

Managing these people is very easy from your side as, once you have established this relationship and they have demonstrated their commitment to you, you can just go with their flow, trusting them implicitly. Offering this on a reciprocal basis to them, encouraging equal reflectiveness on their part, can give you an insight into how they think, what their plans are, etc. Offer the safe space for them to do this with you as well, and suddenly your mutual trust levels go into the stratosphere. They may not be as open with you as you are with them but what they will give you are closer insights into how you can get the very best out of them.

They play their game knowing what they are doing and how to get the very best from it. Copy and imitate them as best as you can, without betraying any of your core values, beliefs and personality, and you will never be far from where you seek to be. You will also then have the chance to become a brilliant leader and collaborator yourself in every aspect of your life if you so choose.

One of the hardest gameplays of them all is when someone

else comes in and replaces this type of leader and they are the polar opposite. You may encounter them at any point in your life and it may be even from the very start. They are high on control and use rules for your game based on "my way or the highway". The culture is known as "JFDI", which crudely stands for "Just f***ing do it". That means that you do as they say or otherwise you are at worst out, and at the very least in some form of trouble. They live in the now, the short term, and want instant results. They "micromanage", have a very blinkered view of the world and ensure a "blame culture" is alive and well in their empire. Any apparent interest in you is false. Their memories are very poor when it comes to what is important to you, and they manipulate the facts to their own game. They will also have a clique of their own people, who are almost like a secret police force, constantly feeding back information to them, specifically finding and probing your weaknesses. The trust levels become very low and information is given by you to them on a need-to-know basis. There are many things that go unsaid between you. You may become secretive, lacking inclusivity with others and find yourself very low on energy. Those around you will see the change as you have to live in the "now" yourself. Their world has overtaken yours, and a daily survival routine kicks in. There is no pleasure for you in looking at the longer view besides the one where you are away from this person. Be very aware that this is incredibly damaging to your game and your physical and mental health.

The best route here is to try and plot a course away if you can. I appreciate that this is not always possible and, if you cannot escape, then find the pleasure in creating small victories. Show your potential at its very best and never compromise on your all-important integrity. You may find that to survive you have followed the route of "If you can't beat them, join them". If this is the case, then you have lost the game unless you choose to change and do it now. You will have been cloned by them.

In these situations, it is vital that you talk to those independent of this situation who you trust and who will listen to you without judgement. Try also writing down your thoughts and what is happening to you. A journal or diary can be a very powerful release of your tensions and, in the most extreme of situations, prove good evidence supporting your case or cause against these bullies.

Always know that the situation does have an endpoint and, like every storm, it will subside eventually. Sometimes a day, though, can seem like a month and a month seem like a year when you are in the midst of this. Context is very important here and what we do when we are under extreme pressure is to blow things up out of all proportion.

Take your life in small pieces. If you have a deadline or target, then break it down into the smallest possible component parts and celebrate the achievements that you have. Micromanagers like this and you will be helping them by taking this approach. Make sure that you have your plans very clear, very transparent, and you provide the person who is governing you with as much information as you can. Beware, though, about disclosing too much, because you want to ensure that the spotlight is not placed on those areas where you are at your most vulnerable or that are personal to you.

It is hard for me to say the words that follow, and it is not a policy that I would normally advocate, but if you intend to protect yourself and stay in the game within this environment, then you may have to divert some attention away from you. Do this by performance, deeds and honest actions and you will be fine. This may help you to cope better in the short term. Be true to yourself and give anyone who you see who may be struggling your support and counsel, if you feel able to do so. You will be aware, though, that sometimes self-preservation has to take precedence over the very best of intentions. Being ruthless with time and courteous with people is a phrase that may serve you well here, whereby you give your time very selectively, whilst being very polite about how you communicate its availability and importance.

Your integrity remains your most valuable commodity. My parting words to my nemesis as I walked away from the worst situation of bullying that I ever faced, or saw in the workplace, was "I am walking through this door with my integrity intact. Sadly you'll never be able to say the same." Finally I got in a punch. A very late and unexpected one, but just saying that helped me in some way, although I did have to go much, much lower within myself before re-emerging, years later, with the help of so many others to get my game back on track.

Where you have a passive or less dynamic leader, you will need to be much more proactive and directive with them. You will feel very free at times, but also very isolated too, as you may not have the relationship or confidence in the person to be able to share, confide and ask questions to seek support. Understanding their game will help here, and finding out how their world works can be one way of unlocking them. You may find, though, that they have no mechanism or desire to be unlocked. In this case, ensure that they give you approval for what you embark on and you have your own back very well covered, protecting against any possible errors on your part. They will be very unlikely to be supportive if you do something wrong. In time this will improve as their trust in you is earned, but, in the short term, self-protection is the most essential part of your game.

A really good example here is when you are new to a task and left more to your own devices. All too often we wish to impress, and sometimes that means making decisions on areas where we lack experience. If you are in any doubt, seek clarification, think through the consequences and keep asking until you are clear on how to proceed. Always know, too, what the expected outcome and result is. The person may get cross with you, but never forget that it is the failure of communication on their part that leads to situations like this developing. Trust in yourself and ask questions. The time pressures that are created are pressures that they bring on themselves, so give them some leeway. Any assumptions on how to do the task by both parties invariably ends in loss, both materially and to your relationship, so never take any chances. Never, ever assume.

There are so many different types of people who will be managers and influencers in your game. Often they are those who are senior in some way to you. I have only covered a few scenarios, but these will help you with many that you encounter along the way and you will come to understand yourself, and them, even better. Your strength for your game is you, your knowledge of you and enabling others to correctly exploit this, not only for their advantage but primarily for yours.

The quick wins and the ladders

- Asking the person "managing you" or "authority" figure how you can get the best from them.
- Knowing who you are dealing with and understanding the different ways to "manage" them for your game.
- Developing a conscious understanding of emotional intelligence and how to apply it to every given situation.
- Talking to those in your trusted circle as a sounding board.
- Never assuming anything and always asking for clarification if you are in doubt.

The traps and the snakes

- Using a "one size fits all" approach to those who "manage you" or are "authority" figures in your life.
- Making assumptions and failing to seek clarification.
- Lacking in a team or collaborative approach.
- Compromising your integrity.

14

Like Dick Whittington, be prepared to turn around and start again

> The Titanic hit the iceberg not because they
> could not see it coming but because they
> could not change direction.
>
> Dean Devlin

There is a wonderful children's story called Dick Whittington, which is often performed in the theatre around Christmas as a pantomime. It tells of a young Richard Whittington, who became lord mayor of London in the fourteenth century. Part of the tale is that as he was leaving London, disillusioned with his life, he turned around to head back to the City after hearing the ringing of Bow Bells. He believed that the bells had told him, by their peals, that he would reach this wonderful position in life. "Turn again" or "Turn around, Whittington, lord mayor of London" seems to be the message that has passed through the legend.

Like with Whittington, what I seek to make clear from this chapter is that if you feel that you are heading in the wrong direction, or walking away from your dreams, opportunities and ambitions, then always stop, listen to the voice of reason in your head, and also take soundings from other people who you trust.

Whether Whittington heard the bells, it was a sixth sense within him, a form of self-talk, or he just simply changed his mind, is open to debate. What is clear, however, is that he changed course and this, for him, was a moment of truth where he actually had the chance to make a life-changing and life-defining decision. Many people will know these as "sliding door moments". These decisions appear in front of us and sometimes we know that they are key moments and chances. On other occasions, though, they pass us by as seemingly insignificant as a glance at a stranger across a crowded street. Looking back with the benefit of hindsight, we can see the difference that they have, or could have, made. This is again another reason why I advocate so strongly for you to be conscious in your game at all times.

Consider too that, as your game develops, you will find that you will undergo regular changes. For example, what was important to you as a younger person with limited experience of the wider world may be so much different as you become older. Your core, or foundation, will always be the same, but the way that you promote and do some things will have changed with the times. Very much like our planet, we are constantly evolving.

You may also find that, as well as changing some ideals and beliefs, you change roles and direction. It is important for you to give yourself permission to change the method of the way you play your game too. I call this "changing horses", and it is ok to change horses so long as you plan ahead and know most of the path that lies in front of you. By doing this you will assess many of the scenarios that you will face and know that you have to change your game accordingly.

Changing horses, though, without warning and consequential planning, not only for yourself and others who will be impacted by your actions, is dangerous and carries massive inherent risks. It may seem the right thing to do in the moment, but always take soundings as to whether this is the right course of action, from those you trust. The chances are that, if it feels right, and you have done as much due diligence as you can, then it probably is. Beware, however, of decisions that are made from the heart, and not from the head, that affect your long-term happiness and welfare as they can be very precarious. If an offer is made to you, and it seems appealing, that offer will still be there tomorrow and the day after that. If it isn't, then you have to question the validity of the offer, whether it has longevity and the overall value that it presents to you and to your game. Walk away, ensuring that subsequent offers meet your requirements.

As you mature, and your game reaches a point where you have to practically consider the various phases and stages of your life, look further ahead down the game board and begin to plan for these times and what you will do when you reach them. Consider phases, perhaps in five- and ten-year blocks. Nothing has to be cast in stone, but it is prudent to begin to prepare in this way and it gives you another chance, in a safe space, to plan and avoid some of the snakes.

What none of us can do is to stop the march of time so, for example, your pension planning will have started at, hopefully, a young age and you will have made financial provision for this. When you reach your forties and fifties, it is important to review and plan for life beyond work. Think about what you will do, where your talents lie, what you enjoy doing and what you specifically want. As I have said, nothing is guaranteed to be certain and circumstances do change, but set down some markers as to what you want life to be like, and above everything else put the health and happiness of you, and those who matter to you, front and centre of your gameplay.

Not to turn around or stop when we are just ploughing on regardless shows arrogance and ignorance and the consequences can be, in extreme cases, deadly. History is filled with examples of people blindly carrying on into dangerous situations believing they were right, without listening to the advice or counsel they were given. Some disaster movies document this well and we should never look at these films as just pure entertainment. They are often educational tools for us too.

As human beings, we seem to fail to learn from history and make the same mistakes over and over again. Far too many times we hear the phrases "History repeating itself" and "We must learn from this tragedy to ensure it never happens again". All too often, though, the event does repeat itself further down the line. This is why history must be in our direct view, no matter how painful it may be for us to see it.

I will also stress the importance of course changes and directional adjustments by putting in a form of "time out", which all good game players do anyway. This will give you a natural break and create clear head space for you to check that you are on the correct course, making the best decision possible with the information that you have available. Effective leaders do this very well as no strategic decision is made or committed to without the effects being known from a holistic perspective. They will never get it right all of the time, but the best get far more right than they get wrong.

Turning around, or changing direction, requires considerable bravery and honesty, especially with yourself. After all, you are admitting that the course that you had plotted was the wrong one, and in fact, you may well have made a mistake. You are laying yourself open to criticism from everyone, including from yourself, and this can affect your inner confidence. However, these shorter-term consequences are far outweighed by you putting your own feelings to one side and showing a more considered train of thought. Some of the greatest strengths that we have come from these experiences, as we develop a sense of humility and a more mature, rounded way of thinking, essential for your longest-term game.

The quick wins and the ladders

- Stopping and listening to the voice of reason in your

head when deciding which direction to go with an enforced "time out".

- Being totally honest with yourself.
- Taking soundings from other people who you trust.
- Learning from history and avoiding any relevant mistakes made previously.
- Planning ahead knowing that your course can be altered or adjusted.

The traps and the snakes

- Failing to turn around or stop when you know that you are just ploughing on regardless.
- Making the same mistakes again and again.
- "Changing horses" without any forward planning or warning.

15

Buying yourself time and the five-second game rule

Delay is preferable to error.

Thomas Jefferson

Decisions have to be made, and we subconsciously make hundreds each day. We cannot avoid them wherever we are, whether it be what seat to take on the train, how we drive, where to walk on the pavement – there is so much we do not give any thought to in our day-to-day lives. And then, when we do make some conscious decisions, we can justify almost anything in our mind to give us say, an extra five minutes in bed, or why it is acceptable to be aggressive on the road, simply because we feel that we are entitled to be. It is an endless list, and one that is fraught with danger for you and your game. How many times have you had a near miss in life when your instant decision could easily have backfired? And how many times have you not? How many people, but for the want of a little bit of thought, have actually ruined their game, and that of others, by making an unconscious decision without thinking through or risk-assessing the consequences of their actions?

As I am advocating throughout the chapters of this book

that you play your game in full consciousness, it is right that every decision, where possible, is fully assessed or prepared for in advance. It is not easy, and is a thought process that will require some discipline and practice, but begin by thinking of the tasks that you carry out in an "unconscious" form. It could be something as simple as walking to your next destination. The next time you do this, try to do it consciously. Give yourself a mental commentary of everything that you do, that you see, and that is happening around you. Think of the threats that could be there and the dangers of the decisions that you make. This will raise your own levels of consciousness, and mean that the decisions you then make are made taking every possible factor into account: other pedestrians, road users, the weather, your visibility, obstacles, both fixed and portable. It is a long list and one that you would usually process unconsciously in an instant, but, by being aware of how you make the decisions that you do, you can then bring this into other aspects of your life.

Police drivers are trained to give a running commentary as they drive. This is often for evidence in trials, and to justify the decisions that they subsequently make. These are often at high speed and they are having to talk through everything that is happening, also describing what could potentially happen. Watch one online, or on one of the many police programmes that are available, and you will see what I mean.

Taking this approach to other aspects of your life will then mean that all decisions that you make have been fully assessed, tested, and made with the best information available to you. You will not get every decision right, but you will get many more right than you get wrong, and you will become more thoughtful of others as well.

Building on this theme further, the importance of a timed space for reflection for you becomes even more important. Yes, many decisions have to be taken at pace so I am making a direct recommendation to you for a self-imposed rule that you may wish to consider. This one I call "The five-second rule". For anyone who may be wondering, this isn't the rule where you drop your food on the floor and it is still ok to eat after five seconds. This is a personal handbrake for you, and another form of time out. It is a method of stopping yourself from doing something and another form of accident prevention.

How does it work? Very simply in practice. If you are about to do something, say something or act in a certain way that you know is an instant reaction (sometimes referred to as a "knee jerk reaction"), a risk and likely to cause an argument, confrontation, angst or harm for yourself or someone else, then stop for five seconds. If it is still worth doing, saying or following through after that time period, then do it. If you are still unsure, though, then add another five seconds to that enforced stop and continue to do so until you are clear in your mind. In electronic terms, this could be sending a holding type of message saying that you will respond shortly. Once you have had that period to analyse your response, if you then feel that it is not worth saying or doing, this is your cue to politely walk away. There is no shame in exiting a situation and, more often than not, your response will give you more kudos and genuine satisfaction. You may also find that you keep your integrity intact. If you were seeking to respond from a viewpoint of pride, or not wishing to be the first to back down, just go through the consequences in your mind to the very end of you acting on impulse and not imposing those five seconds. The potential game play you see ahead will possibly horrify you.

Social media, and the sending of emails, are prime examples where imposing the five-second rule can really win. I had a situation once at work where I wrote an email that had steam coming off it and was, in all honesty, libellous. Instead of writing the email, getting someone to sense-check it or set it aside for a few seconds, as soon as I finished typing I hit send, and then I instantly regretted it. I thought it was not a problem and that I would recall it straight away. I was too late as the recipient had already read it. I awaited his reply and the worry of the action that could be taken against me caused me to lose a lot of sleep. I shared my thoughts with a colleague, who told me to expect a legal case and the possible loss of my job. I started to prepare my defence and even talked to my union representative, forewarning them. I had put my whole game and the security of my family at risk for the sake of waiting for five seconds.

The response to my email came back a few days later, and was full of class. The recipient said that he had taken his time to reply, because he had to have his words checked by a legal professional. He said that, on this occasion, against his legal advice, he was not going to take any further action against me, but he reserved the right to do so should anything else come to his attention that I may ever say or do that was detrimental to him.

In the game I had lost considerable ground. I had lost sleep and some self-respect and I had broken a golden rule. My pride was badly dented, my confidence shaken and I had also lost a week of strong performance as my mind was elsewhere. This was a very, very poor move indeed on my part that makes me shiver even now just thinking about it. And all for the want of delaying by five seconds.

There are times, of course, when you have to be spontaneous, and spontaneity can be wonderful not only for you but for the people around you. It can give you a massive boost to your energy levels, but beware of the cost of "living in the moment" and don't get too carried away, particularly when living beyond your means and overspending.

Some people work to a traffic light awareness system for situations in their life and that, in itself, is a good tip for conscious gameplay. Red means that you stop! Amber means that you are thinking and getting ready to proceed, but with caution. If all is ok, then it is green and go.

Buying time to make a decision is essential, particularly where you are being placed under some pressure and have a dilemma about which way you should go. Always seek to delay for as long as you possibly can get away with. What may be seen as the need for you to give an instant decision may just be because that suits another person's agenda, timescale or narrative. Always clarify the deadlines that you are working to where possible and, if what you come back with is unacceptable to others, then make sure that you get your point across as clearly as you can as to why it is important for you to take your time. It will likely be in their interests too. Avoid aggression and conflict, but politely ask and then use that time wisely. If all else fails, then tell them the tale of why you work to the five-second rule. If nothing else, it will emphasise your maturity of thought and give you more authenticity and credibility. You will have avoided a snake for sure.

The quick wins and ladders

- Creating a five-second break before giving a response, whether it be verbal, written or any other format.
- Applying this, especially to emails and social media, where there is a strong audit trail.
- Never being afraid to be spontaneous although always proceeding with care.
- Self-imposing a red, amber, green traffic light type of system for responses.
- Making as many decisions as you can, as consciously as possible.
- Practising with commentary using situations where you would normally think unconsciously (e.g. walking to your next destination).
- Always buying yourself time and delaying taking action until you have to make a decision.

The traps and the snakes

- Giving instant "knee jerk" responses.

- Pushing the send button or answering before thinking through the consequences of that action.
- Not considering the impact of the decisions that you make on you and on others.
- Forcing others to make quick decisions themselves.

16

You have two ears and one mouth. Try to use them in that order

Why did God give me two ears and one
mouth? So that I will hear more and talk
less.

Leo Rosten

Continuing on the theme of self-awareness, I would recommend this chapter as another essential for conscious gameplay.

I once went on a sales course and had the rather torturous experience of being filmed in a mock client interview situation. I was to play the part of the sales advisor (this was in the days before sales and selling became dirty words never supposedly to be uttered again in financial services), trying to persuade the client (who, by the way, was the course trainer) to buy the products that I felt were the most appropriate based on her circumstances. My job was to uncover all of the relevant facts and to then make recommendations at a follow-up meeting.

I was ready to go, dressed in a double-breasted, deep navy blue pinstripe suit, a crisp white shirt, a red Italian silk tie and black shoes, polished so highly that you could see your face in them. My dark hair was blow-dried for twenty minutes; my quiff was as strong as Donald Trump's, with at least half a can of Falcon hairspray to hold it in place. I was power dressed and ready for action. These were the early 1990s, after all.

After some pleasantries, as the camera started recording, I asked lots of good open questions (ones that do not require just a yes/no answer) to elicit the information that I needed. The lady seated opposite me had a script that led me to understand her circumstances in full detail, and I made good use of summaries and clarification questions (which often do require just yes/no answers). I also paid attention to her body language and eye contact, which told me that she was relaxed and not uncomfortable with the environment that we were in. Her arms remained unfolded, which is always a good sign; she smiled a lot and wasn't shuffling in her chair, which again gave off the right signals to me that I was doing ok.

So, after concluding the fact-finding exercise, we then came to the point where, after a short half an hour break, I was about to close the sale by presenting my recommendations to her at the subsequent meeting. I had quickly prepared my brief and was ready to go.

As predicted, a series of questions and objections came forward from the lady, although nothing too aggressive. My hair was still intact, the creases in my suit were still sharp and I was totally unflustered. My response, though, was to talk… and talk… and talk, often repeating myself and not answering all of the points raised. Even worse was to follow, when I interrupted the client by talking over her. And even when we had got to the point where she was so worn down she said "yes", I still carried on rambling on and on, until in the end she said, "Can I think about it?"

I had broken just about every golden rule in the sales book and learned more in that afternoon about how to play this part of the game, and understand other people's too, than I had in the years before. The video did not make for pretty viewing and, at the end, I realised that my tie had twisted into a very unusual angle, my crisp white shirt looked crumpled and, worst of all, my quiff had lost some of its strength and was falling over my forehead. It was not the sun visor that it had started out as.

What I specifically learned and understood, and that was pointed out to me in two easy sentences during the painful group feedback session, is the title of this chapter – "You have two ears and one mouth. Try to use them in that order". In other words, you should always listen twice as much as you speak.

In the game of life, you will learn more about how other people are playing their game purely by listening to them talk about their strategy and approach. Ask them lots of questions and encourage them to give you as much about themselves as they can. You will come to learn what their strengths, weaknesses, hopes and fears are just by asking and listening. People love talking about themselves and, if you can find the key questions that gets them talking, usually about what they are good at, you will find they are very easily on your side. They will take it as a compliment.

Think of any great interviewer in the media and how they find out as much information as they possibly can without interrupting their guest. They may interject when challenging a standpoint, or forcing their own opinion into the conversation, but mainly they listen, question and summarise.

Forcing yourself to listen and absorb all of what is being said does take time to develop, and knowing exactly when to shut up takes practice and awareness.

As the interviewer or questioner, if you are asked for information by the person you are talking to, please note closely that this is a form of buying signal from the person opposite you. They require more detail from you to clarify their thoughts on your proposition. In the game of life, and game of sales, no matter what you are selling, a question asked of you is a great sign and should be welcomed. "I'm really glad you've asked that" should nearly always be the response, accompanied with a smile, open body language, and a specific clear response.

Once you have answered the question that has been asked and made your point, or gained a position of strength, then, after asking for the sale, shut up, otherwise you will lose your ground, position and also possible cash. If you get a yes, then complete what is needed. If you get another question, then answer that. If you get a no, then ask why. Just don't keep talking for the sake of it. Silence can be golden. There is so much more to this art but as a basic rule this is a good one to live by.

There is a wonderful film called *Frost/Nixon*, which for me shows this process at its very best. It is the true story of how David Frost (one of the great television interviewers of the 1960s, '70s and '80s) interviewed the former president of the United States, Richard M. Nixon. Nixon had been forced to resign from office, in disgrace, after a political and criminal scandal that was known as "Watergate". Frost sought to interview Nixon and, after much negotiation, secured the opportunity. His aim was to gain as much information as possible from him about his life and time in office during a series of recorded interviews. And then, once he had this, he wanted to get Nixon to make a public confession that he had committed crimes during his presidency. This was to be his form of closing the sale.

The interplay, with Michael Sheen as Frost and Frank Langella as Nixon, shows the tension between the two men as all of the background detail is uncovered by the forensic questioning. It is like seeing the peeling back of the layers of an onion. Nixon is allowed to talk and talk about himself until in the end, after hours of recording sessions, it comes down to the final question, where Nixon finally admits to his wrongdoings. He was forced into a corner by Frost, a long silence ensues and Nixon had no choice but to make his confession.

The film is a great watch for anyone seeking to study effective interviewing for results, and how to play this part of the game of life to the greatest effect. Frost gambled everything that he had on selling these interviews to major networks, and could have lost his game completely had he failed to get Nixon to say that he had acted outside of the law. He used his two ears, processed the information that he was receiving, and only spoke when he needed to, but he made his words more powerful than the hours of commentary that came back at him. It is a film that is well worth watching, in my opinion, for anyone seeking to understand the power of the concept of two ears and one mouth.

The quick wins and the ladders

- Listening twice as much as you speak.
- Learning and being aware of open, closed and reflective questions for your gameplay.
- Learning and being aware of body language and reading other people's non-verbal responses.
- Treating any questions asked of you, when you have a proposition for another person, as "buying signals".
- Once you have a "yes" answer to anything that you are proposing then keep quiet.

The traps and the snakes

- Talking more than you listen.
- Not paying attention to the responses you get, or what the other person is telling you, both verbally and non-verbally.
- Always being on your agenda.

17

Telling your story, making an impact and the dark art of the interview

Never underestimate the power of anyone's story... anyone's life.

Abby Johnson

I make no apologies for the length and size of this chapter. You will find that it becomes the most important one for those of you who are in need of help, guidance and support in the arena of self-projection and career development.

For those of you who are mentors, this will also help to save you considerable time in guiding your mentees through the dark art of the interview as it is dissected into manageable sections, taking the whole process of interviewing apart, step by step. This will enable everyone to concentrate on the more important practical elements for you to give support, challenge and encouragement.

I am also conscious that this may come across as something akin to being in a classroom and feel like a "tell" exercise. With so many people, particularly the younger members of our society, struggling to find their way through the maze that this arena can be at times, and with so few clear points of reference that truly analyses each part of the process, this is the only way that I feel I can get the messages across as clearly and concisely as possible. Hopefully it works for you and adds to your foundations and structure, giving you a massive advantage in the game.

You only get one chance to make a first impression

When you meet someone for the first time, whether it be face to face, by phone, online or however it may be, you form an opinion of that person. We cannot help ourselves as it is our human nature. It is pre-programmed into us, and those first few seconds of any interaction with a stranger often shape our thinking about that person forever. You can lose considerable ground and position in your game by failing to make a good first impression. Massive amounts of preparatory work can be done for the whole process that you are embarking on, and yet it can all be lost in an instant by failing to get this element right. This, for your game, is a crucial point, another moment of truth, as you find that the people you are seeking to engage with either become your collaborators and ambassadors or potential assassins working against you, whether intentionally or otherwise.

Starting your application

Begin to look and apply for roles as soon as you possibly can. An application process can feel daunting and it is sometimes difficult to know where to begin. Learning how to tell your story and getting people to want to know more about who is behind the application that you have submitted, is a key strategy in selling yourself and enabling doors to open for you. Your game requires you to achieve your potential, and that involves engaging with others by getting people to buy into you and your proposition. So start early and start young.

The first post or position that you may well see advertised, and wish to apply for in life, could be within your school or college as a school prefect, as a member of a school council/pupil steering group or as a volunteer. This is your chance to begin to develop yourself with applications, and the more seriously you take it at an early age, the stronger and more impactful your approach will become as you get older. Do not ever follow the crowd and seek to replicate the style of others. This must be unique and all of your own work. Take it as if the rest of your life depended on it and, as you progress, you may just find that this first experience is so unique that it helps you to stand out for all of the right reasons.

Experience will also help you to see that roles, titles and descriptions can often be very misleading and not aligned. Never just look at the job title and think it sounds so great that you ignore the actual duties and detail. "An office-based food and drink consultant", for example, could be a tea, coffee and sandwich maker for a group of people. I exaggerate greatly, but to make a point and to encourage you to look deeper at what is expected of you and what your prospects for the future are.

I would always recommend speaking to the person who has advertised the role where possible, in the first instance, as that in itself creates a great impression. It says that you take the proposed position seriously and want to know more. It gives you a chance to make an impression, to sell yourself and, if you are in any doubt about the job, or your suitability, it is a chance to ask your questions early in the process gaining the clarification that you need.

Always do as many full and in-depth checks on the company or the group that is advertising that you can to ensure that the location and place of work is accessible and safe for you. Do they have a stable background and a good reputation, for instance? At the very least, are you certain that they have something to offer that interests you? Be clear as to how they will help with your development, and be equally clear that you can offer them something that meets and exceeds their requirements. It will be part of your own form of "due diligence" and will stand you in good stead as you move further into the process.

A word of warning for the young or vulnerable. Please clarify that any voluntary role or paid employment that you undertake will be correctly supervised and safe for you and that the appropriate certificates are held by those offering the post. If in any doubt, ask or check with the local authorities. Your safety on all levels should never be compromised, and anyone who is a responsible person, or represents a legitimate group, will be only too happy to give that reassurance.

So, having decided to then go for the role, before composing your application, you will need to have a curriculum vitae, or CV for short.

Your CV

A CV is a pen portrait of you and gives you the opportunity to demonstrate on paper exactly who you are, what you have done and what you have achieved. It is the first time that you may have interacted with the person, or persons, who you are seeking to impress and, therefore, it becomes a form of key that opens the door to an interview. It is your chance to make your first impression in writing, as you should have already introduced yourself to the recruiter as I previously advised.

Your CV should be regularly "updated" and "polished". By this I mean making sure that it is current and up to date and reflects you in every way possible. It should also be tailored to each role that you apply for as many will require some different skills and attributes.

Before beginning to write your CV, put yourself figuratively in the shoes of the interviewer. Imagine it is a wet Wednesday, just after lunch, when the mid-afternoon lull has hit and the person reviewing a pile of CVs is in a darkened room, seeking inspiration. They have thirty applications and CVs to go through and assess. What can you do to make yours stand out from the other twenty-nine? How do you make sure that you are placed on their "to interview" pile, and not on those "rejected"?

It starts with the presentation of your CV. There are numerous templates out there and many agencies and online sites will give you excellent advice as to how to present your CV. Take anything for free that is offered and tailor it to suit your own style.

Where I can add significant value is by helping you with its construction and this starts with your profile statement, which should always be the first heading. It should be limited to five sentences as a maximum and not overloaded with words or lengthy phrases. It must be clear, concise and a fair reflection of you.

Although it is only a maximum of five sentences, it can take considerable time to develop and craft. It is right that it does, as this will make the person reading it want to know more about you.

To assist in building your profile statement, I would recommend that you list at least twenty adjectives that you feel describe you. Take soundings from trusted people and ask them to give you some words and phrases that they would use to describe you. To help, I have supplied a useful adjectives sheet at the end of the book. Appendix 2, and this list will also prove useful when preparing for any interviews too.

Once you have the words, you then construct the sentences that include these adjectives. Do not try to write the complete profile statement at this point, but just make lists of sentences, using the words in a variety of formats. I am very keen that this is not something that is plagiarised, or a copy of a template example. The profile statement has to be specifically unique to you. That way it will stand out.

Gradually edit these sentences down, picking out words and phrases until you are comfortable that you have a statement that tells the reader exactly who you are, in such a way that they will feel compelled to read on and want to meet you. Keep the interviewer very much in your mind as you finally complete this. If you were that person, on the basis of the information in front of them, would you want to meet you?

It is vital that you ensure the document is grammar-checked and spellchecked, and the trusted people that you have already spoken to sense-check it with you. This may seem obvious but, for many posts, attention to detail is a key competency, so get it right now.

The font and overall presentation should again reflect you, but please be aware of the impact on the reader. Nothing should be too heavy on colour combinations or multiple varieties of fonts. Keep it simple to follow, easy to understand, easy to read with no small-sized type. It must also be chronological, by listing your present roles and activities first under each heading, hence why a template that works for you may well take some of the hard work out of this. It should be a maximum of two pages of A4 and no more. Ideally it should be one page. You must tell your story in a concise and effective way.

Differentiate it by considering the levels of your achievements, awards, voluntary and community impact and support roles that you have given. Some people really underplay these areas, but once I as an assessor have read the profile statement, I will want to see that consistency is there in the content matching the words as I read on.

If you have volunteered in a charity shop, for instance, then state the role and responsibilities, as well as core skills that you demonstrated. How did you go over and above what was needed, and why did you do this? Again, it opens up your heart and soul to some degree and makes the reader more drawn to wanting to meet you.

No matter what your jobs, education and achievements, list anything that reflects positively on you and the person you are, outlining why you did it as well.

Always put yourself in the reader or assessor's place and

keep asking yourself how you could improve on what you have created.

Your covering letter and what else you provide

So we now reach the point where the advert for the position, or the opportunity you seek, has become available. You then submit your CV, a covering letter, citations and anything else that may be relevant as I have just suggested. Never forget that these are the "door openers" and get you an audience with the decision makers. You may have to go through more than one interview, a selection panel and aptitude tests, but the hard work invested thus far, if done effectively, should get you your shot at the position.

Your covering letter, or relevant section in the application form, is your opportunity to expand on why you are applying for the post, why you have such an interest and to give further detail on your suitability. It should not be a rewrite of your CV but should include some elements of it by way of experience to date and your passion. Say why you have done certain things and give very brief "teasers" of some of your achievements. It is also the chance for you to expand on your interest in the field you are looking at, your ambitions, and also how this fits with your own personal development. Your list of adjectives will again be useful here, as you can pick up and include some that did not make the final cut for your profile statement.

The letter should assist the reader to understand you and to get an insight into the way that you think and speak. My advice would be for it to feel as though you are making it personal to the reader and it's not just another cut and paste exercise, which invariably goes straight to the reject pile. Your sincerity makes it very unique, more readable and genuine.

Beware of a word count limit that some applications may impose. Your covering letter shouldn't be more than one page of A4 at the most, including your address heading, as you do not want to give all of the more granular detail away that will likely come out at an interview.

Keep putting yourself into the head of the reader and, again, keep sense-checking with those who you trust to give you good critique.

There may be a need to send some covering documentation, such as certificates or references, in advance. Don't be afraid to also include something that you are extremely proud of, or send a link to a website, and reference it. It must be something that again, is unique to you, such as a portfolio of work, and a differentiator, but do it as that may give you a further head start over the competition.

Make sure that the people you quote as your referees are willing to act as such and that they reply with urgency when asked, providing a detailed glowing testimonial. These are extremely important and require more than a one-line response. Ideally, they should be people who know you well, have seen you in action in one guise or another, and are responsible, respected individuals themselves.

Finally, and to reiterate throughout this whole process, always, always grammar- and spellcheck everything that you submit.

Caution. Your social media presence

I was once told in the early days of social media that, if you post anything online, you should consider it acceptable only if you would be happy for your mother to read it aloud to you. If not, then consider whether you should post it at all. Many companies and organisations will carry out deep background checks before hiring, or aligning themselves, to individuals or groups. It makes sense to see whether your values, and theirs, are in harmony. A check on what you have posted on social media is often now a part of their due diligence and is almost as good for them as any personal reference. I would also encourage you to carry out the same checks for yourself on their interactions via these sites too, as this will help you to better understand them.

What you post is a direct reflection of you, your values and beliefs. Your game must be played for you, as I have said many times, but beware that what you may have said under your name may just come back as an "own goal", preventing you from progressing as you would wish. I have advised on self-regulation with the five-second rule in Chapter 15, and will continue to counsel against making an instant decision in any arena without thinking through the consequences on you, and on others, first.

You may, therefore, wish to carry out some "housekeeping", which means that this is a great opportunity to remove anything that could reflect badly on you. Never compromise yourself, but anything that is unnecessary and, perhaps written in the heat of the moment, should be considered for removal. It is your call.

Social media can be used very effectively as a force for good and, despite the negativity and fears that I have highlighted, there is much to celebrate about the way that communities and great causes have been brought together by the power that networking sites bring. Everyone's game of life on this planet has been impacted positively in some way and enriched by the knowledge, communication, connections and speed of transmission that the internet has delivered to us. The challenge that you face is to evolve and develop your game so that you harness this power and get the speed of it to work to your advantage on all fronts, whether they be for social or professional reasons. Never let your need to be "seen" on your social media profiles prevent you from your core life activities, though, as these platforms can be addictive. The key influencers on all sites will almost certainly have teams of people working for them to maintain their presence and following, as this is their business. It is a fine dividing line between you being seen and posting for the sake of posting.

Having gone through the process of submitting what is now a stellar CV and a covering letter/statement, you now have to wait for the phone call, email or communication to say that you have secured an interview. Some may feel that I am being controversial here, but always assume that you are going to get one and start preparing as soon as you have declared your interest in the post. You may be disappointed and get a rejection letter, or hear nothing, but by preparing immediately you are getting yourself into a routine and into a train of thought. This time will not be wasted as it will cross over into other roles that you apply for. Write down, record or capture in some way all of your thoughts as they come to you about the points that you want to make and how you will answer the questions that are asked. Carry a notebook or make notes on your phone or portable device. That way you never forget anything that may prove to be of use to you.

Having jumped the first hurdle, you now have to be as good in a face-to-face situation as you will have come across to the recruiter(s) in your submitted documentation. This is why the crafting of your application and accompanying letters must be as reflective of you as is possible. There is no point in claiming that you are an extrovert, and the life and soul of the party when you actually find situations where you are "on show" somewhat intimidating, forcing you reluctantly to come to the fore. It is very important to be true to yourself, and this means that you have not got to live up to a false image or persona that you may have created. If you do make statements that are not truly reflective of you, you then have to act up to this new character creation and this, in itself, puts you under more extreme pressure, making the risk of your game falling down that much greater. Be as close to the person that you really are, both on and off paper. Consistency will always be appreciated, and a skilled interviewer or recruiter will nearly always spot someone who is acting, at some point in the process.

Your interview. Part 2. Selling yourself as a candidate and telling your story

There comes a point in the game of life when you have to tell someone about yourself, usually a stranger, and get them to have so much confidence in you that they will give you some of their time. You have to sell yourself as a person, and interview situations are where, I believe, the greatest test lies. As I have suggested, you may be applying for a place at a school or a college, for a job or for a voluntary position. The list is endless, but unless you choose to be a hermit you will have to talk about yourself at some point in your life. This is a key moment in your game as it often determines the path you take and can shape your ultimate destiny. I cannot emphasise enough the importance of practice and rehearsal for this and, again, the earlier you start to do this in your life, the more that it becomes second nature.

I urge everyone reading this to please finish this chapter and then put down the book, or bookmark these pages and talk to those you know well and trust if you are developing your interview style. If you are a parent, guardian or mentor, then talk to those you support. If you are seeking help and support yourself, then talk to someone else. Seize the moment and seize the day. Ask questions that require more than a yes or no answer. Start with phrases like tell me, why, what, etc. These interactions need to be regular and become an almost daily habit as, then, it will be easier to hold a conversation with a purpose and to talk confidently about who you are as a person.

One of my biggest frustrations when conducting interviews, forums, panels is the inability of the person sat opposite me to talk openly and freely about themselves. As an interviewer I will have had a CV and a covering letter to hand, but when I ask the question "Tell me about yourself", it is almost as though I have sought an explanation for Einstein's theory of relativity. The worst reply that I ever had from someone seeking a role was "So wadda you wanna know?" This was followed by a shrug of the shoulders and a very sulky face. This was someone seeking a job that was to be public-facing as well!

Sometimes there will be a need for you to be able to tell your story before anyone has seen your CV, as you may be in a position where you suddenly meet someone who asks you about yourself. This happens so often, and many opportunities get lost as people are rarely prepared. You never know who you may meet and the chances that they could create or who they know. Never underestimate the power of a conversation and always be prepared.

One good starting point to learn how to tell your story centres around "the elevator pitch", which, legend has it, is named after the conversations that would take place in the old elevators of New York skyscrapers during the early decades of the twentieth century. As the occupants made their slow and lengthy trips to the upper floors, sometimes they would make a sales pitch to other people travelling with them in the lift. The journey could take two or three minutes, hence the name "elevator pitch". There are other versions of how the name originated, but this is my favourite.

For some people, there is a need to write your "elevator pitch" in full and you will have already done this, to some extent, with your CV. Not everyone can articulate easily off the top of their head, and almost need to learn it like a script. That's ok, but make sure you do learn it. Have bullet points or trigger words written down on a prompt card, if that helps you, but practise, practise, practise. Use a mirror to talk into, a friend to listen and to be a sounding board. Record what you say and keep fine-tuning it. Eventually it will become second nature and, as your life progresses, you can adapt and develop it. Be patient, as you will find a style that suits you, so long as you keep working on it and keep it alive in your head. This applies no matter what age you are and, to labour the point, make sure that you regularly talk it through with other people who you know and trust.

When preparing, you may find it useful to have your list of adjectives to hand from when you crafted your CV. If you can tailor these to be specifically about you, this will help you to make your description of you much more accurate, relevant and appropriate.

So, just as for the salespeople with the elevator trips between floors in North America, have a version that is around two minutes long as a maximum, but ideally it should be just over a minute. People can lose interest and their attention can wander after this time. Speak at a normal pace, don't rush, and remember to breathe. All too often the temptation is to try to get the words out as quickly as possible. Consider also the person who is receiving this information. If you speak very quickly, they will miss so much of your vital and critical information and you will also come across as nervous and lacking in confidence. Again, this is why practice is so important and why your delivery should be consistent with your CV letter/statement, and all of your other supporting evidence.

Your interview. Part 3. The importance of your body language and other important non-verbal considerations

As you develop your style of talking about and presenting who you are as a person, there are several other things happening at the same time that you have to consciously be aware of. The first of these is your body language and non-verbal communication. The signals that we send to others help them to make a very unconscious assessment of you, and to "read" you as a person.

This is a science all of its own and, at this stage, I will keep the details limited and very basic regarding what you need to consider for an interview or a meeting.

Your dress and impact

Returning to the message of "first impressions", remember, what people see and experience of you in those first few moments of interaction is defining. It is a moment of truth and how you dress, your physical presentation, your stance and your delivery are all crucial in making the impression that you want. It therefore comes down to a question of how do you represent yourself?

It is always worth checking with anyone interviewing you what the dress code is. If it is formal, then for a man that would mean a suit and a tie. For a woman, something suitably similar. For anyone who identifies in another way, then ask the question and above all else make sure that you are comfortable.

Blue, in formal situations, is always a good colour to wear first time around, as that can imprint on people's minds safety, confidence and security, akin to how people in certain professions that carry some authority dress, like a policeman, for example.

Avoid, if you can, something that would be seen as being loud, unless the role you are seeking requires it. Remember that you are trying here to make a good, confident impression and not seeking to create doubt and conflict in the minds of those you meet. The time for being more outrageous will come once you have secured the position, if that is how you wish to be.

If the instruction is for "informal", in other words to dress how you wish, then my advice would be always to err on the side of caution and to be smart. For me that would mean wearing a jacket, a long-sleeved shirt or blouse (not a T-shirt or polo shirt) or something that would be seen as reflective of you. Casual jeans or trainers would be inappropriate here unless you were specifically told to wear them.

Polish your shoes. Attention to detail, as I am outlining in every section, is crucial to your game. The act of polishing your shoes is one of those small things that is easily missed, yet can tell a person so much about you and your approach. It takes thirty seconds and can often cost nothing besides a rub with a cloth and a quick spray of polish. Yes, it can be old-fashioned, but what have you got to lose by making your shoes look good? Absolutely nothing and everything to gain as they make you look good too. Make a habit of it too, as it is noticed by people.

A good tip here is that if in future you are based in an office and wearing a suit, it is more common now for a tie or a scarf not to be worn. Keep one in your pocket and available at all times, ensuring that it matches your shirt/blouse. Cover your bases. Leave nothing to chance. You never know when someone may wish to see you or you may suddenly be called into a meeting, and strict formal attire is needed.

For those garlic lovers, or spicy food aficionados among you, please make sure that you have some mints available, or have taken precautions not to overpower your interviewer with your breath. It is a very personal call but again be aware of the impact. This can be very off-putting, in some instances, and I hope that those on the other side of the table show the same consideration for you here too. The same also applies to excessive use and application of aftershave or perfume.

If you are on a tight budget and need clothes to be dry cleaned, then some companies will provide free cleaning for interviews. There are also social enterprises and community-based organisations across the world that can assist with recycled clothing, in the form of business attire, so the need to look the part should be within everyone's grasp.

Your handshake

Most of us will have had, at some time, that awkward moment when you meet a person for the first time and think, "Do we shake hands? How should I make the grip?" This is another moment of truth and, strange as it may seem, one for you to again practise in advance so that it becomes second nature and not left to chance. It is part of your first impression and cannot be ignored. If you are unused to shaking hands, then why risk everything without practising on a friend or relation?

Many people will still see a handshake as a gesture of friendship and good faith. In olden times it was to show that you had no concealed weapons in your hand, and were of good intent. And that, to some extent, is still true today. If your handshake is extremely weak, then it can be viewed as a sign of weakness. Grip too strong, with a vice-like squeeze, and it can be seen as assertive, aggressive and dominant. The same is true of holding on for too long.

My tip here would be, on a first meeting where you are the invited guest, to allow the person hosting you to make the first move and they will take the lead. You grasp their hand to match yours. Display a warm genuine smile, make eye contact, say a few words like "nice to meet you" and nod your head a couple of times. If you do this all at the same time it helps to create the atmosphere and air of positivity. Make sure that you let go with a smooth release, after a couple of gentle up and down movements. Don't pump the arm, either, like you are drawing water from a well.

Moving in for a kiss, a hug or embrace, by pulling someone towards you, is a far too full-on approach. I heard a story of a man who was so taken with a famous client he was meeting that, as he shook her hand and, feeling as though he knew her well from her time on television, he pulled her in for a peck on the cheek. Totally surprised, she recoiled backwards, and he was left pursing his lips for a mid-air type of cheek kiss that was very wide off the mark he was aiming for. He realised his mistake, mumbled an apology and then, instead of having the scheduled hour and a half for the meeting, the conversation only lasted twenty minutes. Even worse, her husband was present and was somewhat offended by this display of inappropriate unrequited affection, making his feelings very clear and well known both during the meeting, and then afterwards with a letter of complaint.

Also be careful of the over-enthusiastic "high five"-style grasp and holding on with a magnetic-like attraction. This can be as off-putting for the receiver as a weak low impact introduction. It is also unprofessional and overly familiar, unless you know the person well. Even then it is frowned on in a formal business type of environment.

I would also counsel against the weak and "wet" cling of the fingers. This is only reserved for a meeting with Her Majesty the Queen, in my opinion. If you have sweaty hands, then try to keep them dry, but for interviews most people will allow some latitude for nervousness.

I once had a client who had a bad skin condition and he emailed me beforehand to forewarn me that he wouldn't be shaking hands. We had never met face to face and his concern at my potential embarrassment was really appreciated and actually a good ice breaker to our discussion. Never be afraid to disclose this, or anything else that could be a concern for you if it applies to you.

Coronavirus may well change some aspects of physical contact as we see fist, arm, knee and foot bumps as acceptable in the short term. What the long term holds is not clear but, as a handshake has been with us for centuries, I suspect little will change in time.

The handshake is so important as part of the unconscious inner game that is at play with all parties, so practise, practise, practise.

How you walk and sit

Another important part of your demeanour to consider is how you walk and also how you sit.

If you naturally lean forwards as you walk, then this can mean that you walk with a form of a stoop, and that often indicates to anyone looking at you that you lack confidence. It also signals a disinterest and can also be seen as arrogance. You may be very engaged, and it may be the way that you naturally present yourself, but the unconscious messages that you are sending out indicates the exact opposite. Unless there is a medical condition that prevents you from walking with your shoulders back and your head held high, then try to walk as upright as possible. Learn from watching others, particularly people from a military background or those on the world's political stages.

How you sit is also another aspect to this. When you are "on show" and in an interview situation, as you are offered a seat (wait until you are offered a seat; never assume one will be offered to you), if the chair is an office type of chair that swivels, then you will have to sit upright. Make yourself comfortable and grounded by pushing yourself with your arms, by grasping either the base of the chair or the armrests, to the very back of the chair as you sit. Place your feet apart, parallel to your shoulders, and planted firmly in front of you, with your knees properly bent at ninety degrees. It may feel unnatural, so again practise. The signal that you are giving here is that you are confident, in control of yourself and trustworthy. Please resist the temptation to keep twisting, if the seat has this capability, as that sends so many wrong messages to your host. If you are in a more comfortable style of chair, like an armchair, then try to sit as upright as you can and remain so. This will feel unnatural and uncomfortable, but it will prevent you from relaxing and dropping your guard.

I am going to keep reiterating the need to practise. You are playing a game within a much larger game here. Your future could depend on it and these parts, which may seem insignificant, when all added together form a large percentage of the unconscious assessment that is being made about you.

Your hands

Be very aware of your hands, especially if you are expressive and someone who "talks" with them a lot. This is very challenging for people who use their hands to emphasise key phrases, and to assist with their own message delivery. If you ever watch newsreaders on television, they have to keep their hands below the camera, as otherwise they could be waving them about, and we would lose the thread of the news story by the distraction that they create.

My advice here again is to be yourself, but watch out for any "windmill"-like actions, which can be overpowering and distracting for the person who is listening to your story. If necessary, hold a folder lightly or a notebook in front of you, and consciously keep holding it, as this will ensure you do not gesticulate with your hands. You will, and should, let go of anything you are holding but not too often, and then only to emphasise a point. Practise again as part of your storytelling. If you are uncomfortable with this particular method, then just be aware of your hand gestures and keep them to a minimum.

Beware too of the aggressive "pen point". Holding a pen can be a useful prop to prevent you being overly "talkative" with your hands, but, if you seek to emphasise something that you are saying, the temptation can be to use the pen like some sort of a magic wand. It can appear to the receiver as an aggressive gesture and, again, as part of the unconscious inner game, can be off-putting.

Mirror, mirror

Mirroring is something that we also do unconsciously, but when used in full consciousness it can be incredibly powerful.

If for example, when you are sitting, and the person opposite you leans forward and you lean forward towards them at the same time, this is called "mirroring". You are copying them. It is often seen as a compliment, and also a sign that you both are fully engaged in each other's company. You will pick up these signals subconsciously but only when you are aware of the impact it has will you do so consciously.

This scenario is often played out when someone sitting

opposite you says "Look at this with me" or "I'd like to you to see this". They are encouraging and inviting you to mirror them by moving in, as they share the information with you on paper or on screen, for example. If you observe the person opposite to you leaning back, it can show that they are not interested or have gained as much information from you as they need at that time. You will find that you will naturally lean back too. Just ask a clarification question of them at this time to ensure they have seen what they need and have the amount of information necessary. "Do you have any other questions on this?" or similar wording may be appropriate. Do not be put off when the mirroring breaks, as it may be that you have secured their interest and they have absorbed all of what they needed to from you.

I am not going to go into more detail here as it can create more complexity in an area where I am giving you a considerable amount to act and work on. However, being conscious that leaning in and encouraging people to do this with you (mirroring your approach by, say, sharing a presentation or a document of sorts to look at) can give you an advantage, as this captures those you seek to influence at very close quarters.

Your pace, tone and choice of language

As you develop your all-round package of presentation, it is worth spending some time on exactly how you talk and present yourself verbally before you embark on any external discussions.

The tone of your voice is very important. Too much variation in pitch and you can find that you almost sing your answers. Too little, and you sound very boring and monotone. I have already encouraged you, with the elevator pitch, to record yourself giving your answers as you practise and to listen back. Most of us dislike hearing the sound of our own voices, but this is a pain barrier that you must go through, as you really do feel the impact of what you say and how you say it.

As you practise, please be aware of using phrases and words such as "You know what I mean", "You know" and anything else that can sound, frankly, lazy and just said to fill the noise as you search in your mind for the next thing to say. If you use these types of phrases a lot, then try to use this as a chance to breathe rather than speak. A pause can be more powerful and effective. Less really can be more.

If you do have real concerns with your voice, and this may be from a variety of standpoints including being shy or nervous, having a speech impediment, your accent, or simply struggling to formulate your words, then I would recommend finding a coach. It will be money well invested. If affordability is an issue, then find some free online courses that can help. Either way, do something to invest in you and to help you. This may be the extra one per cent that gets you to your next destination in the game.

Finally, please consider the pace with which you speak and deliver. Your message can be lost if you speak too quickly, and you can be seen as being laboured and lacking in confidence if your delivery is too slow. Breathing is essential and talk as normally as you possibly can without rushing. Give yourself a pause before you speak and take a breath without it being a gulp or an audible intake of air. Again, it is practice, and hearing yourself speak from a recording will show you whether this is an issue for you or not. It is natural to speed up in pressure situations, but try to keep a tight rein on how fast you go.

The danger of drinks and of your shaky hands

It is a welcoming, ice-breaking moment at an interview when, usually as you enter the room, you are offered a drink. Tea or coffee are the usual beverages to be suggested, as a hot drink can be viewed as necessary for sustenance. Always ask for water, though, and never take a hot drink, is my advice for the following reason.

A hot drink can be dangerous to you and your game. It is

an unnecessary risk that you do not need to take. Many years ago I met a candidate for a role who, on being offered a drink, asked for a coffee. My colleague, who was supporting me with the interview, made it from the machine that we had in the room and handed it to her. She immediately put the cup to her mouth, suddenly realising too late that it was still boiling hot, and burnt her bottom lip, which instantly started to swell. She then proceeded to dribble, almost uncontrollably, and became extremely nervous, self-consciously dabbing at her mouth with a tissue that I provided. Note that she didn't have one with her. Another tip here, just in case you need one, have one available. She was unable to give her best and failed to secure my confidence that she would be a good candidate. It was a mistake that she made and one that I am sure she learned from.

Always have water in front of you that you can sip in case your mouth dries, or that you can take a drink from to buy a few seconds of thinking time for an answer. Taking a sip, not a gulp, can really help to settle you. Again, studying those being interviewed in the glare of the media spotlight will show that they always have water to hand in case their mouth goes dry, or they need to buy thinking time. Sometimes just grasping the glass can give you confidence.

Beware, though, of shaky hands. This is a time when you are extremely tense and on edge. Some people (I am one of them) have naturally shaky hands, and holding or nursing the glass or tumbler can again be off-putting for both the candidate and the interviewer. There is also a danger of spillage and this is not good for your confidence, or for the progress of the interaction.

And now it is the time for "the small talk dance". Take your partners, please

At the start of interviews, or indeed any interaction, both parties begin to weigh each other up using the awareness of first impressions, body language and verbalisation. This is when what

I call "the small talk dance" takes place. You've been selected as a partner, and are walking towards the dance floor. Do you know how to dance and do you know what the dance is? Hopefully you are learning as we progress through these sections, but you can't learn to dance without trying it out first.

The lead, in this case, is your interviewer or host. For those of you who have studied dance, or like me, have regularly watched *Strictly Come Dancing* (*Dancing with the Stars* in the USA), you will know that one person seemingly directs or leads their partner around the floor on occasions.

The first step is the opening question asked of you. The more nervous interviewers may ask, "Did you get here ok?" or "Did you find us ok?" Well, obviously you did and you haven't broken any limbs or become lost as you wouldn't be here otherwise. (Top tip: do your homework on the geography and how long it does take to get there. Leave nothing to chance. Get an earlier train, bus, etc.) Just make sure that you have a few polite answers to hand. Again, this is a chance to talk about you in a positive light, so the answer would be that you left early just to be on the safe side and had already tested your route beforehand.

There are so many different ways this dance could go that it is impossible to cover them all. Some may dispense with the small talk all together and just get down to business, and that is again worth preparing for making sure that you are sharp and ready. It is all a test and all a game in itself within the game.

The best advice for small talk that I can give is to say nothing controversial, political or religious and, from one experience that I had as an interviewee, avoid declaring a liking for a sports team. I revealed my allegiance to a certain football club at the start of an interview during the small talk dance, only to find out later that the interviewer hated my club to such an extent that he would never have appointed me to the role. I danced the wrong dance and figuratively stepped onto his toes. Perhaps if I had done my research first and full due diligence then I would have been ahead of this.

What do you take with you, or have available, for any interview or meeting?

Always submit your application on the best-quality paper that you can afford and have printed copies of your CV available, together with your covering letter, application and the job specification. Add to that your certificates, supporting documentation, such as a portfolio of work, any relevant newspapers, online articles and reference material that features you or that you have contributed towards. Assemble a career folder, and have several dividers for each section. This shows to the interviewer that you are prepared, well organised, that you take your development very seriously, respecting the process. It also helps you if you need to refer to anything as the documents are easily accessible and in order. You will have prepared most of these for your initial application, as I mentioned under the "Covering Letter" section. Needless to say, this can also be held on a portable device. Make sure that you reference why you have this and what is on it.

These may seem like little things, but when put together they will give you a competitive advantage as you enter the room. It shows preparedness and full attention to detail. It also gives you something to hold onto for support, and to refer back to if needed, giving you credibility and added confidence. Never turn up empty-handed, as that indicates a distinct lack of interest, preparation and respect for the process. Again, keep in mind the first impression you give.

Finally, practise, practise, practise. If you were a sportsman, an actor or developing a new talent or skill, you would practise. This whole scenario is no different and, to a large degree, is actually even more important. Make all of these good natural habits and embed them into your consciousness so that they are second nature. They then become hard to break, and you are then freeing up your brain to work on all of the other areas that you face and that are coming into play within the game.

As you now know, the purpose of an interview is to determine whether you have the qualities, skills, personality and all-round capability to fill the post or vacancy that the recruiting company or organisation require. This applies no matter what role you seek, from a school prefect through to a global CEO. The objective is always the same.

Having gone through all of the preparation that I have covered so far, you will then be asked a series of questions, which can start with a summary of you and your own back story.

The heart of the interview is then around your abilities and capabilities to potentially deliver for them. Often, you will be asked to talk around scenarios, or situations, that you have covered in your life, and career to date. No matter what age you are, you will have had situations to deal with. These are valuable life experiences, and turning these into positive examples that can sell you and making your own offering a compelling one to another person, is where you will likely secure the role, or not.

When asked about something that you have done, it will often be presented by way of a competency question. This starts with the phrase "Tell me about a time when you…" or "Tell me how/what you have…" This is when you can tell a story around subjects like: leadership; excellence; attention to detail; teamwork; challenging situations; achievements; coping with change; making change happen; making good decisions; demonstrating trust; sales performance; customer service. The list really is an endless one, but these are great headings to start to list your examples. They should also cover most scenarios you will be faced with anyway. Many questions and competencies will cross over, and that is normal. You may well have covered more competencies with one example. Just make sure that you have a good bank of answers ready to be used.

You may be advised of the competencies or situations

beforehand, and this is even better for getting your best examples ready for each heading that you are given.

The formula below will give you a structure for both preparing your competencies and being situationally aware. Stick to this format and the interviewer will see that you have a methodical way of thinking in applying your examples to their questions. It will make their note-taking and assessment of you so much easier, together with their understanding of the story that you are telling.

All good stories have an introduction, a middle or body, and an ending. Your competency answers are no different to any other tale. It just gives it clarity and structure in a more defined way. It is easy to remember as it has an acronym that I have created to help you. It is called **ROWER** which stands for: Replay, Outcome (desired), What you did, Ending, Reflection.

The Replay is the situation that you were faced with at that moment in time. This must include setting the scene for the listener. Describe this in detail, with every relevant fact. Where you were, who was involved, what was the time, how you arrived at this point. List everything that paints the picture as clearly and concisely as possible for the listener.

The Outcome that you desired, including goals that you were seeking. This should be described in one or two sentences, no more than that, and start with the words, "The outcome or goal that I desired was…" Be as specific and concise as you can.

List What you did and the activities that you undertook to achieve the outcome. You should have up to a maximum of ten and again, all of them limited to two sentences each. If you are recalling these from memory, use your fingers to count. Use of the word "I" is very important here – I did, I led, I initiated, I started, I undertook, etc. Assume nothing, listing even the most basic of your actions. It is part of the story as the interviewer may be unfamiliar with your scenario.

The End and actual outcome. Again, this should be clear and start with the sentence "At the end…" You can keep this to around three sentences maximum, making each one a specific achievement and result.

The Reflection is your honest assessment of the process that you have just described. It starts with "And so, reflecting on this, I..." This builds a form of reflection and is something that few people do in interviews. It is a form of conversation with yourself about what exactly happened. Usually the questions that follow from an interviewer after the ending would be, "Would you do anything differently?" "What challenges or opposition did you face?" or "Is there anything that you would change?" By adding this, you are already covering their immediate questions. It is important that you use this for both scenario- and competency-based examples, even more so the latter.

Be honest and share some challenges. If you had the desired outcome and there were no changes that you would make, then say exactly that. Be clear that you wouldn't change anything. However, it is always worth showing some honesty and humility in your reflections, by adding that you may have adjusted or changed slightly one area to give an even better outcome. "If I were to do this again I may adjust/change..." etc.

Always invite questions if there is a silence, and do not be put off by this silence either, as usually the assessor is finishing making their notes and trying to understand fully what you have told them. It is also invariably a good sign that your story has gone well.

Make sure, as I have said, that you have a number of examples to hand for each competency and play your best example to suit the best question.

If you are asked a question, or for an example that does give you cause for thought, then ask for a moment's reflection, take a drink of water, buy some time, consult your notes and then answer. Don't just say the first answer that comes into your head unless you are one hundred per cent certain it is right. Reflection will always be seen as a positive. "I'm glad you asked me that" is always a nice start to the answer and then, to develop your train of thought, initially repeating what has been asked of you. It all buys you more thinking time.

Also, never be afraid to give another example if you feel your first wasn't your strongest, or even stop yourself mid-way and ask to give another one. Some may see this as uncertainty but I view it as maturity, an ability to think on your feet and strong personal awareness.

Your interview. Part 5. Other questions to consider

After the competencies have finished, there can be some direct quick-fire questions from the interviewer or the panel, just to keep you on your toes and to see how you react under some further pressure. Some interviewers may start the interview with these, so prepare for anything. Where will you be in five years' time? What would your best friend say about you? Who is your role model? What is your greatest achievement? There are so many that can be asked.

Consider also turning a possible weakness into a strength. This is a real game changer and can work so well in your favour if you get it right. Some may ask "What is your weakness?" or, more likely, "If you could change one thing about yourself, what would it be?" The key with answering this question is to be honest and sincere, but frame your answer so that it can appear to be a development area that you are actively working on, aiming to make it a strength. It should also never be presented as a negative to the interviewer, giving them the excuse to remove you from the process. You want to give them certainty in their choice. For example, you could say that you are too willing to take on everything, or too eager to please. These are fine attributes and ones that people will warm to if you can naturally show how you are looking to make them stronger.

I would also recommend you to be totally honest about your strengths and your achievements, without appearing self-centred and arrogant or, on the other hand, too self-deprecating. Be bold and clear that you see your strengths as 1, 2, 3, etc…

Make sure that these fit the brief of the role or position that you seek, and be prepared to back up with brief factual examples if asked. These may have been part of your scenarios that you discussed earlier, but state them as concisely as you can.

Your interview. Part 6. RTFQ. Read the full (or f***ing) question, and advice for presentations

I was once asked to do a presentation, after a lengthy interview, for a role that was to be a significant promotion. I had made it to the final two people and was the odds-on favourite to get the job. The post involved a house move to another part of the country, and I was so confident (beware of the overconfidence demon as it awaits to catch you off guard) that I would get it, I had even started to look at houses in the area from the local newspapers. This was before the internet, so you know how long ago it was. I had worked so hard to get to the final round and my interview, I knew, had gone really well. I was in a great place, brimming with confidence. In hindsight, I now know that I was far too confident, bordering on arrogant.

I had the briefing in front of me for the presentation and had fifteen minutes to prepare. I did some flip charts with colour, to demonstrate the points that I was making, and also had some facts that I knew additionally supported the business case further.

I presented for twenty minutes, and at the end breathed a huge sigh of relief and invited questions from the three-person panel. They looked at each other, nodded and I thought that I had nailed it. The person leading the selection team then thanked me for my presentation, for my time and for my clearly demonstrated and obvious expertise. He said that I had all of the qualities they were looking for in this presentation, but they all had one outstanding question in their minds, and they were agreed unanimously on this. He then asked me to read aloud the briefing for the presentation. I looked at the paper that I had been given and started to read. It was at this moment that several expletives went through my head and, cartoon like, I think that my eyes left their sockets bouncing backwards and forwards off the paper in front of me. They had been very generous and very polite in allowing me to finish but, in that moment, I realised that I had monumentally screwed up by not reading the full or, in this case as I have referred to since, the f***ing question.

"I can see from your face that you know your mistake, Andrew" were his words as I mumbled some form of apology and then tried to justify why I had presented as I had. It got worse, as my verbal spade was working overtime as I frantically dug a deeper hole for myself with the panel. Within two minutes I had lost this part of the game that I had worked so hard for, for so long. I had lost my place, my chance, some of my reputation and also my confidence. The panel were no longer advocates but had become detractors. I had slid down a snake of my own making.

The journey home down the motorway was a torturous one lasting well over three hours, with traffic jams, roadworks and accidents causing long delays. I am glad that I was alone, as I took out my frustration by beating on the steering wheel and occasionally shouting obscenities to myself. I think it took me several months to come to terms with my own shortcomings from that day, and by then I had gone so far backwards in the pecking order that the next few years were a struggle to get back to having an opportunity at a role like this again.

In a place of some self-torturing reflection, the one that is occupied only by regrets, I know exactly where I went wrong. I was far too confident and far too arrogant. Life decided that I was not ready for the added responsibility and I know now that life was right. This is a hard admission, but you must be honest with yourself in hindsight, as you will never learn from your mistakes otherwise.

A good presentation will always be like reading the news. Tell them what you are going to tell them (the headlines). Tell them (the body and detail of your presentation) and finally tell them what you've told them (the headlines again but more as a summary).

Avoid giving so much written detail on slides or pages that you simply regurgitate what people are reading for themselves, and try not to present a massive number of slides. Use visuals for effect and keep it simple. Make sure that you don't just look at the screen, or pages, and that you maintain a good pace and look ahead of you, making brief eye contact regularly within your audience. Good, clear lengthy notes or prompts for you to refer to must remain unseen by your audience, and practise, practise, practise. Do it standing up, if you are able, so that you know the delivery will be clear.

Always invite questions at the end, making sure that the person asking the question is happy with your answer, and has enough information from you.

Where possible, if you have prepared this beforehand, provide copies for the attendees at the end and never before, as people will naturally thumb through to see what is ahead. Give a web link too and a one-page summary of everything if you feel it is appropriate.

My final advice here is never to forget, and every time that you have a brief or a scenario to work on, RTFQ! Read the "full" question!

Your interview. Part 7. Killer questions for you to ask. Knowledge is power

Ahh, the end is in sight and your inner sigh of relief is evident. The interviewer or panel tell you that you have reached the end of their processes and ask you if you have any questions for them. You blow out your cheeks, shuffle in your seat and start to relax. DO NOT RELAX! You are still in the interview, playing the game and being assessed. You now have your chance to take them totally into your game, and finally stop playing theirs. This is where you can really win by demonstrating your advanced knowledge and research, to give them some added reassurance that you are the very best candidate. You can even use this to make up some ground if you feel that you have given a weaker answer to one of their questions.

One golden rule here is to not discuss pay or packages unless they do so. That is for another time and another place, in my opinion. Your purpose and mission here is to secure the role or the post. Pay and contractual terms are a fence for you to jump further down the line, if they are to be negotiated.

I have already recommended from the outset the importance of researching the organisation or group that you are applying to. Once you are at an interview (and just to drive this home), you can bring your research to the fore by asking questions about the culture, the team, the company or organisation. Look at its history, its values, ethos, beliefs, what the expectations of you will be and what support they give to your continuous professional and personal development. These are all good lines to progress as you can quote from websites, papers, case studies, LinkedIn, etc.: examples that will amplify your words. It shows that you are not only self-sufficient but that you also have the intelligence, initiative and inner drive to do it. It also further evidences that you are interested and prepared. Knowledge will give you power and confidence, no matter what level of role you are going for and no matter what side the business is.

You may well be surprised that I am having to state, what to many, will be the obvious. Well, don't be, as so many people just turn up to interviews unprepared, believing that in some way they can "wing it". Why on earth go to the trouble and waste everyone's time if you cannot take your own time to research? You will be found out if you fail to do this, so put in the work of knowing the very people who you seek to collaborate with.

If you have yet to cover this during your discussions, then

this is the time to bring out any opportunities that showcase how you could assist and contribute with their commitment to the community. Many companies and organisations will have a responsible approach to society, sometimes referred to as CSR (corporate social responsibility). Stating that you would like to know more about their involvement, support and activities in this area and how they involve colleagues will be music to any recruiter's ears, giving you a massive advantage. For younger people, this is definitely the time to talk about your Duke of Edinburgh Award, or any other such involvement in citizenship, if it has yet to be raised. For anyone of any age, anything else that you can refer to here that adds to your self-development and personal value is well worth bringing out.

Be aware, too, of any current hot topics that may be an issue for them as an organisation. "What keeps you awake at night regarding the business?" is a brave question to ask of any CEO or recruiting manager. However, if you feel confident, then ask it and be prepared for the question back such as, "What would you think it is?" This is a massive card to play if the audience, and the time, is right and you have some idea of where to take the answer. It really would be a positive differentiator.

Ask no more than three questions, and make them count so that you can clearly showcase your preparatory work. It shows the interest you have, your commitment and, again, gets buy-in from those you are seeking to influence. They get to play your game and that takes the interview into your strength areas.

A final consideration would be to ask the person or panel for their stories as to how they have achieved their places in life, or in the company/organisation. This is great learning here for you from them. Not everyone will be open and receptive to this, but you may get a précis of a story as, let's be honest, people like nothing better at times than talking about themselves. Be aware of the time and check that you are not exceeding your allowance, knowing that the interviewer or panel will always overrun for the right person.

Your interview. Part 8. So what if it is a telephone or a virtual interview?

There is no need to reinvent the wheel with this. Do exactly the same preparation as we have already looked at for face-to-face situations. The difference here is in the practice that you do, and that is for you to become used to a virtual environment, or even one where you have no screen, just a voice talking to you. Use a friend or trusted associate to help, and give them the script of what you want them to ask you. If you can (and know someone who has been through this process or has experience), ask for advice and assistance from them, as I can give you the theory but there is nothing to beat "real time" knowledge too. Recruitment agencies are very good at this and it is in their interest, after all, to get the very best candidate into roles as this is how they make money. There is also a lot on the web and on various forums.

The challenge for telephone interviews, and meetings, is that you have no visual signals that you can read from the interviewer as to how they are reacting. Hence the need for you to practise even more.

For any professional phone interviews or meetings, I would always recommend that, if you can you stand up, have the phone on speaker or use a headset, freeing up your hands. The temptation with a phone is to lower your head and talk down towards the ground. You will lose impact with your tone of voice that way, so always stand up and project yourself, if you are physically able. Your hands can then move as freely as they want.

In order to allow you to be as expressive as you can and to keep your brain as free as possible, have visual prompts on a wall. For example, key points from your application and CV, questions you wish to ask, etc. Use a large sheet or sheets of paper (flip chart, ideally) and tape them to a wall in front of you, or above eye level. If you have a complete room, then use all of the space and have everything 360 degrees around you. Know where everything is, use coloured marker pens so the words stand out, and make this as effective as possible.

For virtual interviews (e.g. Zoom, Teams etc.), ensure that you have set the room up to be as user friendly for you as is possible. The area that is visible on screen behind you should be a blank canvas. Even a blurred background can create an impression. Have no messy shelves, controversial posters or visible indications that you are anything but well presented. Remember that the interviewer will not see anything that is out of camera shot so, as I have suggested in the last paragraph, use the wall space for your own prompts. Make your environment work for you.

Be smart and representative of you. What is on show, whether it is you or your surroundings, should not raise any concerns or questions in the mind of the other person.

Check that there will be no interruptions. One student once told me that, during a virtual interview he was undertaking from his bedroom, his mom came in with a glass of water and a snack, thinking he was talking to his friends. She even said hello to the person on the other end.

For anyone with a disability, whether it be physical or sensory, I would say all of the above still applies. Your disability is your strength, and please look at it this way. Please show and present the advantages that you bring with you, not focussing on any areas that you may perceive as a challenge. The person interviewing you may, and should, not have any preconceptions. Prepare for everything as I have described as, whilst some allowance will be made for you, the playing-field overall should be level and even.

Your interview. Part 9. Panels and tests

Your first interview may just be the start of a process so be prepared for several stages of selection. These can include various aptitude tests, group discussions, additional interviews, and anything else that the hirers wish to throw at you. Sometimes it is a test of endurance and whether you have the desire and energy to see this through. Always go as far as you can until they eventually say yes or no to you. It may feel like you are running a marathon, and you may not always be selected, but the experience and learning that you gain from competing at this level will always give you an advantage for your next application elsewhere.

For any other panels and tests that you have to face, my advice is, as always, to be as honest as you can. Questions for psychometric testing, for example, come quickly with, say, one hundred multiple choice questions to answer in three minutes. You have to give the first answer that comes into your head and within this time frame too, which means that you cannot cheat the system. The questions repeat themselves, but with different styles of wording, and this is done so that you can show your consistency of thought. It also demonstrates your ability to make good decisions under pressure, as there will be scenarios offered for consideration too. It is well worth practising these.

One activity that does count massively, and is akin to a gladiatorial contest, is the group discussion. Feared by many and loved by few, it is an hour or so of a round table unnatural conversation, facilitated by one of the selection team with the candidates who are applying for the position. The subject offered for debate will often be relevant to the role and very wide ranging. This is where you see your competition up close and personal, and you effectively take them on in verbal combat, without in any way being seen to harm them. It is brutal and one that you must prepare for, including watching scenarios that are available online.

Here are my golden rules for this activity, as organisations will often look for a certain type of individual:

Be polite and respectful to everyone, and do not try to stare out or intimidate others. Every aspect of your performance will be analysed, sometimes by hidden observers.

Concentrate on you, your tone of voice, your body language, and be relaxed. Do not finger point or aggressively gesture with your pen, no matter how passionately you feel about the subject.

Avoid being controversial and try not to let your personal feelings boil over.

Listen closely to the facilitator, and write down the question posed or subject for discussion, so that it is in front of you. This reduces your brain work, ensuring that you will always stay on topic when others may digress.

The first of the candidates to voluntarily speak invariably loses. They often jump in, keen to get their viewpoint across without thinking through their argument and its consequences.

The second one to speak often wins. This is done by acknowledging the contribution of the first person to the debate and appreciating their viewpoint. You then ensure that your points are expressed clearly and correctly opening up additional debate by the group. You effectively lead and steer the discussion from then on, becoming something of the focal point. You maintain careful control by making sure this isn't your only contribution and that people refer back to you. If they don't, then politely interject and steer the emphasis back.

Avoid conflict, but be prepared to disagree. This is healthy but, again, do it with dignity and respect for yourself and everyone else.

The third one to speak can also win, but it is now more difficult. If this is where you enter the debate, you then have to take over from number two and outmanoeuvre them.

Also, if you are after number three, then you are often introduced by the facilitator, who asks for your contribution. This means that they want to know what you have to say, but you have not demonstrated sufficient strength to force your way through. Be sure that you have real control, if this is the case, as it is very difficult to win from here.

At the end of this discussion, make sure that you thank the facilitator and carry on the conversation with the person who you believe is your greatest challenger. You are always on show and nothing is missed by those observing. Exiting the room is always a good way to take a continued lead here as everyone else relaxes and recovers.

Do not be too downbeat if you come into the discussion later on, as this will only be one exercise of many. However, be aware that this one is crucial for you to show your confidence to get your points across, to participate in a healthy debate, and also to be consistent with your approach.

Your interview. Part 10. The informal coffee chat

So let's quash the myth once and for all. There really is no such thing as an informal chat. If you are invited to one under these circumstances, the likelihood is that you are seriously being considered for a post or position and someone just wants to check out how comfortable they are with you in a less formal setting. It may be that you see an independent person to the recruiter, and it is a process to try and elicit how you react under less stressful conditions. It is often called informal, or just a chat, but do not ever let these titles fool you. This is as important to your selection process as anything else to date, so put in the hard yards and prepare, prepare, prepare. Always check the dress code again and revert back to the sections above, particularly the one that helps you to tell your story. Make sure, as well, that you have continued with your research and that it is very current and fresh. Be aware too of hot drinks, as I have advised previously.

Your interview. Part 11. Feedback, and coping with the outcome

No matter what the outcome is of this intensive process that you have just gone through, you should always ensure that you get feedback from one of the team that you have met. It is a chance to replay the interview and other tasks for you and to see what went well. It is also an opportunity to learn what could have gone better, from their viewpoint. This is invaluable to your game as you can then apply, adapt and improve for the future as, whether you have attained the position or not on this occasion, there will be other times in the future when you will be applying or going through this process in one guise or another.

If you have been successful, then this is a great time to start to talk contracts, terms of employment and remuneration, if you have yet to do so. You should already have an idea about what is on offer, as you would not be applying otherwise, so be prepared to negotiate. For some, this discussion may have already taken place, as companies can be very upfront. Tread very carefully until you have the upper hand. For those where this may be your first time in employment, remember that you have much to lose. Ask the question in the form of you seeking advice such as, "I have never been through this process before, so can you help me with understanding what is on offer?" is a great starting point if you wish.

I did hear one story of a London trader who was in such high demand that a company, to secure his services, asked what it would take to ensure that he worked for them. And so, every morning he went to work by private motorboat across the Thames, avoiding the walk across the streets and bridges of London. This is an extreme example, but the moral here is to know your worth.

Very few situations will be like this, and many companies do have set pay grades and structures, but look beyond the immediate pay too. Do they provide additional benefit packages that include: discounted membership schemes, healthcare, pension enhancements, travel and other incentives? You may find that there is "movement" on the numbers, but be cautious and know where the dividing line lies between asking a question and then losing your advantage by being unrealistic and cheeky.

Unless you have a truly unique skill set, I would strongly counsel you against playing one offer against another. If you have secured more than one role, then beware of letting the other party know that they are in a race until the last possible moment, never forgetting that it is a very small world and some industries and roles have a small catchment of staff. Word can get around for the wrong, and also for the right reasons, about you and your employability. Names are noted and people do talk, no matter how many times you are told they do not. Make sure that you always leave the door open in the best way possible if you reject, or fail at securing, one offer. You never know when you might need to walk back through it.

Using your list of contacts and networks, always keep in touch on an ad hoc basis, say every three months as a minimum. Again, as with all contacts that you have, it keeps your name in their mind. A warmer email, or form of contact, will always be better than a cold one that comes out of the blue. It also shows your professionalism.

If you are unsuccessful, you must maintain your composure and dignity. Displays of negative emotion only justify the decision made to reject you. Naturally you can say that you are disappointed, but never give away your true frustration and possible anger. You may have come second or third and the first two candidates may reject the job, thus placing you first. You never know, so always keep the door open. I saw this happen once with a rejection call (remember that, for the hirer, these are not easy calls either), where the candidate immediately fired off a response that was full of anger and bitterness. It was totally unexpected and, after he had calmed down, he was then told that he had come a very close second. Whilst the first candidate had accepted the role, there was a possibility that another similar job could open up within a few weeks. As a result of his reaction, he was advised that if this situation did arise he would have to apply again rather than being offered the role. A salutary lesson for everyone, justifying his rejection and, needless to say, that when the second position opened up and was advertised he sensibly decided against applying.

Finally, and the last word of caution here, is to be careful what you wish for as you might just get it. Sometimes in life, some things seem too good to be true. Invariably they are and avoid them, knowing that, before you saw it, you did not have it. By not moving towards it, you still do not have it either. You have won nothing and you have lost nothing either. Some roles that you will see in the remunerated and non-remunerated worlds can come into this category, where you find them irresistible, or the package presented is so good that the temptation is too great. Always check, do your due diligence from every possible angle and make a considered decision, knowing that this "leap of faith" is the right one for you. Sometimes what you see that is presented to you isn't what it appears to be. Make sure that it is as right as it can be for you and everyone around you. The risk should always be comparable to the reward.

Final words. Get as much experience as you can as early as you can, even if it is unpaid

Looking at many job adverts, you will often see the phrase "experience required" included in the text. The potential employer is saying that they are looking for someone who can do the job straight away, a "safe pair of hands" or someone who doesn't need a massive amount of training and input from them. This is all to maximise their profits by having minimal business disruption whilst the new employee gets up to speed. In other words, they are seeking an instant game player. Many young people who I have spoken to and mentored find this very off-putting and frustrating. "How do I get the experience in the first place?" is usually the question that follows this difficult area of discussion.

Within the game, you must remember that you can always put your destiny into your own hands. Once you take positive action to seize control of the direction that you want to go in, the stronger you will play.

One way that you can achieve this is to get experience in the field, or fields, that appeal to you. You can physically, or virtually now, knock on people's doors. Have a target list of industries, companies, organisations, or people that you wish to meet up with and begin the process of making contact. Write, email, phone and visit, sending in your latest CV of course. I am not advocating that you carry out any form of stalking, but it is important that you spread your net far and wide. Be ambitious here too. Never be put off by a household name or a big title. You never know what can happen if you make the first move towards them seeking out their support and engagement.

There is a strong possibility, though, that people will not respond to a letter or an email that you send. Sadly, many people choose not to engage. Whilst it is extremely rude, it is to be anticipated. If you expect nothing, then anything else is a bonus. This is why I recommend that you approach as many people and organisations as you can. Follow up with a phone call, if you haven't already called in advance. It may be that you feel comfortable with this as a first option. Any phone interactions of this nature should be done with some bullet points prepared in front of you so that you can talk effectively without having to think of your strategy, the words you will use and any answers to their questions and responses. You are playing the game for you to give you advancement, so plan and prepare. Stand up when you make the calls and tilt your head slightly back so that you look ahead, as I have advised with telephone interviews. Your voice projects clearer and you sound more confident. Walk around and keep your prompt cards stuck on the wall in front of you. Practise with a friend or trusted person beforehand and start with, "Good morning/afternoon. Can I speak to X, please? My name is X and I have recently written to them." You will find your own words to suit your own personality, but the more that you can practise this, and get used to it, the more confident and in control of yourself you will sound.

Quite often you will get a block or a bland response and you will have to go through a filter person before you can get to your desired contact. Be polite and be persistent. This is your future and, quite possibly, you are theirs too. In your eyes you must be the best there is, so ask whether they can return your call or when would be a good time for you to call back. Throw the onus back onto them.

If you are still at school or college and reading this, it is a great time to begin to develop your all-round approach to your future, and this includes gaining experience in different environments. Employers really do have the pick of the best people they want, so please do not just leave it to your teachers, parents, mentors or guardians. Take ownership and attend careers fairs, school work experience weeks, or industry days. Find the local employment and volunteering opportunities. At this stage it is very much about differentiating yourself from your peers and creating your USP.

Wherever you are at in your life and with your game, you will be amazed and surprised, too, at how willing people are to offer support to those who show an interest and ask questions. Despite all of the negativity that the media often create about the challenges of the working environment, the opportunities are out there if you are willing to get ahead of the pack, develop your strategy and put some serious time and effort into you. To keep reiterating, it is your game and you can shape your own destiny.

There is a phrase that says that sometimes in life you have to "give some to get some back". Never has this been more true than for work experience. You offer yourself as a raw candidate, hopefully learning something new by observation (I pray that the days of the tea and coffee maker have gone forever) and then gradually implementing what you have been taught under supervision. Volunteering is a great way to get to this point and also to develop your own ways of communicating, self-organisation and teamwork. Charities and not-for-profit organisations are always good places to volunteer, and often this will be using your strengths for their benefit, not just making up the numbers. There is nothing better for a recruiter than seeing the profile of someone with drive and determination, who has challenged themselves to give back to society, and at the same time used the opportunity for self-development. Any form of work experience will always be one of the greatest ways that you can invest in you.

Beware of long-term internships, though, that seek to exploit rather than develop. It is a tough judgement call to make, but there is a fine dividing line between you getting experience and a company getting free labour without having to offer remuneration. Do your research first and know what you are entering into.

If you find that no one is prepared to give a "rookie" a chance, and you do have the self-belief and feel so inclined, then go and create something of your own. The game is truly owned by you in that case, remembering that every business that has ever started has begun with a person with a spark of an idea.

The quick wins and the ladders

- Making your first impression a good one.
- Paying attention to even the smallest of details, leaving absolutely nothing to chance.
- Being yourself, try not to copy or be someone else.
- Speaking to those who may appoint you ahead of your application.
- Keeping your CV up to date and unique to you.
- Avoiding controversy on social media that may reflect badly on you.
- Being the same in person as you have demonstrated that you are on paper.
- Practising telling your story and developing a strong "elevator" pitch.
- Understanding every element of body language and its importance.

- Use of my ROWER acronym to answer competency-/ situation-based questions.
- Being ready with answers for the non-competency questions.
- RTFQ Reading the *full* question.
- Asking great questions of those who interview you.
- Having a clear strategy for telephone and virtual interviews.
- Being yourself at panels and tests, but also playing the game strategically too.
- Knowing that there is no such thing as an informal chat.
- Showing humility when receiving feedback, leaving every door open for the future.
- Being prepared to volunteer or take on internships to give yourself experience.

The traps and the snakes

- Paying little or no attention to detail of every element of the process.
- Copying/imitating others' applications and then being led by them.
- Ignoring even the smallest of details.
- Not having a unique and up-to-date CV.
- Being controversial whilst highly visible on social media.
- Being unable to tell your story in a clear and articulate way.
- Being unprepared and rambling with answers to questions asked of you.
- Not researching or showing an interest in the people/ organisations that you meet with.
- Dismissing any feedback given to you.
- Not seeking out opportunities for self-development and experience.
- Being taken advantage of when on work experience or an internship.

18

Higher education and
"the University of Life"

Every job is incredibly different, and I love
it because you're picking up skill sets and
experiences. It's the university of life.

Benedict Cumberbatch

Someone said to me recently what their father had told them,
when they questioned why, as a child, they had to go to school.
He said that "education is knowledge and knowledge is power".
So when you consider the game of life at an early stage, the way
to acquire power and leverage, in this gentleman's words, is via
education. This is a statement that I wholeheartedly endorse.
And anyone who has played the game of life with an eye towards
survival and occasional victories will have benefitted from
ongoing development in one form or another. That in itself is
education.

Before embarking on a path towards higher education, and
by that I mean as you approach ages fifteen and sixteen, it is
worth considering the direction that you think your life may
take. This is not to formally cast anything in stone so that your
direction is already decided. It is to have an idea and question

yourself as to what subjects actually interest and inspire you; what areas of life excite you and potentially make you happy; where you feel that your strengths lie. Then start to look at the career options that these subjects can lead towards and begin to formulate some sort of a plan.

For some, the entry into work could be at age sixteen, and many employers will look to support that with an apprenticeship or in-work qualifications. It is an ideal choice if that is the route that you wish to follow, and will always have flexibility attached should you change your mind in the future. You can always choose another option and route. What you will have done for yourself here is to make a clear commitment to doing something, as opposed to drifting into a series of courses and subjects that have very little meaning for you. You will have taken some control over your destiny and, as I have discussed many times here already, this is where you play the game to the best effect for you. Many of the options at this age give skill-based roles and training, which themselves bring lifelong practical qualifications. With, say, a trade behind you, you will rarely be without work. The freedom and autonomy that brings to you in the future is worth so much more than any money you may earn in the immediate short term.

You will also be making your first tentative steps into "the University of Life", where you go beyond the classroom and into the practical and real world. You will begin to understand more of how human beings interact, as the age ranges in the workplace are so diverse, and everyone's motivators and drivers are vastly different. Your learning about people will never end but, with a conscious awareness of others around you, and a developing emotional intelligence, you will find that you make quicker progress here than at any other stage of your life.

For those who move into college, beyond sixteen, regularly check the key factors and questions regarding what the practical qualifications and experience that you are gaining will lead to. Question and challenge yourself as to where you are heading, keeping every option open for as long as you can. Go to careers, college and university events, taking any opportunities for awareness raising that are there. Be aware of apprenticeship schemes and routes into employment for what you seek, and research as much as you can to know what is needed by you to get you what you want. Never settle, and ensure that you have several options available to you, so that when you make a decision you are not pinning all of your hopes on one specific narrow area. Flexible planning of this nature is lifelong learning for the game that you play.

As you do this, keep developing your CV, and keep it sharp by adding any additional extracurricular activities that you do or qualifications that you gain, including voluntary work. Remember your USP? This will help with any applications and also with your personal statement, which is a key for entry into higher education or otherwise.

For any events that you attend, my top tip would be to be aware that you are always on show as this could be the first time that you engage with your next employer, or place of learning. Make sure that you have your CV to hand, that you are well presented and have a great elevator pitch available so that you can talk about yourself. You never know who you will meet and it is vital to be as aware and fully conscious as you can. Revisit the previous chapter in full as the answers are all there.

If you go to university, then make sure that you choose the right university, the right course for you and the right place to live, and that you take your studies as seriously as you can. It is important to have fun, but also to keep the challenge going as to where this is leading, what you will do afterwards and why. Ensure that you make early progress with finding out what is available to you at the end of the period of study, and who can help you with this. The sooner that you start this the more prepared that you will be, as it will help you to be flexible and potentially change some of the direction of your studies if needed. By challenging yourself and engaging with others early into the process, you will get the competitive edge into your game, ensuring that you utilise every possible resource to help you.

You may find that, as you progress, you look at the options ahead and change your mind on where you are heading. Perhaps this is more difficult with vocational qualifications, but, with more people engaged to support and advise you, more options will become available. Always remember that qualifications are the door openers to the interviews and, therefore, never discount anything that may be of interest. It is the person that people seek out to employ, as well as their knowledge and capability.

You may take on part-time work whilst you are studying and should approach this as you would any other role. That way you get good practice for the future process and also the opportunity to add experience and advocates to your CV. For example, if you work in a shop you will have exposure to clients and customers and will be required to deliver a quality service to them. This will instantly give you several skills and competencies to list and develop, such as customer service, communication, accuracy, teamwork and attention to detail. No matter what you do, do it to the best of your ability, and the experience and subsequent references that should follow will then assist you further. This is also true for voluntary roles and internships. Make the most of them to upskill yourself in as many areas as possible and remember they add to your interview examples too.

One question that I always asked graduates who I interviewed was regarding their motivation for taking a gap year out after their degree. This is one to reflect on and be prepared to answer if you have followed this route. There are no right or wrong answers necessarily here, although saying that you needed a rest after your degree did not always sit comfortably with me. It is very much a personal choice, and, as I keep saying, put yourself in the shoes of the potential employer and consider the impact that your answer will have on them.

If you go into work at age eighteen, then there is every chance that you will be involved in an apprenticeship scheme, or have significant training to undertake to become competent with the role and within the company that you work for. Be aware of all dates for opening and closing of applications for the jobs. That way you will get to know the way in which their applications and schemes work. Go to any open or taster days and always follow up with thank-you emails to anyone who has helped you. Again, pay significant attention to the interview section in this book, which takes you through the whole process from application onwards, and have your advocates ready. Be prepared to articulate clearly just why you are the best candidate for the role, and always have a backup plan, which may be that you have several applications running at one time. Do not limit yourself to the one company that may be your dream, as you are severely limiting your options.

As you progress through your career, never forget that the need for education within your own personal and professional development is a lifelong part of the game. This part of the University of Life is one that you never fully graduate from, but know that every situation that you encounter, good and bad, will give you invaluable learning. The more of this that you acquire as you progress, the stronger and more autonomous your game will be and the more ladders that will appear in front of you.

The quick wins and the ladders

- Knowing that all forms of education give knowledge, and that knowledge is power.
- Considering your options early in life, understanding what you enjoy, knowing what you are good at and what sectors you wish to consider.
- Keeping your plans flexible.
- Going to every event that you can that will give you help and assistance, no matter how obscure.
- Constantly seeking to find self-development opportunities.
- Taking ownership of your destiny.

The traps and the snakes

- Drifting into subjects and attaining qualifications without a plan.
- Not seeking to understand yourself or finding out additional help and support.
- Not doing something that you love or enjoy.
- Not learning from being around people.
- Abdicating responsibility for your path in life.

19

It's a very small world.
Networking, friends, acquaintances
and lasting impressions

The world can be very small. That's why you
have to be very careful, whoever you meet.

Bebe Rexha

As your game develops you will meet lots of people, some of whom become lifelong friends, but the majority are really only ever acquaintances. Your true friends are rare and smaller in number than you realise, and can usually be counted on one hand.

We regularly confuse acquaintances with friends, but keep in mind that, within the various available definitions of a friend, you usually find words including affection, trust, love, understanding, longevity. A friend is someone that you know very well and can safely share your innermost thoughts with. How many of your friends do you know that well and implicitly trust? Equally, how many of your acquaintances do you know that well and trust? It is a dilemma and one that the unscrupulous may seek to exploit.

Acquaintances, though, become very important to your game strategy. They are people who we meet and get to know, but usually only know us by what they see on the surface. They will give away as little of themselves too, and similarly we to them. This form of social and professional sparring starts the moment that we enter environments where there are other people, and interaction with them is needed. You can probably remember your feelings within school, where you met many people, but probably only found two or three true friends if you were lucky. For those who left their education several years or more ago, can you, without referring back to anything other than your memory, recall the names of everyone in your school classes? Let's go further: can you remember the names of everyone you've subsequently worked with or may have encountered since? Of those that you can remember, how many have you retained any form of contact with? The number will be relatively small, although the development of social media means that we can now be more connected than we ever were. Even then, how many of your connections remain effectively dormant?

So, consider just how connected you are to others. Is that contact just superficial or is it something that we really want? What is it bringing to your game or possibly even taking away? By this I mean the energy that you could possibly give to something else that is more productive and beneficial. What I am advocating is effective contact for mutual benefit with those acquaintances that we make, and the power of networking.

I once knew a man who collected business cards like an avid fan collects autographs and memorabilia. Every possible networking event that he could attend, he was there, and everyone he shook hands with or spoke to, he exchanged business cards with. On the back of that card, or somehow, he made a brief note about the person and one key thing that they said, even if he had not made a formal date for a future meeting with them. On leaving the event, as soon as he could, he usually went somewhere quiet and wrote more details into his notebook to capture his memories of everyone that he could remember. Over the coming days he would ensure that all of their details were entered onto a spreadsheet that he maintained himself and, in one form or another, he would contact them. The final three columns of his sheet were his next contact dates and how he would make that interaction. He assessed everyone's usefulness to him and also, vital to note here, whether he could be of benefit to them. Another column had possible ways in which they could help him to unlock doors to people that he wanted to meet. It goes further, in that he had colour-coded them for 30-, 60-, 120- and 365-day contacts, so as soon as they appeared amber or red he knew he had to do something with them, whether it be a call, an email, a letter (he believed in personalised letters and handwritten Christmas cards) or to arrange a meeting.

It all sounds very labour intensive, but the reality of this was that it was not. This was his business and professional networking and, as he called it, "for mutual benefit". He believed that, by giving something back to those that he could help, good would also come back to him.

Now, this may feel very much like a type of stalking behaviour, but consider this, as an "acquaintance" of every website you've ever signed up to, online survey that you have completed, product you have purchased, etc., don't you get follow ups that are designed to keep you engaged?

Needless to say, the hour or so that was invested in this means of contact every day saw our man become very successful, and he owned his game. He also owned the games of many others as, by giving something away where he could, he knew that thirty out of one hundred would have the conscience within them to give back to him in some way too. And, if they were unable to, he was ok in saying something like, "Do you remember me introducing you to… Well, I'm after a link into…" It meant his business development was taken care of and he never had to cold call. Was he successful? Materially, yes. Was he successful personally or in the whole game of life? I guess so, although that is ultimately between him and his own conscience. He did much for other people, local communities and he helped me with my game too.

For many young people, I would see something like this as a critical skill to starting your professional life and education. We may be great at learning a subject, but the hardball game of life we are very poor at, and these are the kinds of skill that are needed beyond those of the prescribed learning.

If you are serious about controlling your game, and can see the benefits of doing that, then develop a spreadsheet or system that can help you with your contacts. For example know who can give you a reference and vouch for you; know who can coach you with interviews, panels, your CV and job applications; know who knows who in the industry that you want to get into; know who can help you with gaining work experience; find out who knows who, etc. Trust me, it is time well invested and well spent "network weaving", as another contact of mine calls it.

Never forget that it is also a very small world. You never know who knows who, who is connected to who and how often people talk. Nothing is more apparent than when people ask, "So you work at XYZ business" or "You went to ABC College, didn't you? Do you know X?" Once an affirmative answer is given, there is no end to where this conversation can go and how this can affect your game, either positively or negatively, if it is your name that crops up. Leave a role or a position with a bad feeling, or under bad circumstances, and it may at some stage come back and "bite you". You cannot always control this, but never forget when you might need someone for your game, whether it is to provide a reference or testimonial or to be a door opener for you.

Whenever you leave an organisation, no matter what role it is that you may be resigning from, try to be remembered for how you have left and the dignity that you have shown. It may not be that simple, but you never know when you may need that particular door to be opened again one day. People remember the last interactions more than any other, and will always appreciate gestures like a letter, a card or an email of thanks. It is more networking, and in that you are absolutely controlling your game and destiny.

I have already explained at length about first impressions and, once you have clearly imprinted into your psyche that you only get one chance to make a first impression, you then need to follow the same process to be familiar with lasting impressions. This is often around consistency and massive attention to detail from you, including making sure that you always deliver, and where you can, to over deliver on your promises and timescales. That way you present yourself and your work in the best manner possible. The moment that you drop your standards and become inconsistent is the moment when you put your game at risk. It will be noticed by someone, somewhere, sometime, and that will get around into the network. It is a very small world full of snakes and ladders.

The quick wins and the ladders

- Differentiating between who is a friend and who is an acquaintance and treating them differently.
- Keeping an effective up-to-date contact list for mutual benefit.
- Knowing that it is a small world with many people who are interconnected and talk to each other.
- Making good lasting impressions.

The traps and the snakes

- Not differentiating between friends and acquaintances.
- Not keeping in contact with people or making good use of your contacts.
- Not caring about the impressions that you make on others.

20

Going it alone. The brave and the bold business creators, I salute you!

> The most important characteristics you
> need to succeed in business are resilience,
> determination and persistence.
>
> Karren Brady

For some people, the prospect of working for or being supervised by another person is simply too much to bear. The lack of freedom and autonomy and having to play someone else's games by their rules is just an unacceptable concept. I have known people who have felt they have been almost enslaved by their employers, and one even described how their therapist diagnosed them with the early stages of a type of "Stockholm syndrome" with regard to their working environment. This is where hostages begin to develop an empathy with their captors, taking on their ideals and beliefs.

I spent all of my working life from the age of eighteen with one company, and never seriously considered going it alone at any time. I could have, but, being completely honest, I was never that brave. I liked the safety and relative security of the job that I held with the company that I worked for, and only cut the cord to leave once I knew that I was financially free. Even then, I still felt something akin to a bereavement. Perhaps, again, reflecting on my upbringing, it was drilled so deeply into me that I must have a "job for life", as my dad put it. I know now just how lucky I was to survive with the company, and how unusual it is for anyone these days to work under only one banner for the length of their career.

More and more people are turning to online and innovative ways of earning these days, with trading sites such as eBay, Amazon and many others. These can be extremely lucrative if run correctly, and a great way to learn about and to fully understand all aspects of business, including expenditure, income and profit, and sales and marketing.

If you, like me, seek safety and security from a job requiring a regular income, together with the associated benefits that can be available, then that is fine. Just make sure it is a job that suits your game, that you enjoy and that you can never become trapped or tied in, so that you need them more than they need you. Keep your network alive and never take your pay cheque for granted.

If you have a talent, an idea or a concept, or even just want to go it alone as a businessperson, then I salute you as you are brave, bold and playing the game of life very much on your terms.

Take as much advice as you are offered and that you can gain, particularly from others who have also done it for themselves. They will share with you, if they have a generous nature, what they did well and also admit to some of the mistakes that they made. Very few get the recipe right first time around. Never commit until you are certain that the timing is right for you, and make sure that the areas that you are weakest on you have covered with the strongest attention to detail. By this I mean that you may be the greatest designer, say, in the world, but, unless you have the "basic but criticals" – or BBCs – sorted and in place, such as finance, trading terms, legals, etc., then you will potentially fail. Again, remembering that failure to prepare means prepare to fail.

Some of the very best leaders, business owners and company directors that I have encountered invariably surround themselves with people who are more talented than they are. What this means is that the supporting team are experts and specialists in their chosen fields. True entrepreneurs have vision and holistic thinking, and can see, engage, drive and take the calculated risks knowing the people they have around them can make it all possible. They are the glue and the facilitators. They never miss any detail and trust only themselves and very few others. They often know a lot but do not always have the granular detail across the whole of the business or organisation. They just know how to make each competent part work so that the total output is greater than every individual contribution.

Here is a list of some things to look at and consider as you formulate your plan. It is in no set order and is not a list of barriers. You do not have to do everything here. It is a series of considerations and guidelines for you to reflect on, which will help you to have a great start in building your own business and to be able to present proposals to those who can also help you:

- Business plan. Always have one that is available and evolving. There are plenty out there and to download from any supportive site. Developing your own "SWOT" type of analysis (strengths, weaknesses, opportunities and threats) is a great place to start.
- Seek help and support. There is lots of help out there including local and national government, various trade organisations, forums, business groups, charities, social enterprises and chambers of commerce, to name but a few. Many are free and will help you with networking too.
- However you set your business up, involve if you can your bank, accountant, financial advisor and solicitor

(if you have them) from the outset. Think of them as a shadow board of directors for you. Their input will be invaluable. Also ask them for client introductions. One thing that has always frustrated me with some who take fees for their sage-like advice is their inability to see the business-to-business opportunities that exist.

- Know your competition. Who is out there, what are they doing, how do they differentiate themselves and what can you do that will mean you will get a greater share of the market?
- Premises. Do you need them? Consider whether the spend for an online presence will outweigh the cost of a physical site.
- Protect your ideas with the use of patents and also be aware of the intellectual property that you may have.
- Vehicle(s). Always talk to your accountant and bank manager about the various ways in which you can best finance transport (if you need it) to suit your business model.
- Employees. If you are taking anyone on as an employee, intern or supporter for you, create a culture of professional learning and that you are able to treat everyone so that they feel like an individual.
- Regularly ask everyone you engage with, including clients, suppliers, employees and your advisors, for feedback about what you need to do to keep improving the company and environment. It is important that you are transparent with the outcome and have a visible plan for continuous evolution.
- What is the USP of your organisation? Be able to articulate this as clearly as you would about yourself.
- Do you franchise out or become a franchisee yourself? This can be an excellent way to set up a business with an established brand behind you. Be aware of the need for capital injection from you at the outset, though.

- Many of those with talent are brilliant at producing and creating their output, but often forget to pay as much attention to their finances. The business graveyard is full of wonderful concepts that have failed for want of proper financial planning.

- Always think big and be like a multinational organisation from the outset. What do they do that gives them sustainability? Research and, where possible and it is legal to do so, replicate into your plan.

- Never settle. Be restless, different and curious. Constantly seek to innovate and develop, as your competitors will.

- Never rely on one big contract. Landing a huge deal that gives you eighty per cent of your income may seem like the answer to all of your prayers, but relying on one company is fraught with danger as they effectively own you as a subsidiary and can dictate their terms to you. Be aware of the risks that you take, your potential loss of autonomy and also the potential business loss if they cancel your contract. Be aware, too, that close alignment to them means that if they fail then so too do you.

- Advocacy. Get as many people as you can to sing your praises from as many rooftops as you possibly can, with online reviews, letters of recommendation, telling friends and family, etc. Make sure that you also acknowledge every time those who support you in this way.

- Network, network, network. Go to as many events, virtual and physical, as you can initially, to showcase what you do or to learn how others do it. There are so many out there that you will find your level and what works for you. The cost can vary, so ensure you use as many free or low-cost "taster" opportunities as you can. Also have a comprehensive follow-up system, as I have discussed previously, and a robust system and strategy to follow up all contacts. You may get to meet the people you need to help you move forward at these. An active social media presence is also critical and again make sure that you are fully aware of how it works. There are many tutorials, coaches and experts who can help. Some will cost but it can be well worth it.

- Tell your story. You will have read in the chapter covering interviews about "elevator pitches". It is important that you can clearly and concisely articulate to an audience what you do, remembering that some people who are not technically minded may struggle to grasp a complex explanation. Always keep it simple and make sure it is told well. Again, pay for this if necessary as lack of professionalism with presentation is lazy and costs you sales.
- Celebrate the successes. Never forget why you are in business, or why you are doing what you do. Be your own greatest cheerleader and celebrate when it goes well. Nothing extravagant is needed here, but something that gives you a boost as a reward for your efforts.
- Create a culture that reflects you. Do you and your business act ethically and responsibly? Your business integrity, like your own, should never be negotiated away. Set your values out very clearly from the start and make sure that everyone who works alongside you, in whatever capacity, signs up to these. They must own them as much as you do.
- Be aware of your responsibility to your locality and the communities around you, even if you are home-based. The people there will support you. It can be something as simple as donating the odd prize at local events, school fetes and the placing of adverts, even in, say, a parish magazine. These gestures can often pay for themselves many, many times over.
- Prepare, prepare, prepare. Start preparing and planning as far ahead as you can. The more you do, the greater the chances of you achieving success.

- Know what success looks like for you specifically, what your definition is and, even at the very start, know when your exit point will be. This is both for any profit that you make or for any loss.
- Set aside a percentage of your income to cover taxes and to give your pension a start. Your advisors will help here and this may be a good point to seek out a good financial planner if you do not have one. It is never too early to begin these conversations.
- Insurances. Sometimes this can be neglected, but make sure that you have everything covered, including yourself against death, accident or illness, never forgetting of course public liability.
- Work from home? For those who may consider doing this, be aware that this is also your refuge and castle, and may have many distractions, lacking the "work feel". However, embrace it if you can to make it work for you. Certainly it reduces the commute and your carbon footprint.
- Get to know who your local businesspeople are and who are successful. Try and meet them, remembering that people like nothing better than talking about themselves. This is a tip for anyone showing an interest in, or studying business. These people can make great mentors and are often found via a chamber of commerce.
- Never forget the duty of care that you owe to yourself and your loved ones by looking after your physical and mental health. Establishing a business and then keeping it going will be an assault course on your own well-being at times. Help is there and never be too proud or independent to seek out support in the same way that you would for other aspects of this.
- Finally, case study the entrepreneurs, including the survivors and big individual players. Know what they do, how they started, what mistakes they made and what

victories they have had. All will have a tenacity and an inner drive that has meant they have never given up. You may not like them, or agree with some of their methods, but there is no doubt that they have a story to tell and you can learn from them. There are so many interviews, books, biographies and articles within the media about "dragons" like Cher Wang, Steve Jobs, Bill Gates, Mark Zuckerberg, Oprah Winfrey, Jeff Bezos, Lakshmi Mittal, John Caudwell, Alan Sugar, Rupert Murdoch, Jay Z, Richard Branson, Peter Jones, Deborah Meaden, Anita Roddick. Read their stories and understand their drivers and also their mistakes. LinkedIn is excellent for providing short summaries and profiles. I would urge you to watch programmes like *Dragons' Den* and any business-related documentaries, news and films for even more learning.

The quick wins and the ladders

- All of the list above.

The traps and the snakes

- Failing to plan or prepare, just diving in to follow your idea.
- Not paying attention to or understanding the basic but criticals (the BBCs).

21

Talk, be a human being and stay sane

> Speech is a very important aspect of being
> human. A whisper doesn't cut it.
>
> James Earl Jones

How many times do we avoid a conversation with another person by choosing to text or email them instead? It is easier and less effort to do the latter, I suppose, as you can "talk" in this way at a pace and in a way when you choose. You never have to worry about those uncomfortable silences that can often occur when you are distracted by your surroundings, and you can do so many other things in the interim that feels more important to you. And you are still engaging with the other person, so that makes it ok, doesn't it?

We are all guilty of disregarding the power of our ability to talk, and the positive impact that it can have upon us. Does texting, or any other form of non-verbal communication, actually save us time and make us more effective human beings? Does it raise your spirits and touch your inner soul in the same way that a voice can?

Just before Covid restrictions came into force in 2020, I overheard a conversation where one person was talking in a shop about how difficult it was proving to arrange a prescribed time for a text exchange with her friend, so that they then could arrange a night out together. Surely the easiest thing to do would be to just pick up the phone there and then?

The point that I am seeking to make here is that one of the fundamental qualities that separates our species from the others on this planet is our effective and clear method of verbal communication. We use so many different sounds, tones, and complex formation, of sentences in ways that other animals cannot. We have such a variety of languages, dialects, speech, customs and ways in which we adapt to our changing situations to get our messages across. And we always seem to find ways of changing our words with people who perhaps struggle to understand us. The power of our speech and verbalisation is a way that we can simplify and cement our relationships. Even if we lose our speech or our hearing, we have developed many other ways, such as sign language, that can still make the act of communication possible. We can still "talk" to one another.

Part of this is knowing that talking is also very good for us too and plays a key part in our own daily therapy. Coronavirus has taught us, especially during lockdown, that we need not be so isolated if we are able to harness technology with virtual interactions. Many are still able to work remotely, and most of us can easily socialise in this way, but it is just not the same as receiving the signals that we take from being in the immediate vicinity of another human.

And here is another thing to consider: you will never get the same feelings from a phone or a keyboard chat, although they do really help in-between. The handset, or tapping out of characters, does not fully help you to detect the body language, smells, eye contact and other sensory perceptions that we pick up unconsciously during a face-to-face chat. We have so many of these coming at us and they, again, help with the whole process of raising our spirits.

Sometimes you can end a call and have more questions about

how the other person reacted to you than you have answered. This is because you were unable to correctly read them as people, and you were not in possession of all of the unconscious facts that you would pick up face to face. It is like finishing a jigsaw and finding, to your great frustration, that there are two or three missing pieces. For those who are housebound or lacking in company, then these ways of communicating become a lifeline, vital to their mental well-being, and we must always try to find at least one way of creating a physical contact of sorts.

Keeping your sanity is crucial for your game, and is not easy to do. As I have consistently said, there are many people who will want you to succeed and who you can trust, you just have to find them, but they are there. Similarly, there are many who will seek to undermine you and play with your emotions. You must talk to those you trust, love and who care for you. The cost of not doing this is too great to your and to their games, as you are important to them too. Talking is everything and there is no problem that a true friend will not be able to cope with or help you to try to resolve.

If you are feeling low, then find a way of expressing it and say, "Have you got a few minutes to talk?" We are not good at this and retreat into ourselves using all sorts of excuses for not talking to others, often assuming that they have too much going on in their lives to talk to us. Many simply say, "I'm ok", when actually that is the last thing they are. This was, and still is, especially true of the pre- and post-war generations.

The next time someone asks "Are you ok?" or "How are you?" try to answer as honestly as you can. You may be on top of the world, so tell them you are and exactly why. My uncle used to say to me, when I asked him how he was, "If I was any better I couldn't cope." I love that phrase as it is full of humour, it always draws a smile and, with him, you knew that he meant it. But equally you may not be at your best and explaining why you aren't could actually help you and the other person too.

Your game needs face-to-face "talk" wherever possible, in

addition to the virtual lines that are open and essential, both from you and from others. It is a way of venting, a way of sharing, listening, learning, helping and coaching. You will laugh, cry, show anger, compassion, love – possibly all of these in the space of one conversation. It is vital for your game to keep your sanity, and you will also help another person's too.

So, my final question for you to consider here is, "Are you ok? Do you need to talk?"

The quick wins and the ladders

- Having a conversation wherever you can, knowing that talking is great for your well-being.
- Being honest if people ask you how you are.
- Trying to make more face-to-face interactions.
- Using virtual, phone or keyboard conversations if you are unable to speak face to face in the interim.

The traps and the snakes

- Not talking or having open conversations.
- Keeping everything to yourself.
- Avoiding physical conversations in favour of alternate means of communication such as text.

Talk, be a human being and stay sane

22

Laugh, for goodness' sake, laugh, and at yourself too

If you can't laugh at yourself, you don't deserve to laugh at anybody else.

Charlie Murphy

One of the most challenging things we find as people is to be the butt of the joke, and it's even worse for us if we are present as it is taking place. It hurts when people snigger behind your back, but actually to your face? Now, that is a very tough test of character. Get this wrong, bite back, or object and you are considered to be lacking in humour and overly sensitive. Go with it and allow the joke to continue for too long, and you are then considered easy game and become a regular target. And then when you finally snap you are told that you cannot laugh at yourself or take a joke.

So where is the happy medium here and where is the line drawn so that it never goes as far as bullying? This is a game changer again, as you can easily lose advocates and acquaintances if you seem to be lacking a sense of humour. Note, though, that friends will always be there for you regardless, so for your gameplay to be truly effective know who is on your "team" and who specifically are your friends.

My view on this is that, if you can force some self-deprecating humour by turning it to a strength, then people will pick on you less. If they still choose to be challenging, then they can make themselves look overbearing, giving you an advantage.

Sometimes, just sometimes, it is worth following the example of politicians down the ages and selecting some appropriate "fake news", or even creating it. Make it uncontroversial, funny, and one that paints you in a good light, remembering that someone will always pull out the story at some stage, making you front and centre of the discussion. The skill then is to go with it for a while, making sure that it then leads onto what you do really well. It is an art form and one that I have worked on for many years, never quite perfecting. It creates legends and reputations. It gets you known by populations that otherwise would never have heard of you. If you can make these stories forces for good, without compromising your integrity, then you have currency and collateral in the game. You must cash this in.

One gentleman I know who is now over seventy years old, paid for lessons to learn how to do stand-up comedy. It had been a lifelong ambition and finally he achieved it. He described the final presentation at a comedy club in front of an audience of one hundred people as one of the scariest moments of his life. He also said how rewarding it was as he made people laugh, and used stories of his life and unfortunate occurrences to do so. He made fun of himself, not to enable others to pile on more humiliation but to laugh with him. He chose a visit to the doctor as one story to tell that was also linked to his age, where a rather "intimate" examination had to take place. The detail he gave was graphic, but not crude or rude. He painted a picture of one that is seen every day across the world in doctors' surgeries, and broke down the barriers of his fear and embarrassment with his funny story. People laughed, cringed, cheered loudly and applauded him off the stage. He did this within seven minutes of coming on, from a cold start where very few people in the audience knew him. Inspirational stuff. I am sure that there was some exaggeration for effect and a modicum of "fake news", but it certainly got me laughing and cheering him on.

There are others who just cannot bear to hear anything but positive words spoken about them, and they get borderline aggressive when challenged. Be very aware of who these people are as they do not make for good friends. Their game is their own and they have little in their kitbag to give anything to yours. Upset them at your peril as they are fierce, unforgiving enemies who will throw you, figuratively, under the bus without thinking. You cannot put a foot wrong with them, and always feel in their debt. Avoid them especially when they are fuelled by alcohol, lack of sleep, or both, at all costs. This is when they are often at their worst.

Finding things to laugh at unites us as people. It helps to create common ground and increases the flow of all of the happy chemicals that move around our bodies. The act of smiling uses fewer muscles than frowning so is less hard work. Laughing is infectious, and does make you feel mentally stronger and more able to take on what is ahead of you. It brings people together.

Keep in mind, though, that laughter can also be cruel when your happiness and those around you is at someone else's expense. Know your audience, sense-check if necessary, and always be compassionate if you realise that the recipient of your humour did not appreciate or welcome it. I apologise via this medium to the friends and colleagues who may feel like I took the jokes a little too far at times. Writing this has made me realise that what I said perhaps made me feel very good in the moment, and gained me some applause and accolades, but I realise now that some of it was simply wrong.

The quick wins and the ladders

- Being prepared to laugh at yourself.

- Making sure someone is ok with you creating a joke against them.
- Knowing how to make people laugh with you.

The traps and the snakes

- Being unable to laugh at your own shortcomings.
- Not realising that taking a joke too far at someone else's expense is bullying, pure and simple.

23

Finding your religion... or not

I always say that people should not rush
to change religions. There is real value in
finding the spiritual resources you need in
your home religion.

Dalai Lama

Whether you believe in a superior being in whatever form that
may take, or whether you have a passion for some cause that
is almost religious in your devotion to it, many people on this
planet choose to follow someone, or something, in some way. For
these people, this can be the principal reason for their existence.
Look around the globe at the millions who make pilgrimages
every year to shrines, and the devotion shown daily, and weekly,
by those attending their places of worship. Remember, too, that
not all of these are representing recognised religions or icons
either.

There are many who choose not to believe in a "god"-
like character, retaining an open mind on the subject or
classing themselves as agnostic. As humans, though, we are
almost pre-programmed to have a belief in something and to
question as deeply as we can the reason why we were created.

If you look back through all of the known ages of man, there has always been a presence of some god, or icon of sorts. This has been true of every culture and society since time began, with their deities often being earthly in their shape and revelation.

This belief, through time, has been a blessing and a curse. The ancients believed that anything good that was happening was at the pleasure of "the gods", and, similarly, anything bad meant they were upset and angry. Offerings, sometimes in the form of sacrifices, were meant to appease them and, again, this can be seen from recovered scrolls and writings from civilisations across the globe.

Even now, religion can be used to justify almost anything. Going back to my school days in the 1970s, my morning assembly started with prayers. The headmaster stood in front of us warning that eternal fire and damnation awaited us unless we improved our ways that very day. Scary stuff, to say the least, to ten- and eleven-year-olds, and he usually did this whilst pointing aggressively with his cane and holding the lapels of his black cape. He really was the embodiment of the teacher created in the video for Pink Floyd's "The Wall", staring over the top of his half-moon glasses. All of the staff stood at the sides of the school hall, scanning the audience for anyone not assenting to his cry, ready to admonish those who weren't acquiescing. He really did relish the authoritarian role and never lost the walk of the captain that he had been in the Second World War, with his favourite stick under his arm. Woe betide anyone who stepped out of line and failed to respect his authority. If you held other faiths, it was tough, as you were still expected to sing "All things bright and beautiful... the lord God made them all". The fear of God was literally drilled into us, and it is little wonder that so many rebelled when they had the chance, rejecting his form of Christianity.

Religions do, though, support our need for commonality and togetherness. At times it is compelling, drawing us closer into the community that it creates. This is where religion is at its best – as a force for good and holding that spirituality in your heart, in itself, can give you massive support in your game.

I am not advocating here that you rush out and find the first religion that catches your eye, as communities and excellent causes are everywhere around us. If you are comfortable with not believing in a religion, or a faith of sorts, then that is ok. What I am suggesting here is that finding your religion can be about finding out how the power of people, coming together, to share a common theme or cause, can help your own game in the short, medium and long terms. A cause that gives you a sense of well-being and inner harmony will only enhance all of the other areas of your life that you seek to develop. It will help to create a clear space in your head for you to consciously plan your game. You may also find that your inner human need to belong is satisfied.

Let me explain more. In times of emergency, say, where war or disaster have struck, people will often turn to a religion for peace, comfort and support. They do this because they know that they will not only get relief at the time that they feel they most need it and are most vulnerable, but they will also be with others who are feeling similar to themselves. They have a united struggle where they gain and give strength to and from the people that they are among, often by prayer. Think how many times you have said "Oh my God!" or have muttered or thought of a silent question, hoping for a positive answer in some way.

A friend of mine recently talked to me about how she finds personal comfort at different times in her life by visiting various places of worship, not only when things are difficult for her. She will go in good times as well as bad. She will sit and listen to the teachings offered whilst experiencing the atmosphere, the music, the fellowship, and the peace. Some of what is said she cannot understand because of the languages used, but the themes are very much the same, and the warmth of the welcome is always strong, regardless of the creed and colour.

She used a phrase when we met that her father had given to her when she was younger. "There are many doors to the same house." This resonated with me and made me realise that, when you may go in search of your religion, you do not necessarily have to find one, as religion may not be what you are after. By being among other people in different settings, you will have found a lot of what you seek simply by the togetherness that is offered there. The door that opens you to the feelings, emotions and sensations can appear in many different ways. In the end, as she so clearly put it, "You end up in more or less the same place as everyone else."

Her questioning continues, with her search for the answer to "What are you doing in this life?" This is the question that dogs many of us throughout our own existence and often makes us seek out quick-fix answers and solutions. Going to the places of worship is where she finds the personal space and variety of thought that help her to find some of the answers to questions such as this. It makes her game so much stronger.

For some, their religion is a form of commitment, and this can involve following certain influential individuals, sporting allegiances, politics and current affairs, and can even see the evolution of cults. It can be a defining part of your identity.

As people go in search of the deeper answers and solutions to the questions that they have, it is very easy to become influenced and indoctrinated. Keep questioning and never stop doing that, by always being curious about the motives of those who seek to influence you. If you are ever faced with a salesperson, remember that, if their product is as good as they say it is, then they will have no problem in letting you take the information away and comparing it with others. Quality always sells and has longevity. Therefore, please beware of the salespeople of religion, or anyone who claims to represent a group that can have all of the answers to the questions that you have. Invariably they want your money and to have control over you. They will seek to do this very quickly, as they want to own you, your game and those around you by dividing you from them. Walk away and consider the proposition at your leisure. Seek out alternate views and, only if you are sure after time, then commit.

Forms of religious cults can appear as individuals or as groups, and often find people at the most vulnerable times in their lives, when the promise of escape and answers can prove irresistible. The mind control techniques can be very subtle and seem very light to begin with. Be very aware, though, that this is bringing you and your assets into their world, and at some pace. Give your time, your energy, your conscience, and your hard-earned cash sparingly, remembering what you have gone through all of your life to accumulate everything, both tangible and intangible, that makes you the person you are.

Is it important for you and your game to have a religion? No, but if you replace the word religion with phrases including inner harmony, peace, love and a positive contribution to your own world including the well-being of your fellow man, then, yes, I believe it is. Respect, too, of other people's right to believe or follow as they wish and for their respect of what you follow is surely at the crux of what any religion of any definition is truly about. Whatever then leads you to that place is a path well worth following.

The quick wins and the ladders

- Enjoying the power of togetherness of other people.
- Being curious and questioning.
- Visiting many different places until you find where you are most comfortable, whilst retaining an open mind.
- Avoiding a "quick fix" mentality to your life.
- Respecting other people's right to follow and believe.
- Accepting that you may not need a religion in your game.

The traps and the snakes

- Being drawn into something that seems to be the answer when you are most vulnerable.
- Not questioning in depth the motives of others.
- Failing to accept others' viewpoints or respecting their right to believe.

24

Understanding what you and everyone else wants from the game

Realise that the game of life is the game
of, to some extent, being taken advantage
of by people who make a science of it.
Whether they are in government or personal
life or in business, they're everywhere.

Walter Kirn

Once you reach the point of consistent conscious gameplay, you will have a series of plans formulating, evolving and ever changing. You will start to look at the game of life in a totally different way. You will begin to question more of what is being asked of you. You will question why a certain direction or path is developing, and that word "why?" will constantly feature into much of your reasoning and decision-making. You will take longer to respond to requests made of you and, as a result, people will try to rush you, becoming impatient as you seek more answers than they are prepared to give. They want you to play their game in their way, and not to have to give their own full account for this, as people invariably want to keep some of their strategies to themselves. Giving full disclosure on their part could potentially reveal a weakness or a hidden agenda. If you are uncomfortable with what is being asked of you, and have not received full satisfactory explanations, then do not head down that route. If you are subsequently faced with a "just do it" type of response, then you know that the situation is likely to be detrimental to you, and it is only for the benefit of the person giving the instructions. They are choosing you as their risk taker for their game.

Sometimes you will be faced with instructions, or situations, where time prevents you making all of the enquiries that you would wish to. This is when you make a considered and calculated judgement call. These can be unavoidable on occasions, but make the decision as consciously as you can, fully aware of consequences of the outcome, both good and bad.

I did this once where, in my first week of a new management role, I was desperate to impress my team. I was asked to make a snap strategic decision that adversely affected another business unit. I was not in possession of all of the facts, had not asked enough questions and made a call that I knew was risky. I should not have made it, but I put my own desire to impress and my own team's immediate needs ahead of everyone else's. It was no surprise that within half an hour I was being hauled over the coals by my new boss and had to backtrack. It took hours to unravel the problem that I had caused across the organisation and, whilst my immediate colleagues thought that I was a hero for making the decision that saved them considerable time and work, I knew that I had called it wrong. It took several weeks for me to regain some credibility with the wider business, and memories are long when you have caused other people stress and additional work through your own poor decision-making.

Constantly pushing back and asking questions of others can lead to a perception of militancy. It can cause you to be alienated and to be seen as someone who is not a team player. It is a fine line to tread between asking questions, being persistent and just being plain awkward. Put yourself in the shoes of the person, or persons, you are seeking information from and think how they will react to your approach before you begin. Always consider your level of persistence versus their level of resistance before you embark on your strategy, and the best way that you can to elicit the result from them that you seek.

By doing this, you will begin to see more of what others want from this phase of the game, and probably start to see their longer-term requirements. You may be surprised that someone who you perhaps thought was very much on your side is actually "playing you" for their own advantage. Be prepared for people who are as in tune to what is happening as you will now be.

Honesty of conversation at this point, as to what you both want and where you wish to go to, can not only save everyone time and energy; it can help you to reach a level of understanding with others for mutual benefit. There is a high level of trust required as you show more of your hand than you would like. You will find that you "fence" a lot – not making your strategy obvious at first – but you will know when you find a kindred spirit who is on your level and on your side. They then become one of your collaborators and, likewise, you become one of theirs. Think of the names of Henry Royce and Charles Rolls, who formed Rolls-Royce, a combination and brand that most people are familiar with, early in the twentieth century, and you will understand just where this can potentially lead to.

The quick wins and the ladders

- Questioning anything that is being asked of you, and only make your decision when in full possession of the facts.
- Making "why" your watchword.
- Knowing that any resistance to answering your question/ questions invariably means there is something hidden.
- Being realistic and respectful in how many questions that you can ask of others.

- Making judgement calls only if you have enough information and you have considered the full outcomes, both good and bad.
- If you find a like-minded person, then make them at the very least an acquaintance. At best, and in time, they may become a friend.

The traps and the snakes

- Not questioning and blindly trusting, hoping everything turns out ok.
- Making snap, risky judgement calls without the full facts. Doing so can negatively impact you and others in the short and longer terms.
- Asking too many questions without good reason, thus alienating others.

25

Coping with the bullshit, theirs and yours

Welcome to the world of bullshit, my dear.
You have arrived.

Elton John

A lifetime of experience has taught me that effective gameplay requires an ability to spot what I call "a wrong'un". Someone who is not telling you the truth. Even now, after hearing just about every tall tale going, one can still get through my net, but not so many as there used to be.

There is a saying, "The older that I get, the better that I was". Nothing is more true than when hearing some people describe their sporting prowess. Go to any youth football match and listen to the dads on the sidelines comparing notes on how close they came to getting a trial for any named football club when they were youngsters, and you will understand just what I mean.

And this applies to many situations where people reminisce about the past through rose-coloured spectacles saying just how good those times were. People roll stories off the tongue, actually believing they are real. Sometimes they themselves cannot distinguish between their fantasy and their own reality, and the truth becomes blurred. They seek kudos, admiration and credibility, giving them more right to bring you into their game so that you can play it in their way. They convince themselves that their stories are true, and thus their own legends are created.

Let us be honest, though, we all "bullshit" at times for effect, and can embellish a story with additional detail that can make it sound truly amazing. Listen to any accomplished speaker or observational comedian tell a story, and the picture they paint in your mind is very graphic and clear. This means that you are there with them, reliving the event as they want you to see it.

People who sell concepts and products that are intangible, like insurances for example, will also do this, as they have to make you see and feel the benefit and peace of mind that they bring to your world. You cannot touch or feel their product, as it is not like buying a car, for example, but the really good ones will have real-life examples to draw on, and there are so many now. Most people understand the concept. It then comes down to trust and the quality of their advice. I speak from many years of experience in selling intangibles.

So how do we cope with this and trust, or bring someone into our world based on what they have said? Even more importantly, how do we avoid a commitment to them and their game merely on their words? "Due diligence" and "buyer beware" are two phrases to keep very much in view here.

"Due diligence", as I have already mentioned in previous chapters, is about you doing the essential background checks to ensure that the person, or persons, that you are engaging with are who they claim to be. Is their proposition exactly as they have said and are they presenting themselves in the way that you believe that they should? Will they play your game for your benefit, or just for theirs? Do they have a hidden agenda, or do you suspect that they do? Most people are actually quite harmless with their stories and can be sometimes very entertaining. The ones that you have to really be wary of are those who are seeking to get you to commit to them in some way. Wherever possible, take a recommendation from a trusted source.

"Buyer beware" applies to any situation where you buy a product, a concept, or the person who is brokering the relationship. The more background checks on a person that you can do, the more secure you will be with your decision to trust them. If possible, always go with a recommendation from a known and trusted source.

If you have any doubts or warning signs start to appear, then walk away. In business you would likely RAG rate according to a traffic light system, which is red, amber and green, which I have already mentioned in a previous chapter. Just like driving on the road, green means go, amber means caution and red is a must-stop instruction. Put this into your questioning of yourself and you will find that you have a formula for sense-checking yourself, and thereby giving a form of independence to your assessment.

Be aware that often the game for some is specifically wanting your cash in their pocket, and to do this they will give you a glowing picture of what life will be like with them in your world. The promises will flow, one of which is that you should soon be living a utopia that they presented. But the reality is often so very different. Once they have your cash, then you are at their mercy, and the unscrupulous will take advantage of the situation.

And here is a lesson for your game, and a sidestep you can easily make when faced with a person who ends a sentence with "I won't let you down". The harsh fact is that, if they feel the need to say this, then they will always let you down, so be aware and walk away. Your game is better without them, and for your personal well-being too. You do not need that level of stress.

There are occasions where you will find the need to embellish and "polish" a story yourself. As I have said, never compromise your integrity, but sometimes it does help to have a few phrases and words available to give you some additional commentary to a situation. This is your bullshit, and how far you go with this is very much down to you and your own personal conscience. My view is that, if you need to do this, then keep it very light, often humorous and without any form of malice. The best advice, though, will always be to always stick one hundred per cent to the true and known facts. That way you only have to worry about the bullshit of others in the game and not your own.

The quick wins and the ladders

- Paying strong attention to "due diligence" and "buyer beware", knowing exactly the people you engage with.
- Red, amber, green (RAG) rate situations that you encounter to decide whether to stop, proceed with caution, or go.
- Knowing where your own reality starts and ends.

The traps and the snakes

- Buying and believing the bullshit of others without having done any form of background check first.
- Bullshitting others yourself for your own benefit and to their disadvantage.

26

The one called "the rescue movie". Finding your escape from the game

Escapism is survival to me.

Johnny Depp

There comes a point in everyone's day, week, month or year, when you need to escape from yourself and from the game. You cannot be in play all of the time, and actively need to manage the downtime that you have. Anyone who has worked constantly for seven days a week for several months on end, without a break, will tell you that fatigue sets in after a while and your body and mind need to rest and recover. Sometimes you have to force yourself to do it, but do it you must, as leaving the rest period too late can lead to burnout, illness and loss of game position. You can become careless, too, lacking in concentration and unnecessary accidents or mistakes can happen. Never forget your impact on others by you not being sharp or at your best. This also includes the example that you set if you are a leader, by taking the appropriate breaks and sticking to them. I worry immensely, for example, about the pressure that the "macho"-style work culture can have on people where, if you are not on your emails 24/7, you are seen as lacking commitment to the cause. This is also now known as "presenteeism". There is always a payback, and your body and mind have their limitations.

There are some professions, such as lorry drivers, where it is against the law to work in a fatigued state and over your legally set hours. There are directives laid down in legislation about how long people should work for, but mostly people will work to a specific shift, or are left to self-manage.

For everyone, I would advocate recognising the signs of fatigue and anxiety, putting in a self-enforced break. Turn your phone off, train yourself to resist the temptation to keep looking at your screen, and then find your escape. Your game, and the game of others around you, is dependent upon it.

Some people will use sport, hobbies, vocational work or outside interests, but all of these often require interaction with others and use of your energy for a purpose or goal. What I am talking about under this heading is complete downtime, an imaginary off switch that you can push safely to enable you to fully recharge. Remember as well, though, that this is not the competition part of the game. However, many do forget and place competition in the true relaxation category. These activities can sometimes be as draining, if not more so, than your other daily pursuits. If that works for you, that's great, but be very self-aware that 24/7 competition to beat others, or even just to beat yourself and your own personal best, is simply unsustainable. You cannot always play in this way. It is unhealthy, both mentally and physically. Your game will genuinely suffer.

One way to completely "zone out" or, in game terms, to "miss a go" is via something that I call the rescue movie. It may be a film, a programme, a book, a podcast or a piece of music that you know so well that you do not need to concentrate too hard, and it does not matter if you fall asleep midpoint and lose the plot or the thread. It is one where you feel safe and can wrap yourself into, so that you forget the outside world, close the door, dim the lights, turn off the phone and computer, put on comfortable clothes and simply relax. Isolate yourself from the pressures as much as is physically possible. It requires little effort and something to look forward to and that you can create in an instant.

Some people may also use relaxation techniques including hypnosis, water therapy, massage, reflexology and many more. There are also apps designed specifically for this purpose. All of these are wonderful if they work for you. Spa breaks, in particular, are seen more as a mini holiday and a great way to treat yourself, although they do often need planning and effort. The wealthier Victorians and Edwardians visited spa towns across Britain and Europe, "taking the waters". They were regarded as medicinal and necessary for their physical and spiritual well-being.

Unlike those times, ours is one where we have a need for instant communication, so escaping from the "tech" in our lives, by switching off, is also a "must do" part of this. All too often you see people at leisure who are still "switched on" to work, or another activity. Complete downtime is absolutely crucial.

If none of this resonates, then take these opportunities to find your "happy place". What I mean by this is the place in your mind where you know you were the happiest and felt safest in your life. It may be from your childhood, a holiday, or anything else where you had the very best of times. Recreate that moment by remembering the scenery, the sounds, the aromas, the people and the inner happiness that you felt. Close your mind to everything else around you. This is best done when you are alone and able to shut your eyes and have no other distractions. It is a great way to fall asleep and to relax. I have heard of others recording themselves (for later playback) talking about how their positive past experiences made them feel. This helps them achieve a state of calmer relaxation. It is a form of self-hypnosis and touches also on cognitive behavioural therapy (CBT), which is an important part of helping you to quell an inner doubting voice of anxiousness. Both of these I would fully encourage you to research and take professional advice wherever possible.

Ultimately it is whatever works for you. Keep experimenting, as you will find something in time that helps to give you the escape from the game to recharge and face again the board, the dice, the ladders and the snakes.

The quick wins and the ladders

- Finding your escape, i.e. a "rescue movie", ensuring you have complete downtime and can create the mental space for yourself in an instant.
- Switching off all tech and communications at some point for complete downtime.
- Knowing your triggers for fatigue and anxiety and knowing how to escape the game when these hit.
- Knowing that competition or competitive activities are no way to truly relax.

The traps and the snakes

- Having a hobby, or outside interest, that merely substitutes the environment that you need to escape from for another similar one.
- Not switching off, including your technology, when you are tired, fatigued and anxious.
- Living a 24/7 lifestyle with no enforced rests.

Choosing your teachers, mentors, coaches and cheerleaders

People need to be in charge of their development plan. They need to seek out their sponsors and their mentors and be very strategic.

Denise Morrison

From birth, the path for many people across the globe is that you are raised, you go to school, you may attend a college and possibly venture into higher education. From then it's into a working environment before retiring. You may take on some other roles in society and you may become responsible for another person (e.g. if you become a parent), and the circle starts again. The baton for assisting you with your development is passed, almost unconsciously, from parent to teacher, to lecturer, to employer and finally to just yourself. There are constant presences there, but if we consciously seek out those who can help to make us the very best versions of ourselves, and for our children too, our true potential must be realised. We cannot just wait for things to happen; we must make them happen. We cannot just do what is asked and set for us; we must seek out our own horizons and see what then transpires. We, as individuals, must break out of the figurative tramlines that can be set for us, and then begin to reach for the stars.

At school, we learn, we are taught, we are coached and mentored to a level and a degree of intensity that is more and more of our own choosing. If we opt to drift, then we can, and the world of opportunity will pass us by. And that is ok if that is your conscious choice. This continues through life as we develop our education and learning. We can progress at levels that we feel comfortable with and, again, we may choose to opt out knowing, however, that the chances to improve our circumstances are limited.

A famous quote from the children's author Dr Seuss sums this up for me. "The more that you read, the more things you will know, the more that you learn, the more places you'll go."

The role of teachers, mentors and coaches is ever more important in our world, and their impact can never be underplayed. They set a standard in every area of life, from helping us to define our own values, right the way through to giving us aspirations, goals, objectives and opportunities.

We must never lose sight, though, that they are not solely responsible for a person's full development. As teachers, in a formal school setting, they will see their pupils for a maximum of twenty per cent of their waking hours. The responsibility for the extra eighty per cent rests with the pupils themselves, their parents, guardians or anyone else they encounter. All involved have the chance to become a role model and a hero for the young people concerned. But there is a hard, uncomfortable truth to face as everyone progresses down this particular road. There will come a point where those who raise children (as the most significant people in their life since birth) may not be the best people to completely take them forward. They will then move to the role of supporter and cheerleader, as their own skills, knowledge and experience may be insufficient to enable the person to be the very best version of themselves that they can be. Recognising this is a moment of truth for everyone. Keeping the environment safe, secure, happy and enjoyable becomes their critical role here from this point on.

Finding teachers, mentors and coaches is not easy, as not everyone gets on with everyone else. A person who may inspire one may have exactly the opposite effect on another. However, they are in the position that they are because of their experience, knowledge and qualifications. Take what you can from every person that you encounter and develop your game, not in spite of them but because of them, whether you agree with them or not.

In school, the staff who teach you are largely non-negotiable. Unless there is genuine conflict, you have to take and accept the person that is given to you as a teacher for your subjects. You will not like all of them, and that is a fact, but you will find that they are there to help you to be the very best that you can be. You may not see the point of studying some subjects or elements of subjects either, and may actually take the view, "What is the point of this?" I remember thinking exactly that with some parts of science, and certainly some of the more complicated maths. However, as you grow older you will realise that the issue at hand may not prove to be the relevance of that aspect to your life but the discipline of learning. You will naturally begin to seek out more knowledge and that is the life skill that you are also being taught. It is then up to the teacher to ignite your flame of desire to learn more, and in that respect to help you to grow, mature and become curious.

Coaches and mentors can be the same, but invariably one is there to improve your performance in a specific area or discipline, and the other is there to motivate and direct you. There are certain crossovers, and a great coach will often be an inspirational mentor and vice versa.

No matter what age you are, the chances are that you will have had the opportunity to participate in an activity, whether it be drama, music or sport (these are usually the main ones). Someone will have been the lead figure in the organisation of this, likely occupying the role of coach. They will have helped you to find your way in the activity, and be specific in focussing on developing your strengths and abilities. Coaches become even more important as you become stronger and more skilled, and it may be that you have and need more of them for every aspect of the discipline as you progress. They know you as people and how to get the very best out of you. Once you find one that works for you, then hold them close as you can, as they are as important to your game as anyone. They will take you to being the best version of you that you can be and therefore make your game so much more rewarding for the rest of your life. They will help you to survive and sometimes to win.

I often use sport as a comparison when seeking to explain certain aspects of life, as we can learn so much from competitive and non-competitive sport. How many coaches, for example, does a top golfer or tennis player have? And how often, when you hear them speak, do they give credit for their performance to their coaches? They are never ashamed or defensive about this. They may be at the very top of their game and yet constantly seek to stay there, learning about every way in which they can be the best. They use diet, fitness, control of the racket or club, relaxation, and life coaches, to name but a few.

A great coach will also never miss an opportunity to coach. Seeing programmes on some of the greatest football coaches, you realise that their ability to find the moments that matter were often "in the moment", when they saw something that they knew they could develop or improve on for the player. It is the same in every walk of life, and if you can give a better direction to someone, then do it. Just make sure that the coaching intervention is welcomed and appreciated first.

In my working life I had a boss who held regular monthly meetings for all of his managers. Quite often a scenario or situation would be presented to us for discussion, usually sales-related, with a set time limit to provide the strategy and solution. "People, the answers are in the room", he would say assertively, and we all knew exactly what he meant as he had told us that many times before. We had the variety of skills, experience, knowledge and talent between us that meant that, as a group, nothing was insurmountable. We actually coached each other at times and had a strong, unwritten mutually agreeable contract to do this. As Aristotle said, "The whole is greater than the sum of the individual parts."

As another example, one person whom I have recently assisted with interview preparation knew that the question "What have you done to prepare for today?" would be asked. She wanted to know whether it would be seen as a sign of weakness on her part to reference the discussions that we were having, and the fact that she had sought out a coach. "Absolutely not" was my reply. It is a massive strength and it shows that you have taken the process very seriously, seeking to be the best that you can be. It is a true commitment to yourself and should always score highly, in my opinion.

Coaches and mentors are everywhere. The key is, as I have already said, finding the ones that work for you. Some will place themselves purely as advisors, but make no mistake – they are just as important as you get older as when you are younger. They will likely have particular specialisms that are specific to your circumstances at that point in time. The mistake that many make is that they reach a point of competence or experience and thinking that they do not need anyone else around them, as they feel by now that they should know it all. What many forget is that this is the exact point when your game is at its most vulnerable, as you will have reached a stage in life where you have a considerable amount of experience and knowledge, but not necessarily of what lies ahead of you. You can guess and make big decisions, but never be too proud to accept or take help and advice. That is when your game can really fall apart if you are not careful and you do not have good, competent people around you.

Mentors, as opposed to coaches, are often much less subject

or area specific. They seek to merely help you question and find the best way forward for yourself through the minefield, of the role or task that you have ongoing, including life itself. They are people who you trust implicitly, and it is very much a relationship of mutual trust too, as they often will share their own experiences with you.

The best thing a mentor does is to take you outside of your situation into another form of holistic thinking. When done really well this, again, makes you look at yourself from a totally different viewpoint.

The power of a conversation is something that a mentor understands, and the use of "pregnant pauses", which are silences allowing reflection on both parts, is an essential component of that. A good mentoring discussion is very much 40/60, whereby at least sixty per cent of the talk is done by the mentee (the person being mentored). Put another way, it can also be considered good counselling.

It does not have to be a formal contract either. If you say that you will meet every week, then you could be entering the realms of coaching. Mentoring should be more ad hoc, in my opinion, albeit with some structure. An agenda for the discussion does help, as does some written output, though neither is essential if both agree. What should be clear beforehand are guidelines and possible desired outcomes, with any pushes and calls to action, coming from the person who is seeking support.

I have been fortunate both to be a mentor to some exceptional people and to be mentored myself by some extremely talented individuals. I have never been what I would call "subject strong", like a teacher. I lack the desire to delve deeply into the specifics of any one area, hence why I also do not consider myself to have been a particularly good coach. What I learned, though, from all of my mentoring experiences, and still do to this day, is the importance of questioning behaviours, and then reflecting on someone's impact. By doing this in the right environment, such as via a mentoring discussion, you can safely replay situations and go through all possible outcomes. The mentor can make the person feel better about themselves and come to value exactly what they bring and create. The mentee will then answer their own challenges and questions if this is done effectively.

Another aspect of this is the acceptance of responsibility for your own destiny, and, in the game of life, I encourage everyone in this area to be single-minded and, to some degree, selfish. The latter is a trait that I struggle to advocate, but, when it comes to you and your performance, you have to be very clear that, if everyone else's game around you is to develop, then you have to be at the very top of yours. Therefore, having a coach, a mentor, a collaborator or just an honest, trusted sounding board is essential. This then leads you to demonstrate even more of your own true abilities, unlocking more of your talent and potential.

If you want to be taught, coached and mentored, then you will learn, develop and achieve. You will survive and you will sometimes win, as you will realise your potential, enjoying yourself more along the way as you go. The key is finding the desire within yourself (and at the earliest age you can) to be inspired and encouraged. It begins with those who raise you creating the very best of environments. This is the responsibility of parenthood and there is no greater responsibility in life that gives so much reward for getting it right.

If you are blessed to have a natural talent and a natural aptitude for something then, even if others cannot create the environment for you, you must be relentless in seeking out ways in which you can showcase what you have. Some of the greatest exponents of their talents have been those for whom it has not been easy. The push, the drive and the determination to realise their ambitions have often seen them fight even harder to be even better. If they have retained their core values, and not lost sight of who they really are, then these are the greatest of all role models.

I would recommend reading autobiographies of anyone who has survived, and who you perceive to be a success. This will help with your understanding of what is needed, and how to play the game as effectively as possible. You do not need to imitate them or copy them completely, as you are an individual, but you will learn from them some of what they did and how they did it. It does not matter what background people are from, either. It is their desire and of those around them to help to get them to realise their true potential that must be unwavering. Talent is recognised, but even more important is the need to shape the character of the individual to have all of the attributes that we have talked about so far: to cope, to survive and sometimes win, never forgetting that winning is often about survival.

One final trap to avoid is the win-at-all-costs mentality. Those who follow this usually lose sight of reality and forget others around them. They compromise their values and integrity and sacrifice friendships to get there. The "at all costs" mentality of victory, winning or even survival is just not worth it. You will always lose in the end and slither back down the longest of the snakes that lurk in the shadows of the board.

The quick wins and the ladders

- Finding out who the people are who can help you to be the very best version of you and making the most of all of their knowledge and experience.
- Realising that all learning has relevance to your game, either now or in the future.
- Knowing when, as an influencer (e.g. parent, teacher, coach), you must step back and hand over your responsibility for development of the person you support to someone with more skill than you.
- Finding out what you like and are good at.
- Trying out everything that you can.
- Learning from others who have survived and sometimes won.
- Avoiding a win-at-all-costs mentality.

The traps and the snakes

- Not seeking out additional support and help.
- Passing responsibility to others for your own development, without first taking some ownership yourself.
- Passing by an opportunity to support and help another.
- Ignoring opportunities to learn and not stretching yourself.
- Having a win-at-all-costs mentality.

28

Big picture and holistic thinking. Be the helicopter that hovers over the board

Holistic Thinking is a combination of analysis,
Systems Thinking, and Critical Thinking

Pearl Zhu

For those of you who wonder why some people seem to have eyes in the back of their head or three-dimensional vision, here is the answer. They look at the whole picture for their game from a vantage point way above the board of play. Imagine for one second that you are in a trench and you put your head over the top to have a look. All you can see is what is above you, in front of you and around you if you rotate through a full 360-degree circle. What you are unable to see is what is happening from a bird's eye perspective, and as a result you cannot accurately calculate movement, speed, distance and time. This is why air supremacy is so vital for armies in battles and wars.

Holistic, or helicopter-like, thinking and vision, is exactly that. It is assessing everything from a position above the game board rather than being on the board itself. Having this perspective gives you a competitive advantage over others. It is your very own navigation system to help guide you from point A to point B as effectively as possible, constantly assessing and recalculating your route. This way you can see far more clearly where the snakes and ladders exist. Like all systems, the more that it is programmed, the more sophisticated and better it becomes.

It is not an easy skill for a person to acquire and takes practice, time, patience and some understanding from those around you.

As always, the first starting point is awareness that you need to develop this skill, and acceptance that it will make a fundamental difference to you.

Next, think of a situation where you have reacted to something with a viewpoint, or opinion, taken only on the facts that you knew, or that you took at face value. The best one to reflect on is where you had a different stance to the one presented. It may have been a situation at home, at work, at college, with family or friends, something you have read. It could be anything.

Now, consider whether you knew all of the relevant facts and reasons behind the opposing side of the discussion to your own. Did you appreciate and have an awareness of the pressure that someone was under, and any other pertinent factors that you could have taken into account? Were you conscious of your own body language and how your response would be received? Did you make a judgement call without knowing everything?

Constantly questioning, and looking at all angles of your subject, will begin to give you a process for developing holistic thinking.

Once you think you have all of the facts and the information, you can then start to present your case, argument or strategy in the best and most logical way. You will leave no stone unturned.

Sometimes you have to do this at pace, but always try to buy time to allow your brain to process what is coming in and think like you are a helicopter in the sky. Ask questions of yourself such as what is invisible to you by being on the ground? What else could you see if you were up above? Why is someone reacting the way they are? What are your options? What are the consequences of your various decisions? There are so many but these should help if you are under pressure for a quick reply.

The next time you see a helicopter in the sky, imagine the view that it has and just how much more information the people on board have versus the information that you on the ground have. This will give you the understanding of why holistic thinking becomes so important to your game.

The quick wins and the ladders

- Thinking as though you are a helicopter in the sky, hovering over the game board, observing everything.
- Making judgements only when you have all of the facts, by constantly asking questions, until you are able to say that you have everything that you need.
- If you are making decisions at speed, then having a ready-made bank of questions to hand to help you.

The traps and the snakes

- Taking things that you are told on face value without questioning.
- Failing to ascertain all of the material facts before making key judgement calls.
- Making unnecessary snap decisions and judgement calls.

Making mistakes is ok

> If you're not making mistakes, then you're
> not doing anything. I'm positive that a doer
> makes mistakes.

John Wooden

Having continually championed the need to prepare thoroughly, I must clearly state that, even with the strongest of attention to detail, we all make mistakes. So often, when we have got something wrong that has affected others, we trip out the standard phrase "We all make mistakes, don't we?" as though it is normal, acceptable and just human nature. It is designed to soften the blow, to reduce the heat of responsibility, and to make everyone affected feel better about what has happened. The hands held with palms face up as though in a form of surrender or confessional pose, accompanied by the words "I am so sorry", is the way that this usually plays out. Sound familiar?

Making mistakes is actually ok and in many ways it is the only way that we truly develop and improve. As young children we learn to walk by falling over. It is a concept similar to riding a bike and almost any other task that can be named. We accept it and encourage development by telling the person learning to try, try and try again. With toddlers learning to walk, they get up and keep having a go. We smile at them and use all of the encouraging signals such as cheering, applause and words of support to help with their confidence. We say that the first attempt may have failed but its ok to keep going and to keep on trying.

In the current environment in which we live, the quest for perfection seems to be everything, with the margin for error and acceptability for making mistakes significantly reduced. Tolerance for errors has disappeared, and the health and safety, politically correct conscientiousness that seems to have become forced upon us has taken away any potential for risk. How else do we develop and learn if we are not allowed to have exposure to some degree of risk or error?

So, with that in mind, why are we so lacking in tolerance when people of all ages are trying to learn a new skill or task? Why do we berate them, shake our heads and look disappointed? I am not advocating a cotton wool world where there can be no criticism. Far from it. But the way that we respond can, and often does, have lifelong effects.

I remember coming home from school when I was around ten years old and getting ninety nine out of one hundred for a spelling test. I was top of the class, with several others, and was absolutely delighted. I had worked hard, revised and taken it very seriously. I ran home from school and, out of breath, proudly told my mom, "Guess what? I came top in spelling. I got ninety nine out of one hundred!" Now, instead of saying "Well done" or some other form of praise, her instant reaction was, "So which one did you get wrong?" The focus was taken away from the achievement, the work and the pride in the outcome, with the attention placed heavily on the negative. It was another example of how easily trust can be broken, and that their quest for perfection in me was relentless.

My dad came home from work later on, and, before I had chance to tell him the result and seek his approval and praise, my mom had already told him that I had got a question wrong. Only as an afterthought was the peer group position revealed, but the happiness, positivity and emphasis were completely lost. The moment was tainted and, with it, another sliver of trust disappeared. Add to that, I was told to write the word out ten times just to make sure that I did not make the same mistake again.

The word, by the way, was "lieutenant". It was pronounced phonetically by the teacher as left-tenant, as this is the English way of saying it. It is a word that makes me go cold, even to this day. As I type this sentence I can feel my lip curling and my fingers banging on the keyboard. Funnily enough, some of the nicest and most community-conscious people I know are deputy lieutenants, but their title still makes me reflect on that event even now.

The mistake itself was ok, and it is one that I have not repeated since on the few occasions that I have had cause to write it. The reaction to the result was not ok, though. It sought only to divide and to undermine my own confidence. It set a pattern for economy of the truth and a loss of communication and openness. Information was, in those days, more on a "need to know" basis, with that becoming the norm over time. The chance to support and celebrate with some positive coaching thrown in was lost.

Making mistakes is the only way that we truly learn, particularly in our formative years. However, once we are clear on what went wrong and have learned from the mistake, it is important not to keep making the same mistake again. People will be forgiving the first time but less tolerant to a second-time offence. However, it is the reaction to the mistake and the understanding that goes with it that is equally important. Also, putting the error into perspective around the error. Was it really that bad after all? With that perspective you can finally, finally give acknowledgement to just what else has actually been achieved.

The quick wins and the ladders

- Learning from mistakes without then repeating the error.

- Taking risks at times is the only way that you learn.
- Giving credit for achievements, not just focussing on errors.

The traps and the snakes

- Having no tolerance for mistakes in others.
- Making the same mistake over and over again without ever learning.

30

What doesn't kill you makes you stronger

That which does not kill us makes us stronger.

Friedrich Nietzsche

This is a well-used phrase that is thrown around society these days like confetti at a wedding. Face any difficult situation in life, emerge still alive and, no matter how grim your plight may have been, there will often be some wise old sage who will say, "You know what they say: what doesn't kill you makes you stronger." And people like that always seem to pick the time when you simply cannot tell them to "shut up", as they are invariably in a group and are seen to be "helping" you. The assembled crowd, no matter how large or small in number, will nod in admiration and agreement at the statement as though it is the first time it has ever been said. They feel like they've witnessed Moses receiving one of the ten commandments on Mount Sinai. I exaggerate considerably for effect, but I think, if you have ever seen this played out or been on the receiving end, you will get my thought process here. My goodness, it can be annoying, and yet it is so often said in such a well-meaning and sincere way.

The people offering this advice are sometimes the ones who

have never offered you any significant support, and somehow seem to be viewed by the world as regularly going out of their way to help. Their game is seriously warped in their favour and they are a whole book on their own. Be very wary of over engaging with people like this. They have a unique agenda.

Oh, and here's a thought, no one ever says, "Well, that didn't kill me and I feel a whole lot stronger because it hasn't." It just doesn't sound right.

So, before slapping the people down or walking away to punch a wall in frustration at just what has been said to you, think on just what strength it does give to you and your game.

The statement in itself is one hundred per cent true, in that what has happened has not actually killed you, for you are still living and breathing. It is an event that you will have gained massive experience from, on-the-spot life learning about you, those around you and how to cope, in many instances, with real adversity. You may well have made mistakes, too, and the memories of these will be so raw you will be unlikely to ever make them again. You may also have achieved and done things that you never dreamed possible, and taken on some massive positives during your reflection. You are a stronger, more powerful and well-rounded person as a result.

Now, if the person saying "What doesn't kill you makes you stronger" added "because…" and then explained why you are stronger, then that would be much more acceptable than a broad-brush soundbite statement. Backed with a clear example, it would be a real compliment. It would take you out of recovery and much quicker towards acceptance helping you to regain your confidence.

If you are ever offered these words, take them as a form of a compliment and then disengage from whoever has offered them to you, even if they are the nicest person in the world, unless they add something else that justifies it. Reflect in your own time and take the learning at your pace, not when someone else is running the airwaves and trying to monopolise your thought process.

Oh, and never forget... What doesn't kill you... You know the rest.

The quick wins and the ladders

- Taking this phrase as a compliment.
- Saying it to others but backing it up with facts about the person you are directing it at, knowing the positive effect it will then have on them.

The traps and the snakes

- Saying it as a soundbite just for the sake of something to say.

31

Is this a hill worth dying for or worth dying on?

All human actions have one or more of these
seven causes: chance, nature, compulsions,
habit, reason, passion, desire.

Aristotle

I have read of many accounts of people fighting for a hill in battles and in war. This is the highest strategic point possible, which, when captured, could materially change the direction of the conflict. Do you die for that hill and that position? Is it that important that you would give your life for it, and potentially the lives of others? Or do you walk away and fight another day in another way for the same hill, or possibly for another one?

Every now and then we find a cause in life that stirs our blood and makes us give more than just ranting commentary from our armchairs. We see an injustice, or spot something that is simply wrong, and away we go. Everyone has a different trigger that sets them off, and be aware that these do change as you get older and your circumstances and responsibilities change.

Within your game, it is extremely important that you are aware of what these triggers are, and pay close attention to just how deeply involved you are getting into the argument.

Is this something that you have a genuine and real passion for, or are you pursuing the disagreement and drawing it out to unreasonable lengths? Is the position that you have found yourself in so entrenched that you find it sucking the very life out of you and taking you away from your own game? You may be in a no-win scenario, but your own pride will often prevent you from backing down.

There are numerous examples of this quoted in the press. One I recall concerned two neighbours who had a boundary dispute over who owned a six-inch strip of land between their houses. Eventually it went to court and the loss for one couple was over £500,000. This represented their life savings and the cost of their home. In their game, they lost thirty years plus of financial progress, and all for fighting for six inches of land. They lost so much more as the stress it caused them had affected their physical and mental health. They may well argue that their cause was just, and I have no doubt that it was, but where is the line drawn at what is a reasonable fight? What if it were six feet of land? Wars have started for less, people have died for less, and we should always be conscious as to how deep and how far this goes.

I would encourage everyone to exercise a degree of caution and common sense when choosing which battles become the ones where you put absolutely everything on the line for. The ones where you put your game, and the game of those around you, at risk. You will have worked hard to get to a position where you can stand up for what you truly believe in, and that may even be at a relatively young age.

Make sure that you do all of the research and look at the whole picture. Look from every possible viewpoint at how the various opinions and arguments have been formed. In an actual wartime battle, generals assess the risks of assaulting a hill to capture it from the enemy. What are the risks and the dangers, and does the outcome of capturing that hill justify the possible losses? In other words, is this a hill worth dying for or worth dying on? In your case, and the cause or argument that you are pursuing, this is your game of life and everything can potentially hang on it. Do you continue with your attack on the hill or retreat to a safer point to reconsider? Once you have done your assessment, and if you have done it objectively without any form of prejudice, you will know whether there is a point where you may walk away. If you do, then you will have to set your pride aside, and that can hurt, but pride is repairable. Stay, fight and win or walk away, knowing that in time you will fight for the hill, or another one again, with better knowledge and a better strategy.

The quick wins and the ladders

- Picking your arguments and causes that you fight for so that you only fight for those that are just.
- Knowing that if you pursue the fight you could place your and your loved ones' whole game at stake.
- Doing your research and knowing the ground that you are on from every angle.
- Knowing exactly when to walk away from the fight.

The traps and the snakes

- Being ruled by your pride.
- Fighting on regardless of when you know that you should just walk away.

32

Regularly sense-checking your progress

> If you are going to achieve excellence in
> big things, you develop the habit in little
> matters. Excellence is not an exception, it is
> a prevailing attitude.

Colin Powell

One conscious action you can take that will help your game is to give yourself a regular personal review. This is an appraisal of your own performance – in other words, where exactly do you feel that you are positioned in your game? This is different to the short in-play "time out" that I have advocated in previous chapters as this is an opportunity to figuratively draw breath and assess your progress with your ongoing life plans. This is the time to turn off your phone for a while and to make yourself almost invisible. The key to this is time, and not to put it off as a task for another day that can wait.

Sense-checking your progress means a period of extreme honesty with yourself, and also a chance to be self-congratulatory. Very few people will tell you that you are doing well, as they are all so caught up in their own games and lives. Therefore, if few people are telling you that you are doing well, who else is going to be a cheerleader for you besides you?

The time period that you take is entirely up to you, and is largely determined by your own personal circumstances. It may be that an hour will do it, and at other times it may be a day or even longer. You can pre-plan these times in advance, knowing where you will be, what you will do and how you will assess your own performance. You may be lucky and have the flexibility to make a spur-of-the-moment decision to get away from it all for a couple of days, but, whatever you do, make it effective. Others will wish to regularly assess your performance too (having started when you were at school), so why shouldn't it also be you who appraises you?

So why do we plough on through life facing multiple challenges without giving ourselves this conscious break, when at other times in other situations we are forced to? The answer lies simply in the pressures on our time and the pull that we feel to do other things, whether it be compulsory or not. We seem to be good at living in the moment and creating the moment, but not at creating the time for us to consciously and objectively coach and appraise ourselves in an organised and constructive manner.

In the past, many people kept a diary, or a journal, and updated this at the end of every day with an account of what had happened. It would say what life was like for them at that specific point in time. Fewer people do this now, but for those that do it really is a great way to remember, reflect and to have something to look back on at a future date: you can be sentimental about life, but the real commentators are, and have been, truly independent of thought about them and their world. What pleased them, displeased them and what emotions they encountered as they faced certain situations. It is rarely shared as it is a private recollection, but it is also a great way to learn. People under massive stress have done this before as part of their own counselling and support. It is another way to create a review or break.

It is important, as well, to consider how you are performing in other people's games. You will be aware of their strategies and where you fit in, so think about their game plans and how you will then be a better friend, a better family member, a better member of society, a better employee, etc. By doing this with complete honesty, you will also help yourself with your all-round holistic vision. This will enable you to assess your own performance from different viewpoints, thus positively influencing your own game plans. Some of what you will see and learn about yourself will help to form your game plans and, as a natural consequence, you may change some of the direction that you choose to go in. Don't leave it to a New Year resolution. Do it now.

What the output of this looks like is very personal to you. You may choose to call it a mid-term review, a state of your nation – it may even be a career break or whatever title works for you. But do please take the time out to assess your own progress within the game.

The quick wins and the ladders

- Giving yourself a regular objective review of your performance in the game.
- Taking time out to review your performance with no distractions.
- Keeping a diary or journal to capture what has and hasn't gone well so that you can make changes and improvements in future reviews.
- Reflecting on how you are doing in the games of other people who you have relationships with and who you are close to.

The traps and the snakes

- Not setting aside time to review your own performance or recognising the importance of this.
- Not being honest with yourself as to your own performance and progress.
- Treating it as a New Year resolution that invariably gets broken.

33

A letter from you to you, and to those who have gone before

> Everything is a railway junction where past
> and future are sliding over one another, not
> touching.
>
> Timothy Morton

As part of the personal growth and development contract that you have with yourself, one piece of guidance that you can consider is to send a letter, or a series of letters, from you to your future self, all to be opened at specified dates. These will serve several purposes, including you being able to describe your life at the date you sent your letter, and your hopes, your dreams, your ambitions and your fears. I would also recommend listing your values and beliefs too as, whilst these will naturally vary over time, the core of what makes you the unique human being that you are should not. It will be a chance to write your future game plans and tell yourself the way that you have played the game so far, giving yourself advice for the future: who you should side with, who you can trust and who to avoid. The snakes that you have avoided and the ones that you have fallen down, as well as the ladders that you have found and climbed.

It will serve as a form of time capsule, and remind you of a period in your life when you were different. It may just help you to recalibrate if you are not making the progress that you wish. It could also give you confidence in knowing that the game plan you are following is the right one.

It differs from a diary, or journal, as that is more of an "in the moment" reflection of your day, and the events that are current. These letters can be extremely therapeutic and, if you do it, keep to the discipline of it, as they really help you to learn from yourself.

Writing a letter of advice to your younger self serves to be more introspective and is a chance to look back at what has gone well, and also as to what could have gone better. It's also a chance to look forward too, with counsel and experience, at whatever you feel may lie ahead for you.

Writing to those you love and care for can help their gameplay too. You can outline your successes, share your feelings and talk about your disappointments. Be as honest as you can and avoid putting a gloss or a polish on it. Write from the heart, sharing the joy and the pain. It is another leap of faith, but it means that you have a framework for a discussion and a chance to possibly share your experiences without being seen as overbearing. It can facilitate conversations that you may otherwise not have with them and can help to repair, rebuild and positively develop. Either way, what have you got to lose by doing this?

I asked my son, who was leaving his teenage years behind at the time, to tell me what he would say if he wrote a letter to his younger self. I was surprised when he immediately said, "It's a good life, remember the moments, listen and make as many friends as you can rather than enemies."

I asked him the same question but to imagine he was writing, this time, to his older self. His words staggered me with their maturity and wisdom. Summarised, he said, "Happy equals success and success equals happy. Minimise the regrets, get maximum joy and love from life whilst having fun, and do it now whilst you can." I hope that he continues to reflect and look forward in this way. It is great advice.

Ellie (who was the catalyst for the writing of this book) and her partner, who are both in their early twenties, gave me some of their thoughts on this too. One great phrase they both used was, "To keep ten per cent in your personal fuel tank and do not run at one hundred per cent all of the time as it is unsustainable."

Another was, "Just because you have missed an opportunity doesn't mean that you miss out."

The final words from them, as we ended our discussion, were, "Don't trust everyone. Keep your circle tight and close." Good advice and, if you have got this far in, you will know that this is a message that I fully endorse.

Writing to a loved one who has died, is missing or is in some way out of contact is another part of this cathartic process, and one that took me by surprise as to the healing it can bring. This may not work for everyone but, again, if we are to make our game as strong as we can, learning from experiences like this may just help you at a time when you need another viewpoint.

When my dad died I really struggled with the sudden and unexpected loss. I threw myself into work and, with so many other massive life events happening for me at the same time, the grieving process was unconsciously put on hold. Several years later, when I suffered with stress and depression, my doctor sensed that it was not just work that was bringing me down, although that was what I knew was the root cause. He suggested that I see a counsellor and arranged for a consultation. At this stage I was getting desperate for any solution, so I put my ego to one side and, a few days later, was lucky to see a qualified therapist. She was a lady in her late fifties who just instantly made me feel relaxed and confident that my deepest secrets would never leave that room. She reminded me of my favourite auntie, and that was the way that I thought of her from then on. The connection was made.

After a few pleasantries I sat back in the reclining glossy

black leather chair and made myself comfortable; she said in a very calm voice, "Tell me all about yourself, Andrew." A great invitation for me to talk about my favourite subject, so off I went.

The room was so quiet. I remember that there was a smell of lavender in the air. I could hear birds singing just outside the window and some beams of sunlight came in through the partly closed mustard yellow curtains and bounced off the pale cream-coloured painted walls. There was a picture of a wooden rowing boat beached on a shingle estuary that I seemed to be drawn towards. For some reason, I instantly felt safe. A few minutes into my monologue, she interrupted and said to me, "You have talked a lot about your parents. I know they both died, but I cannot quite understand when you lost your dad. It must have been very recently?"

"It was six years, three months, two days and around twenty-two hours ago," was my instant response, and I started to talk some more.

She interrupted me again and said, "Can I just stop you there and ask you to reflect for a moment on what you have just said, and especially that passage of time, which, by my understanding, seemed like only a few weeks from the way that you had previously spoken."

It was in that moment that I began to realise that I had not grieved at all for my dad and, as though a dam had been opened within me, the physical pain really began to come through as the enormity of his sudden and unexpected loss from my life hit. I had blanked it out because of the intensity of work, home life and everything else that was happening. For the first time, I had to deal with my grief and loss, before I could put everything else right in my head.

After a very emotional discussion, the counsellor recommended that I write a letter to my dad as part of my grieving process. I remember saying to her, "What's the point of that? He's never going to read it." Her response was, "You seem quite practical, Andrew; what have you got to lose by doing it?"

So one morning, a week or so later, I woke at 3am, got out of bed, went downstairs, grabbed some paper and a pen and started writing. The words just came, and so too did the tears. By 7am I had written eighteen pages of A4 and said everything that I wanted to, including dealing with so much from my childhood, and how proud he would be to see his grandchildren. It was deep, personal and written from the heart.

From that moment on I started to get better and continued to occasionally write to him, including some poetry that I had never written before or since. The pain eased over time, but even now, over twenty-five years on from his death, I can still feel it.

Your game of life is one where you never quite know what unexpected turns are there for you, and just how lacking in control of events you can be at times. If you can control the events, rather than the events control you, then you have more of a chance of survival. Knowing how to cope with the unexpected by counselling yourself and others who you care for is a critical skill to acquire, and being prepared to give your thoughts to a page can be a part of that. After all, the page in front of you has no opinions and doesn't ever judge you.

The quick wins and the ladders

- Writing a letter or letters to your past and future self, with advice, reflection and guidance.
- Writing to a deceased loved one expressing how you feel can help with your own therapy.

The traps and the snakes

- Disregarding any advice that you are given, or have available, as you never know when you might find it useful.

34

Today's news is tomorrow's fish and chip paper

Stacking all of this paper, dawg. I like to call this shit old news.

Wiz Khalifa

Some reading this may just be old enough, like me, to remember when you went to the fish and chip shop and your takeaway food was wrapped in newspaper. Some posher pubs and restaurants these days serve fish and chips on newspaper-style greaseproof paper that is meant to replicate those times. My nan, who was born at the turn of the twentieth century, used to have several phrases that included, "Today's news is tomorrow's fish and chip paper." For me, this has always meant that what is headline news and read today is quickly forgotten, as it will be used to wrap up fish and chips tomorrow.

Think about how quickly the news changes, even more so now, with the 24/7 thirst for information that we have. What was news only a few hours ago is often quickly forgotten and everyone has moved on. The physical newspapers become out of date almost as quickly as they are printed, and can now be seen on many occasions to serve no other purpose other than as a reference as to what happened at that particular point in time.

We may all have a time in our lives when we are dragged reluctantly to be the centre of attention. We have a moment in the spotlight, or at least we perceive that we do, and possibly for the wrong reasons. We may have done something such as making an error, or a bad decision. At the time, it may feel as though the eyes of the world are upon us and opinions are being instantly formed. We feel vulnerable, and very low in confidence. The reality is that it is probably magnified only by a few people and, even then, they have more important things in their world to focus on. But in our own mind's eye we blow the issue up out of all proportion. Keep a sense of proportion, though, as it does not last forever. Soon it will be over, another day will dawn and the world will have moved on. The headlines and spotlight will likely be about, and be on, someone else, and you can regroup. Yesterday's news is confined to the pages of history and you start over again.

I appreciate that not all problems or circumstances that we create are closed down in this way, and what I am saying could be seen as a soundbite written for effect. But please remember the title of this chapter if you are encountering a difficult period, whether self-inflicted or not. Take all actions that you can to put the situation right, refer to the chapters in this book, engage with others as positively as you can, seek out counsel from those you trust, and keep your core values front and centre of who you are. If you have made a mistake, then own up to it, never layering it with confusion or trying to cover it up. Make sure that the adverse headlines last for as short a period as possible. Your game needs it, as otherwise your energies will be misdirected for far too long.

My message to those of you who worry and continually stress over what you say, and how others perceive you, is to please keep all of the above very much in mind. Your game is being played out daily and you need whatever support you can draw on to help you with your own "self-talk".

So, rehashing the headline to suit our modern time and environment… Today's newspapers are for tomorrow's recycling.

The quick wins and the ladders

- Remembering that what is news today will not necessarily be tomorrow. Do not dwell on it for too long.
- Seeking out support to help you understand your position.
- Owning up to your mistakes as soon as you can.

The traps and the snakes

- Overthinking an issue and forgetting that people move on to other things very quickly.
- Covering up your mistakes without admitting to your error.

35

Coping with and embracing change

*Change is inevitable, change will always
happen, but you have to apply direction to
change, and that's when it's progress.*

Doug Baldwin

The pace of change comes at us faster than ever these days. No longer do we have the luxury of having time to consider some situations for as long as we once did. Our position within the game moves on, driven by the speed of communication and the instant need for information. Look no further than the world of politics, where not only do those reporting the news set the pace but those making it do too, with instantaneous messages and outpourings via the various available media. We have seen how Donald Trump, as president of the United States, used Twitter to announce policy changes and his innermost thoughts. It is almost unheard of for a world leader to behave in this way, and so overtly as well. By doing so he changed the playbook, drawing the opinions of others out with this fundamental strategy change. He played the game exclusively for himself, and everyone else had to play along, or otherwise they were excluded. People struggled to cope with it, but this is how it always will be for him, and by rising to his bait in whatever form that takes they feed oxygen to his publicity and controversy. Thus, inadvertently, they embrace the change by actively responding to it.

Coping with change is essential to your gameplay, and I would go one stage further with this and suggest that you positively embrace it wherever and however you can. Change can be frightening, but it is often an unstoppable force driven by others. So, unless you are looking to completely prevent the change happening, you will probably have to go with it in one way or another, making the very best of it that you can. Influence what you feel that you can influence, but the more time that you spend in denial that the change has happened, the less energy you will have for your game to move forward positively. I am not advocating a complete U-turn of human nature here, and to totally undo our attitudes and reaction, but the sooner that we can exit any form of denial, chaos and confusion that the change delivers to us, progressing into an acceptance, the less of your energy that will be lost for your own gameplay. It is a hard concept to get around, and one that will be seen as controversial by some reading this.

There are so many causes that people fight for, and so many that are right and just. It is a personal judgement call as to how hard you fight and resist and goes back to a previous chapter: "Is this a hill worth dying for or worth dying on?" However, when your desire for change is at the cost of other people's freedoms, liberties and individual rights, surely it is better not to die on that hill but to fight another way. In this age of instantaneous and impersonalised communication, where people learn about life events via social media and messaging, moving quickly into acceptance wherever possible without ever compromising ourselves is a change I would advocate that we must seek to embrace.

There is a model for change called "the Change Curve", which was originally developed in the 1960s by Elisabeth Kubler-Ross, a world-renowned psychiatrist, to explain the grieving process. The curve helps to practically show several stages of human reaction to change and is shaped like a valley in an extended "U" shape. There are many versions that have developed over the years, which broadly say the same thing, and I would encourage everyone to look at all of these in more detail where you possibly can.

I view change as following several stages, and these for me are:

Stage 1. Denial and anger that the change is happening.
Stage 2. Blaming yourself and others for the change.
Stage 3. The chaos, confusion and lack of understanding that the change brings to you and your life.
Stage 4. An acceptance by you that the change has happened.
Stage 5. Making sense of the change, with practical actions to show that you are making it work.
Stage 6. Resolving any outstanding issues that prevent you moving to the final stage.
Stage 7. Finally, moving on with your life, ensuring that the change does not hold you back anymore.

We go through change every day of our lives, and will run several change processes in our minds contemporaneously. Some will run through to stage 7 very quickly, almost instantly, whilst other reactions to change may be ongoing in our lives for years at a time, possibly never reaching resolution.

To try to make this come to life, here is an example of our reaction, in the moment, to change and some phrases that we may use. This could be where a change is enforced upon us and is suddenly out of our control, like a public transport delay, in the example below. These phrases could also be relevant for any other type of change, but this gives you a feel of how you could think when change hits you:

Stage 1 – Denial and anger
"I don't believe it. It's happened again. I am so cross and angry."

Stage 2 – Blame

"This is all their fault. They are useless." "If only I had done something else. I'm going to complain…"

Stage 3 – Chaos and confusion

"What am I going to do now? How on earth will I cope? This is causing me so many problems."

Stage 4 – Acceptance

"I suppose I'll just have to make the best of it, and after all I can…"

Stage 5 – Making sense and practicality

"Ok, so by altering one thing in my plan, here is what I will do now…"

Stage 6 – Resolution

"So that means that in future, just to be on the safe side, I had better…"

Stage 7 – Moving on

"I am still cross about what happened that day, but that is in the past and is behind me now."

This is a very simplistic and basic example to demonstrate what are very often extremely complex dilemmas for us, and I do not wish to downplay just how challenging change can be. Think, for a moment about your life and the changes that you have experienced. Reflect on how you and your game were affected, and how aware you were of the process of change that you were undergoing at that time. Our pre-programming as human beings with emotional intelligence means that some experiences of change will still be ongoing throughout our lives never to be fully resolved, and this is normal. Bereavement is a prime example where acceptance can be many years away, if indeed it is ever reached.

It is ok to have outstanding issues, but know where you are in the process. How do you then react to change? Consciously coaching yourself through it is a critical part of your game, as well as enlisting the help of many others where you possibly can. One thing is for sure: you know that change will happen in your life and your best laid plans will often have to be adjusted at a moment's notice, so be prepared.

The quick wins and the ladders

- Knowing the stages of "change" and being aware of them.
- Knowing that you will have several changes happening at once and you will be at different stages with each one.
- Influencing what you can influence, retaining your positive energy for your game without compromising your values.

The traps and the snakes

- Being unaware of how change affects you and how it occurs.
- Losing energy to changes that you cannot directly affect, unless they are a non-negotiable cause for you.

36

Rolling with the punches and 360-degree feedback

Adjusting to the passage of time, I think, is a
key to success and to life: just being able to
roll with the punches.

Dolly Parton

Progression in the game can often mean that sometimes you have people blowing sunshine at you, and at other times they bring the dark clouds and the rain. Occasionally these can come within a few minutes of each other too. The more responsibility and profile that you have in life, the more negative feedback that you will receive, whether you like it or not. Coping with feedback is a skill in its own right, and is one that I have always known as "rolling with the punches". This is more than just developing a thick skin. This is about being able to deal with the bombardment of criticism or commentary that will be directed at you from all different angles, and knowing how to safely and effectively protect yourself. You may choose to deflect them away or to actually take onboard what has been offered.

You must protect yourself at all times (as a boxer would when pinned on the ropes) and know when is the best time to break away, and even then to develop an attack strategy, always remembering my advice that attack is not necessarily the best form of defence. This can see you swing wildly at fresh air and miss your target. My advice regarding your overt consciousness and planning ahead is essential to keep in view here, as then you can assess the best moves to make and when. Never give an instant reaction, unless it is to say thank you. Buy yourself time, like a boxer would on their stool between rounds, or resting on the ropes. Say that you will give a response shortly if one is needed. Otherwise be very polite, humble and respectful that others have taken the time to feed back. Do this even if it is good, bad, indifferent or even unwelcome. An aggressive, angry rise to the bait is occasionally what people seek, which then justifies their commentary of you.

As I have already covered previously, individual feedback comes in a variety of forms – it can even be anonymous. Put any form of opinion out there on social media and be prepared for the appreciation, and also for the criticism. My advice to you is still the same. Do not rise; buy yourself time and then respond. If you have made a mistake then admit to it, apologise, say thank you where appropriate and move on. If you have been proven to be right and what you have said is true, then take the applause graciously and humbly... and then move on. Always learn from the experiences, take any constructive phrases into consideration but never get into a battle over feedback unless you have the strength, experience, courage and character to keep going. It is a no-win situation for you, as many of the world's political leaders, I am sure, would testify.

For the truly brave, gaining 360-degree feedback is where your real gold lies. This is where you can interact with everyone who you know, and who you possibly work alongside. Some companies and organisations will do this as a corporate body, and often you as a consumer, will be asked for feedback on your experiences with them. You may have done some "experience surveys" or even been a mystery shopper. They will do the same with suppliers, staff, and everyone else who they interact with. It gives them a holistic view of the perception of them as a business, and from there they can develop their strengths, understand their weaknesses and develop their strategies going forward.

Leaders often do this in their own right, where they will ask the same questions of their team and those that they report to, and will be curious as to how they can develop and improve. This is often done anonymously, as there are people who may not like what they read and others who would not be truthful if named. If you are serious about your development, and by reading this I assume that you are, I would encourage everyone to go through this form of exercise (a 360-degree profile) at some point, whether formally or not, just to get an understanding of how you are rated and regarded. In other words, what do you do well and what needs developing?

The very first 360-degree feedback that I did was after I was appointed into a management role, and it was scary. I was eighteen months in and it was a new concept at the time for everyone within the organisation. The feedback for me was done formally, and also anonymously by colleagues at all levels, including my boss's boss. I then went away on a three-day residential course to discuss and learn about myself, reviewing the questionnaires in granular detail. It was intense and very strange to take this time out to be so introspective. I was delighted with what some people whom I worked alongside said about me, particularly regarding my approachability, and how I could make that even better. One thing, though, did bother me and still does to this day. Everyone had said that I often sought approval for decisions that I made. In other words, I would make a decision and then seek out a form of sanction. "Was that ok with you?" and "I hope you're ok with what I have done here" were two phrases quoted that I often used. I have been conscious of this ever since, and have nearly always discussed it openly with my teams and my superiors as it is a trait that I have wanted to lose.

When the facilitators drilled down deeply with me on this, it all came back to my childhood and wanting to please my parents, particularly my dad. It was probably the case that I feared a decision made when I was younger may have caused him some displeasure if it was the wrong one, and resulted in me showing a lack of courage and belief in my convictions. I therefore needed supporters to tell me that what I had done was ok. Even more importantly, I was seeking approval from my line managers, who the course facilitator said were further representations of a parental figure to me.

It is something that is hardwired into me and has adversely affected my game on several occasions, resulting in me not making the right decision, or appearing to dither and delay. Once you consciously become aware of the issue, then it is easier to start to deal with it. However, beware just how exposed these aspects can make you and who you choose to share it with. It comes back to trust, as it can be perceived by those who seek to be unscrupulous as a way to undermine and destroy you. Trust only those who you know will respect your honesty and integrity, but share you must, as this will help with your overall gameplay.

In my case, I shared my awareness of my need for approval with a new line manager before getting to know him and exactly what his hidden agenda was. He almost destroyed me, using this as one way to further his game and subsequently ruin mine. This was a very hard lesson learned and one that I share with you by way of a note of caution and a snake you can avoid.

The quick wins and the ladders

- Having a thick skin and being prepared for both the good and the negative aspects of feedback.
- Knowing that attack is not always the best form of defence when it comes to receiving feedback.
- Being polite and respectful to those who give feedback to you, no matter who it is.
- Seeking direct and open feedback from those who you

trust and who will look at all aspects of what makes you an individual.

- Where possible, gaining 360-degree feedback from as many people as you interact with to see what you are doing and what areas need development.
- Building the feedback into your ongoing professional and personal development plans.
- Being cautious who you share this with.

The traps and the snakes

- Giving aggressive and instant responses to negative feedback.
- Lacking honesty when feeding back to yourself about you.
- Focussing constantly on another person's negatives without ever appreciating or recognising the good within them.
- Betraying confidences or misusing information about another person against them.

37

Pay it forward, give it back

> It's like "Pay It Forward". Everyone has
> seen that movie. If someone teaches you
> something that helps you in your life, why
> not pass it along and help the next person?
>
> Kyle Lowry

Every now and then, you watch a film or see a programme that makes you think about the world in a totally different way. It can inspire you to strive for more, stretch the boundaries of your own capabilities and motivate you to achieve. It is an uplifting time when your energy levels rise, your imagination is fired and you move towards a positive place in your mind that sends the serotonin, endorphins and the other chemicals, which I call "good-quality brain juice", into overdrive. The feeling doesn't always last, but sometimes it does. Either way, it gives you an inner warmth that you did not have before.

There was a movie released in the year 2000 called *Pay It Forward*, which did this for me. It featured a young high school student, played by Haley Joel Osment, who was set a task by his teacher to try to come up with an idea that would change the world for the better. For every good spontaneous deed you do for another person, they then have to "pay if forward" to three others and they then pay it onto another three, and so on. In other words, good begets good, begets good. It is an ever-multiplying number of acts of kindness and generosity that becomes a national movement. The film is very sad in places and was largely panned by the critics. I am a sucker for a "weepie" type of movie, so I loved it. Watch it if you can as it is a film that does stay with you once you have seen it.

I remember thinking just how amazing it would be if we could be so generous of spirit to create random acts of kindness like that. Every now and then I do think of that movie and it spurs me on to further support a cause that is close to my heart in some way.

The closest that I came to seeing "pay it forward" in action was when I worked alongside some of the charities, social enterprises and voluntary sector in Dudley Borough. My role was as a business connector for Business in the Community, one of the Prince of Wales' charities. I was seconded to work for them by my company to assist the communities within the area using my business knowledge and skills. What I experienced, many times over, was a wave of human kindness that went beyond networking, connecting and creating mutual benefit. I met people who volunteered and gave freely of themselves and their time, purely because they felt that it was the right thing to do. Communities are reliant on these people to function, and I had never truly appreciated just how much good there is out there. This was not just limited to a corner of the Midlands, either, but replicated across the nation, as my fellow business connectors would all testify. Sadly, though, the full concept of paying it forward often seemed to stop at the receiver, and therein lies one of our challenges as a society: how can you on receipt of a good deed give something back to another person? Of even more consequence is how you then recruit them to do something good as a result, and then they with the next, and the next, and so on, as happened in the film.

It can happen, though. I was privileged to hear about a

personal epiphany for one man who worked in a call centre answering phones all day and having conversations with customers. It was a massive building, very modern in its design, and, as you walked into the lobby there was a great atmosphere and you just felt that everyone was pulling together. The large open spaces with floor-to-ceiling windows and warm lighting also helped, as it had a non-aggressive corporate feel.

The gentleman I am referring to, like his colleagues, worked from 9am until 5pm, five days a week. He always took a full lunch hour, but unlike most of them never did any more than he was ever asked or contracted to do. He never attended out-of-hours team events or charity functions, and never socialised in any way with his colleagues. He was occasionally seen as a militant, a loner, and he gave away very little of himself.

He attended a meeting about the community support that he and his colleagues could provide, by his own admission, purely to get away from his job for half an hour. In that time he heard how everyone was being offered an hour a week of their contracted time to speak on the phone to local people who may be lonely. The company happily provided the employees and the cost of the calls as part of their corporate community programme, liaising with local voluntary organisations to source those who may be in need of a chat.

"So let's get this straight, I can sit at my desk during the day and make a phone call to someone and talk about absolutely anything for up to an hour, or possibly longer? And I'll still have my full lunch hour? And I'll still get paid for that hour that I am talking? And I can still start at 9am and finish at 5pm? What's the catch?" he said with a look of genuine suspicion. "There is no catch," was the reply. "It is simply the right thing for us, as a company, to do."

After a few weeks he had observed how his colleagues were making these calls at various points during their week. They were actually laughing more, talking about the state of the world, in fact anything other than business, and having a "full hour off", as he called it. He could see there was no hidden agenda so he signed up. The following Tuesday at 10.30am, he logged off his work calls and dialled the number of an elderly person who was expecting someone to ring. He introduced himself via a loosely worded script that was provided to him, and he talked for over an hour, putting the world to rights and finding common ground with a pensioner who had no relatives and was housebound by his disabilities. For the first time at work, the staff in his team heard their colleague laugh.

Spin forward a few weeks more and a meeting took place within another team based in the same building to introduce this concept to them. I was told that leading the way with great enthusiasm, and being a massive advocate for the scheme, was our once-militant employee, paying it further forward in his own way. A huge transformation had taken place. He has since increased his own productivity, his engagement with his colleagues, and become an employee award winner. Every week, I believe, he still calls the elderly person who helped him to find out how he could give something back. His game changed for the better and as a result he influenced many others to change theirs too. More than that: he makes someone's day every week.

Another great example of this comes from two dear friends of mine, Chris and Karen Cronin.

Chris and Karen are custodians (their words) of the Walled Gardens at Croome in Worcestershire. They also have a manufacturing business in Birmingham and are "go-to experts" producing bespoke staging for events such as concerts, festivals, sporting-related events, or anything where a large audience is present. If you have ever attended such an event, the chances are their engineering and specialism will have likely made it possible to happen.

On the face of it, people will look at them and see a success story, and they would be right. What differentiates them from others, though, is their desire to help to build a legacy for people to enjoy for generations to come. It is a unique approach that they have to life, and how they personally pay it forward.

Their back story is one of some challenge and, like all of the people that I feature, they know real hardship and personal difficulty. The building of their business alone has been many years in the making, with considerable hard work, sacrifice and commitment. Businesses like theirs do not just happen, and, once you reach a point of some success, the even harder part is then staying there, and also being ahead of the competition. The workload, if anything, can get greater and more demanding.

I first met them around 2005 in a professional capacity. Their business was already well established and, with their daughter grown up, they had embarked on a property development. This is not unusual for some people approaching the midpoint of their lives. This was no run-of-the mill property, though. This was a complete renovation and partial rebuild of the house and walled gardens that sit within the National Trust Estate at Croome Court, in the heart of Worcestershire, totalling some seven acres.

To understand the scale of the project, it is probably best to look at their website, https://croomewalledgardens.com, and see the progress they have made since 2000, when they completed on the purchase. I hope it may even make you want to visit them.

For many people, a project like the rebuilding and renovation of a property would eventually see the sigh of relief on completion and years ahead relaxing, whilst enjoying the fruits of their labours. It would be done at pace and to a strict timetable.

Chris and Karen were very clear from the outset, with me and anyone else, for that matter, who became involved with them on this project from the beginning. They were making a contribution to the continued history of the UK that would last long after they have gone. The renovation was not just a personal project; it was a legacy and a responsibility that they both took on, knowing it would take many years to complete, if indeed it ever did.

Chris is a bundle of energy, always smiling and truly passionate about everything he does. If he starts something, he commits one hundred per cent to it and sets a very high and exacting standard for everyone who engages with him. Karen equally has the same level of passion and enthusiasm, with a phenomenal eye for detail. They are an amazing team, and it is little wonder that they have made their business the force that it is.

I remember standing at the very top of the gardens, on my first visit, looking down towards the house. The Malvern Hills were in the background and rolling green fields spread as far as the eye could see. The sun was shining brightly over what really is the heart of England. You understand fully when you are at Croome why Elgar was inspired to compose so much incredible stirring music in this part of the world. And yet, as I took in this incredible vista, I had so many mixed feelings. The professional in me said that this was a challenge so great and complex in itself that many people more qualified than Chris and Karen would never attempt it. I would certainly have to write a report about the project and to do it justice in that format would be a challenge. As you have found now, reading this, it still is. The property owner in me said, "This scares the living daylights out of me and run now. It is just too much, and too great a commitment." The human being in me said that, "This could be one of the greatest single acts of selflessness and charity that I could ever witness in my life." I realised that I was among people who were prepared to lay almost everything that they had on the line, knowing it would be a lifetime's work, to eventually give back to others.

Chris stood next to me and drew the pictures in the air with his hand. He told me what would go where, what had existed previously that they knew of, showing me certain landmarks and talking about Capability Brown, a famous English landscape architect of the eighteenth century. He told me about how the walls were used for heat (amongst other things), and what they expected to find during the work. "The Visitor Centre will go here and we expect to open to the public within six years," was the last thing he said after telling me about his desperate need for bees.

Karen was further down the very long grassy bank beginning work on a new greenhouse: a very, very long greenhouse and one of three that had been recently restored.

My senses were overloaded, and the thought of their home being overrun by the public was the final point where I knew that I could not take in anything else at that point.

It was clear that they understood in minute detail the scale of their commitment and what their vision was. I realised that this was not just a hobby or a project. This was to be their legacy.

The human being in me was right, and ever since then the project has developed and continues to do so. Historical finds, and the learning that has resulted, have taken the significance of the gardens to our nation to a new level. Visitors come, volunteers help, produce from the gardens is sold and people also come to learn. This is their home too, and I can think of very few people who would be so generous as to allow this level of openness. They truly understand just how much the gardens can offer to others and I think they get as much from seeing people like me (whose jaw hits the floor every time in wonder) as those who visit, help, volunteer and gain a genuine inner peace from being there.

Karen takes particular delight in ensuring younger people from inner cities, or those with little access to green spaces, get to see vegetables, plants and flowers close up. She gives them an understanding that food can be grown and doesn't just originate from a takeaway shop or in a package from a supermarket.

As the final capstone was laid on the kilometre of walls, twenty years after the work started, it will come as no surprise that Chris has taken on another project as well. This time it is to help young people who wish to study for a career in the musical entertainment industry. Together with other like-minded people, he has helped to develop and create the very first centre

Chris and Karen Cronin

in the UK for students who wish to specialise in all aspects of musical production. "Resonance" is an amazing addition and offering to the West Midlands' educational landscape.

Chris and Karen are truly inspirational people who I am proud to call friends, and who have set a standard in life for me to aspire towards. They are people I truly respect and who I have looked to in the writing and development of this book. They have really paid it forward to me, and also with other acts of kindness. I know many others feel the same about them, with the development of the Walled Gardens, and now with Resonance. They do what they do because they want to create good. They wish to be part of facilitating a better world, leaving something behind for generations to come. They have taken unique practical actions to give back in an altruistic way, whilst allowing space for others themselves to also pay it forward too.

The quick wins and the ladders

- Regularly sense-checking how you can help others, and then encouraging them to do the same, by "paying it forward".
- Following and emulating the role models that exist in our communities who seek to make a difference for the better.

The traps and the snakes

- Not taking the opportunities to help and support others when they are available.
- Receiving help or support and then choosing not to give back yourself.

Pay it forward, give it back

38

Magic moments

No act of kindness, no matter how small is
ever wasted.

Aesop

One of the amazing and visionary leaders that I worked with
(Peter B, please take a bow) proposed to the team (of which
I was very proudly a member) one day the concept of "magic
moments". This was awakening us all as to the opportunities
that we had to find the moments in life that were special for
our clients and to recognise those times in some way. It may
have been a birthday, an anniversary, a holiday, a party, a family
event – anything. It could also be a sad occasion and a chance
for us to let them know that they were in our thoughts. What
we did then was to send the clients a handwritten message, a
gift – or just something that said to them that we cared, that
we thought about them and we were not just another financial
institution or transactor. It was a differentiator for us, a unique
selling point and also a way of further cementing client loyalty
and our relationships with them. They, after all, paid our wages
and without them we would not exist, so why not try to do
something that was different?

Magic moments are very important in our lives and come

along all too rarely. We move at such a fast pace and forget to acknowledge along the way just what is truly important, and what really matters the most. We fail to smell the roses as we walk by them. When someone else recognises a milestone, significant life event for you, or demonstrates that they care, it makes it even more powerful and special.

This is the shortest chapter in the book, and deliberately follows the "pay it forward" concept, as it is another way to create the chance to give something back. Do it "en masse", or in any way that makes it feel as though it is from a corporate machine, and you will miss the moment, the point and the impact. In fact, you could have the exact opposite effect from the one you seek to achieve by generating some form of cynicism and losing advocacy.

The chance you have, in whatever capacity you hold in life, to create a memory for someone, to simply say thank you, or let them know that you are thinking about them can be priceless. It will give strength, sustenance and support to your game as well as to theirs.

The quick wins and the ladders

- Using spontaneous "magic moments" to recognise someone in some way that makes them, and you, feel good inside.

The traps and the snakes

- Being less than genuine and original when making a gesture, e.g. using a template or just going through the motions for the sake of it.

39

Money. Try playing the game without it

> Money makes your life easier. If you're lucky
> to have it, you're lucky.
>
> Robert De Niro

We all need money – fact. Yet, "the love of money is a root of all sorts of evil", according to the Bible. And it is as true today as it was in the times of the apostles, when it was written.

Unless you are living totally "off grid", self-sufficient from the land and a virtual hermit, I would challenge that everyone else on the planet needs money, or a currency of some sort to survive. Therefore, playing the game of life means that you have to work with and use money for the most basic of items such as shelter, food, water, clothing and warmth. Even in ancient times, bartering, where one tradable item was exchanged for another, was a commonplace transaction.

Most cash is derived from a service being provided or goods being sold for a price. The price is usually set, or may be negotiable, and that determines your own level of income and potential expenditure.

For young children it can start with pocket money, possibly for a series of home-based tasks that progress through to part-time jobs. Surprisingly in this digital age, paper rounds continue to be one of the popular ways young people can derive income.

Like all things in life that can be boring, energy-sapping and time-consuming, your personal budgeting and financial planning can be something that you put off for another day when you are "more in the mood". *Don't!* This is one of the most important of all tasks, as, without your money working correctly for you, your game is uncontrollable and you are always forced to play by the rules of those who supply you with the money, and also those who then take it away from you. I add this to my list of BBCs, also known as "boring but criticals".

The game of life is so much easier to play if you have sufficient money to meet your requirements for happiness, your goals and your ambitions. Just make sure that you acquire it legally as otherwise your game is compromised and you will ultimately lose.

The list below will give you some clear pointers for you to have as close to absolute control of your game where money is concerned:

Day-to-day management and budgeting

Use any form of spreadsheet or tracker to ensure that you know where you are at any one moment in time with your finances. If you were a business, for example, you would have to do this so why not do it for yourself? This will also help with managing your spending, making sure that you do not live beyond your means. Know what is coming in, what goes out and the running balance. There are so many available online; just choose one that you feel comfortable with.

Plan

I encourage everyone to look at their short- (within the next year), medium- (within the next five years) and longer-term plans (five years and beyond), together with using an appropriate and qualified advisor(s) along the way. Generally, the older you get the more complex your financial needs and requirements become, and so taking correct advice from a suitably qualified person is crucial and ultimately cost effective.

As soon as you possibly can, start to plan for your retirement. This may sound strange to, say, a sixteen- or eighteen-year-old, but the earlier you can start to build up a pot, even for just a minimum payment, the more time that money has to work for you. The game of life is played at a pace that, whilst we know there are 365 days in a year, the hours and minutes somehow seem to go quicker as you get older. They actually don't, but it does feel that way sometimes. Putting it off for another day means that you will be unlikely to take action until it is absolutely necessary, and that means that your future plans run out of your control. The cost of making up for those lost years of inaction can cause massive pressure in the years that follow.

Understand from an early age why making a will is so important, and also ensure that you recognise your responsibilities for those whose financial positions you may have to take care of after their passing. These are far from easy conversations to have but they are essential as, at the time of maximum grief, the legal and financials can be challenging and confusing to grasp from a cold start. Mistakes can be made and decisions taken under pressure (which are often irreversible) must be made with a clear head. This is a key move for your game and for those you love.

Review

As with a car, there is a need for a regular service. Never put it off. Sit down and do a complete health check on yourself. Once a year try to review your finances and position with a professional, whether they be from a bank or any other advisor. Your game deserves and demands it, and so do you to protect your autonomy. Always listen to a maximum of three advisors and go with the one that you feel the most comfortable with. Never be price driven, and always ask, as a minimum, what they will do for you to earn their fee. It comes down to trust in the end, and often a recommendation from a reliable source goes a long way.

Insurance

A word that can act faster than most anaesthetics, in my experience. Make sure that you regularly check whether you have yourself, your family, your property, your car and any other assets protected in the correct way. Again, always seek out professional advice where you possibly can.

Tax

Unlike insurance, which can put you to sleep, tax is a word that in my opinion can have a quicker effect on people than laxatives. The tax authorities of any jurisdiction play the toughest of all games, and charge you for playing the game of life at certain levels in very different ways. They are very much like a snake along the way for your game, and to progress to the next stage you have to make sure that you pay your taxes. These taxes can differ for every person, so it is well worth researching and, if your affairs are complex, again pay for good advice. Always speak to the tax authorities or correspond with them. They have a job to do, but they are a necessity for our society to function. There is a phrase in finance about "never letting the tax tail wag the dog". This means that you must never put the need to save tax ahead of your own financial objectives and goals, otherwise you can lose sight of making income and may follow some schemes that can be on the edge, or the wrong side of the law. Stay on top of it and always set aside some of your earnings to cover your tax, if the way you pay is not through your earnings directly.

Loans and financial agreements

There will be times when you look at taking out a loan, a credit card or a financial agreement to borrow money in one form or another. My advice here is very simple. Do not take out anything that you do not understand or cannot explain to someone else. Always check the rates of interest, cooling off periods and penalty clauses. Know what happens if you cannot meet the payments at any stage. Take advice if you are in any doubt, and ensure that what you are spending to service the debt is not so much that you are unable to live to the levels that you would like to play your game effectively for you.

Notes of caution

Beware of what may appear too good to be true, otherwise known as get-rich-quick schemes, as they invariably are not as good as they seem. The same applies to gambling. Always question if someone is offering you an amazing deal. These "one-offs" rarely are what they appear to be, and your game can be lost by trusting someone who you have never met. In the same way, do not buy cold from the door, in the street, via an email or a phone call. Any reputable person will happily make an appointment, send you details of their product, explain how they are regulated and not subject you to unnecessary pressure. Remember, you are the consumer and if you are in any doubt then don't.

Do not ignore your post, emails or any other communications. Check your bank statements regularly and know where you are day to day. It only takes a minute to check online, say once a week or monthly, to review and reconcile exactly where you are with that.

Do not do what your friend says or does, as the advice for them may not be right for you. Seek out the professional help and support that is pertinent to you and to your specific circumstances and then act on it.

Finally, make sure that when you have money you enjoy it, keeping your expenditure under control. A later chapter on rewarding yourself will help you to understand why this is important to your game.

The quick wins and the ladders

- Paying attention to your finances.
- Having a plan or a series of plans for your money.
- Taking professional advice and not buying impulsively from anyone with a get-rich-quick scheme.
- Reading and implementing the recommendations from the list above.

The traps and the snakes

- Ignoring your finances and not planning ahead.
- Gaining funds from illegal sources or taking on get-rich-quick schemes.
- Spending beyond your means.
- Not reading the above list or implementing some of the recommendations.

40

Four stories of people I regard as role models, survivors, winners and great game of life players

However difficult life may seem, there is always something that you can do and succeed at.

Stephen Hawking

All too often we focus our energies and attention on seeking to be someone else. We are told by the media almost daily that we should never be satisfied with who we are. We should try to be slimmer, we need to carry more weight, be more giving, be more selfish, be more outgoing, be more reserved and so on. You see daily the bombardment of contradictions in magazines, TV programmes, adverts – it is everywhere and there is really no escape from the confusion created about who, and what, we should aspire to be. It is little wonder that we all have lost some of our own identity and take on parts of those flung at us by so-called "role models". We become a hybrid of multiple personalities, and seek to find a form and shape that is acceptable to what we think that society demands of us.

One sad consequence for me is that the pressure on people in the public eye is even greater than ever, and, once they are held up as an example or given a media profile, some do struggle to cope. What is ironic is that the media will then knock them down, having built them up, for being human and making mistakes. So then they are vilified – no longer a role model but an outcast instead. Their game will have seen a rapid rise up the ladder, only to hit a snake and fall straight back down the moment they are no longer "perfect".

The successes when they happen are amazing. I genuinely admire anyone who can find fame, live with everything that goes with it, remain level-headed and survive. It is a responsibility, and one that should never be carried lightly.

Within this chapter I am profiling four people who I know and who are, in my opinion, local heroes in our communities. They are survivors and winners at the game of life. They all have incredible back stories and have demonstrated qualities that I can only look on in admiration and awe.

They have several things in common too. These include the desire to give back, to recognise that they can make a difference, and to take personal responsibility to facilitate positive change in society for the betterment of others. They play their games selflessly, yet with a clear focus, and they recruit like-minded collaborators, with ease, to buy into their vision and ideas. They own their lives and their respective destinies, without asking for anything in return except an open mind from everyone who they encounter. They do not moan and have an inner peace of mind that few of us truly know. Whether consciously or not, at times, the game of life that they play is one where we can all be beneficiaries if we choose.

I want to share their stories with you, as all four are "normal" people. They live among us, often anonymously, yet make massive differences to the world. They seek no adulation, are extremely humble people and have all known and faced adversity in their lives. I am proud to call them friends, honoured that they have trusted and agreed to help me with this book, and privileged to share their personal stories with you.

Steve Waltho MBE, local councillor and former mayor of Dudley

Steve Waltho

These titles are the official ones. Steve is also a father, a husband, a grandfather, a brother, a son, a friend, a volunteer, a walker, a climber, a runner, a traveller, a football fan... the list is endless.

Arriving at Steve's home, on a new housing estate in Kingswinford (in the heart of the Black County), which he shares with his wife, Jayne, on a dark, damp September afternoon, I find that he has just returned from another morning volunteering, this time at a local hospital supporting the drive for more people to sign up to the Organ Donor Register. He is wearing a bright pink T-shirt promoting the message for people to put their names to the list, and the warmth of his welcome is as genuine as his smile.

Steve is a man of the people. My words, not his, as he is far too modest to use terms like that. His diary is one of events and meetings that bear this out. He is in his mid-sixties and yet, at a

Didn't anyone ever tell you? It's all a game!

time in his life when he should be thinking about slowing down, he seems to create hours that simply don't exist. "If I need to be in ten places in one day, then I can," were his exact words as we discussed his largely unpaid workload.

Listening to him talk, as I have done many times, I realise for the first time just how Steve's mind works. He thinks deeper than most, and with a need for full 360-degree awareness of every viewpoint before making a decision, or committing to any form of opinion. "Mmm... interesting," were his words when I explained my idea for this book. He still had yet to glean all of the information that he needed, so was unable at this point to give his unconditional endorsement and a thumbs-up to my project.

As we speak about his life, it quickly becomes apparent to me that his biggest influence and role model was his late father Jim. Jim was a man who had worked hard to progress from a sheet metal worker in post-war heavy industry, operating dangerous machinery, to becoming the factory manager. That was some achievement in those days. Steve proudly describes how this man was totally non-discriminatory during a period when the country was full of post-war bigotry and hate.

Steve's childhood was based in Smethwick, near Birmingham, which technically makes him a "Brummie", as Black Country folk refer to Birmingham residents. With a growing multicultural community in the 1960s in the area, his dad would find jobs for genuinely hard-working people irrespective of their race. Jim carried a massive social conscience, and Steve recalls men wearing brightly coloured turbans calling at his home with gifts to thank his father sincerely for giving them a chance of work. The gifts may not have been valuable in themselves, but they were symbols of respect and appreciation for what the man gave to them. Jim did it regardless of reward and recognition. He set an example for Steve that became ingrained into his very soul. The need to do the right thing by other people and to be a humanitarian are qualities that have seen him follow a need to publicly serve, for no other reason than it is the right thing for him to do. "Fairness" and "equality in life" are phrases that he uses many times when reflecting on this time.

Steve felt his childhood was unremarkable in many respects. His dad, as previously stated, worked a hard manual job, and his mom, Doris, was a very traditional family woman, but was also an accomplished legal secretary. She gave up work, as many women did in those days, to look after Steve and his sister Alison when they were born.

His earliest recollection of a significant life event was surgery in Birmingham to correct a "lazy eye", as a five-year-old. He was subsequently labelled "four eyes" by his friends and had a patch on his round National Health glasses. This kind of label would be seen as bullying at the very least now, but in those days it was the norm.

School was never a great challenge, as he was able to cope academically, although his advice to his younger self would be to be more serious about qualifications and the positive impact that they can have on your life.

Sunday school, the church choir, practical science lessons, sport and a love of the outdoor life all made for a happy and simple childhood. Steve describes this as "life-defining" for him because there were a number of people who helped him to find out more of who he actually was. People who were friends, acquaintances, and also involved in the local community. And all of the time there was Jim's guiding hand on the tiller, helping Steve on his journey, which included supporting his son's amateur football career. This became the backbone of Steve's sporting and social life in his twenties. He played over 800 matches in local leagues, with a full trophy cabinet as evidence, before suffering a serious knee injury sustained on a charity parachute jump. He just could not give up the football, though, and, as he was unable to play, he chose to referee instead.

You are probably reading this and thinking, so how did this normal lad become someone who many, in the Black Country and beyond, regard with such respect and admiration. It is an everyday story of a normal man's life.

Steve's principal change began as he progressed into higher education, studying A levels. He recognised that he struggled to retain information easily, and he modestly admits that concentration was always a challenge. Self-deprecating as always, he said it was the chance to captain the first 11 football team that was the real reason he stayed in education. He was very practical and knew his key strength areas. We are back into the arena of self-awareness, consciousness and an inner knowledge of yourself, as I have discussed so many times in this book. He took the advice from his father (which he never regretted) about not going to university but instead starting a career as a trainee chemist at a large chemical company. He listened, reflected and accepted where he should begin. This ability to see all sides and have holistic vision is critical to his story.

Steve's awakening into public life and the local council came via the sad loss of his father at the age of sixty-one. Jim was in a National Health Service hospital on a ward that Steve described as resembling scenes from a Second World War concentration camp. It was full of men in striped pyjamas, all looking very ill and being given, in his opinion, substandard care. As Steve talks, the scene is clearly one that still haunts him to this day, and he said in measured tones, "It was just not right that he came to an end in that ward."

This sad event has shaped Steve's life ever since, and he left the hospital asking himself, "If I can change the world for the better, what mechanism can I use?"

He took soundings from many people (this theme of all-round vision and questioning is ever present), including his then wife's family, who were strong socialists. It was from there that he joined the Labour Party, where he felt his political home was. He then began campaigning to save a local hospital, and subsequently stood for election to the local council.

He had been true to himself and his commitment to facilitate change. For many, the story would end there, with the person fading into the background of politics, possibly being voted out at a subsequent election and feeling that "they had done their bit". And, let's be honest, that alone is more than most of us do.

For Steve, though, this was just the beginning, and the list of service and achievements from then on is breathtaking.

To date he has:

- Served for over twenty-two years on Dudley Council, representing the St Thomas Ward.
- Sat on countless committees including being cabinet member for housing and social services.
- Gained a degree with the Open University that he started in 1994, finishing in 2010.
- Held down a responsible job, working for the same company for over forty years.
- Held positions within the company extra to his twelve-hour shift, with duties including member of the works fire brigade, charity committee secretary, trade union shop steward, and company magazine reporter.
- Tried for the SAS as a territorial reservist… and nearly made it.
- Been a trustee to several large charities, and a fundraiser for many others. This has included walks, bike rides, mountain climbs (he has just done Ben Nevis again).
- Been a mentor to newly elected and younger councillors, regardless of their party, in Dudley Borough.
- Been a member of a local male voice choir, who also do considerable charity work.
- Been mayor of Dudley. Steve and Jayne (his wife and mayoress) completed and attended over 450 events in their year in office. An amazing achievement, and to do all of this he took a year out as an unpaid sabbatical from work for this.
- As mayor, raised a then record £55k for local charities.

He was also the first Dudley mayor to run the London Marathon and to climb Ben Nevis in his year of office.

- Been awarded an MBE for all of his incredible community work and service in the Queen's New Year Honours at the end of 2017.

And all from a moment of truth in a hospital ward in the early 1990s in Birmingham.

Steve came out with some amazing quotes when we met, in addition to those I've already used:

Never judge who you've never met.

My dad was my hero. He was a good honest, decent, solid character.

A principle I have for my life is fairness and equality.

I was a late developer; it's never too late to start.

Black Sabbath helped with the difficult times.

Live for the moment. (I was surprised when Steve said this, bearing in mind his cautious approach, but it makes sense as the moments for Steve are always risk-assessed in his mind first.)

I don't use the word regrets; I prefer disappointments.

I asked Steve what his greatest achievement in life was, fully expecting him to refer to his MBE or his inspiring charity and council work. No, it wasn't. It was climbing Mount Kilimanjaro with his son. The pride burst out of him and he just about held back his emotion. It was evident that this had a deeper meaning for Steve. He said very little after that as this was a very personal memory that was not to be shared and would stay deep within for his own personal safe keeping.

Steve would have made a remarkable Member of Parliament, but he decided not to go down that route. I think if he had done so he would have had to compromise on several of his strongly held values at some stage and, for him, that would never be an option.

Steve's advice to play the game of life as effectively as you can is as follows:

Be true to yourself.
Don't pretend to be someone else.
There is absolutely nothing wrong with having old-fashioned values.
Do unto others as you would have them do to you.
Don't have recriminations.
Be consistent.
You do not have to believe in God, or a superior being, to embrace the values of Christianity.

My takeaways from listening to Steve are: his tenacity, resilience, self-awareness, holistic vision, drive, determination, ability to get people to buy into him, unflappability, and incredible humility. Above all of that was his desire to listen and to take advice from those who he trusted and saw as role models, most notably Jim, his dad.

And so finally, as we ended our discussion, I believe that I finally gained the endorsement for this project that I was seeking from him at the outset, as he revealed what he describes as "the four cornerstones" of his life. These being football (playing and also being a lifelong Liverpool supporter), rock music (inspired by Black Sabbath), charity work/community service and climbing/hill walking. At the inner core of these sit his family, his friends and so many people that have shaped his life. And in Steve's own words, "At the very, very centre of all of that is my soulmate, and love of my life, Jayne."

Thinking of his life like this is typical of the thoughtful, deep man that Steve Waltho is and why he is such a great example as a survivor, and sometime winner, who plays the game of life very much on his own terms but in a totally selfless and altruistic way.

With this description I can see that his 360-degree holistic vision of life is essential to making him the man that he is. His world is very much sealed with a protective wrapping of activities and values around it, with his most precious and sacred of all possessions safely held tightly in the centre at the core of his very being.

The Ceri Davies story

Ceri Davies BEM, social entrepreneur and disability rights campaigner

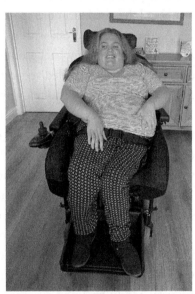

Ceri Davies

I first met Ceri a few years ago at a community meeting one evening in a local civic hall to arrange a series of Christmas events for a local town in the Black Country. She was a person with a disability who I instantly felt sorry for. She was in a motorised wheelchair, and clearly was struggling with her mobility and movement. She looked in pain and real discomfort, and my heart went out to her and also to her family too, who were with her. At the time, I was seconded to the Prince of Wales charity, Business in the Community, working within Dudley Borough. I felt that I could do something to help Ceri with her social enterprise and charitable work that she spoke so eloquently about. We agreed to meet at her home to get to know each other, and to explore whether there was any way that we could collaborate on any upcoming projects. This was my role – to connect people and groups within communities to make a material difference. Ceri was just the sort of community person I knew that I could help.

A few days later I went to her house, and met Ceri, her mom, Denise, and her then personal assistant, who was also her part-time carer. Another meeting with another person, or so I thought. It turned out to be one of the game changers of my life. It was an hour and a half that I will never forget.

We sat in the living room of the bungalow that was being altered to cater for Ceri's disability and to give her more comfort. The building work had been ongoing for some time, and was constantly evolving as her condition changed so quickly. Their home required everything to be open plan to accommodate her chair, and the need for more space was immediately apparent.

As usual I started out with my elevator pitch, stating who I am, what I do and my background, and ending with my usual offer to help. This extended version lasts a good five minutes and is one that I can adapt and tell with real ease and comfort.

The three ladies listened intently and then, as I picked up my rapidly cooling mug of coffee that had been kindly given to me, I asked Ceri to tell me her story. She was sat in her motorised wheelchair, which looked like it had technology from a Formula 1 racing car. She adjusted her position and faced me square on so that she could look directly at me. As the sofa I was sat on was quite low down, Ceri's eye level was probably a good eight inches above me so she had to look down as she spoke. Then, without hesitating, she told me her story in a very unemotional delivery, rarely breaking eye contact (she has a poker player's stare). It was an articulate, clear, concise, factual and very hard-hitting description of her life to date, detailing her disability, the numerous challenges that she has faced from birth and also her many achievements. She is rightly proud of the difference that she is making but she never once came across as boastful, which would have been easy to do. She also stated exactly what she wanted from me, which was my time and my advice.

When she finished after ten minutes, there was a silence and I felt compelled to speak. I tried and no words would come out. I knew what I wanted to say but the lump in my throat just would not move. I have never before or since been faced with this in a "business-type" meeting, and I have had some very emotional ones. There has never been one, though, where I just was unable to speak. I tried again to say thank you and then started to cry. The impact of Ceri's story had reduced me to tears and, as I gathered myself, I looked around to see the three ladies all shocked. I have no idea whether anyone had ever asked Ceri her story in that type of environment before, but her mom, Denise, said this was the first time anyone had reacted that way to Ceri. I suspect others have, but have had the ability to cope better with their emotions than me.

I am not ashamed to say that I cried, and it was not because I felt sorry for her. Far from it. I simply felt privileged and humbled to be in her presence. I have never thought of Ceri as disabled since that moment. She is actually one of the most able people I know – unfortunately her body prevents her from doing the things that the rest of us take for granted. Her mind is razor sharp and woe betide anyone who is not at the top of their game when meeting her.

So what is Ceri Davies's story that reduced a hardened old bank manager to tears on a Tuesday morning in Dudley? And what is it about Ceri that makes her one of my heroes, a survivor and a sometime winner in the game of life?

Ceri was born in 1989, and from birth has had cerebral palsy, scoliosis, and tethered cord syndrome. A list that means she should not have survived childhood. These conditions have presented, and continue to present, challenges for her and her family beyond what most people could imagine or endure. She needs twenty-four-hour care. The fact that she is still alive is in no small part down to her own burning desire to live, to make a difference to the lives of others, particularly children, and the incredible selfless support of her family, who love and care for her twenty-four hours a day.

Ceri said that as a child she hadn't been aware that she was different, and went to mainstream schools with all of the other children locally. It seems that some of those who were in charge of her care and learning, though, may have inadvertently helped to feed her strength and determination by saying that she wouldn't achieve anything. This was at age six. Listening to Ceri and her mom talk, they had no bitterness, which is remarkable, considering the language and tone used at the time. They felt sad, however, that people in authority could be so thoughtless and disparaging. They also agreed that the people making these statements were also frightened, and ignorant of Ceri's condition and her ability to fully integrate into what many would class as normal school life.

For every doubter, though, Ceri mentioned a number of teachers and supporters along the way who gave her the belief and confidence that she could achieve and be anything in life that she wanted. These people have been crucial as cheerleaders for helping Ceri to be the best possible version of herself that she can be.

It was clear to Ceri from an early age that she wanted to work with young people, and she knew by her teens that this was where her ambitions and her future career path lay. She said that her greatest achievement in life had been to make children smile. It's staggering to me that someone who faces so many personal challenges every day can be so giving.

As well as progressing through school and achieving good qualifications, she had gained a 2:1 BA honours degree in early childhood studies, joint with sociology, from the University of Wolverhampton. In October 2015, Ceri earned a postgraduate degree in youth and community work at Newman University. These are wonderful achievements for most people and for Ceri it was even more so as the learning was interspersed with long periods of hospitalisation and recovery.

Her public service also led her to win numerous community awards including "Build-A-Bear Workshop Huggable Heroes Award". In 2005 she was given a Princess Diana Award for being a courageous citizen, and in 2009 received the rare accolade of their golden award.

From age thirteen she has been associated with several youth participation teams throughout the country, including the Dudley Youth Council, becoming the youth network leader for the Arts Award Youth Network and completing her Silver Arts Award in September 2012. She was part of the National Council for Voluntary Youth Services, sat on the National Youth Forum and was a regional co-ordinator for O2's Think Big in 2012.

The Think Big role then led, in October 2012, to Ceri delivering a speech on disability rights and inequality at the One Young World conference in the USA. Travelling there was a feat of organisation, but, as always, her mom and dad ensured that she had the platform to follow her dreams and to make her mark on the world. This was Ceri, taking her game to an international stage, inspiring more people and showing them just what they can do when facing disability issues head on.

It was following the deaths of two people very close to her in a very short period of time that Ceri started her community interest company, More Mascots Please (MMP). The aim is to enhance the lives of disabled, disadvantaged and terminally ill children and their families, using her own branded character mascots. The play-themed parties, trips and activities do exactly what Ceri set out to achieve when she was a young child, and that is to make children happy – especially those facing real challenge in their lives. She is constantly looking at innovative ways to assist and, via some good effective networking and use of social media, receives some local business attention and support. MMP was also one of the mayor of Dudley's causes to receive financial support during his year in office in 2015/16. To date Ceri has helped over 500 children and those people who care for them.

Also in 2016 she received an award for inspirational women in the West Midlands, and was heartbroken that illness and a life-threatening sepsis infection prevented her from being there personally to receive the award. Her dad, Dave, her mom, Denise, and her sister Rhianna received the award in her place. I think that, with their incredible dedication to Ceri, giving her the platform for her to live her life to the fullest extent possible, this award was their award too. They are all remarkable, selfless, dedicated people.

Despite her numerous health setbacks, Ceri stood as a prospective candidate for the Conservative Party in the local council elections around this time. She received over 400 votes, which considering that she was too ill to campaign and debate, endorses further her ability to engage with people. She laughs when she says, "This wasn't my finest hour". I disagree, as she took a decision to try and serve the community and public from an even more visible standpoint, and this bravery in itself deserves recognition. The fact that she has subsequently reflected, and realised that this path was not the right one for her and would not help her to achieve her goals and ambitions, demonstrates her own self-awareness and inner consciousness even further.

It was wonderful to hear from Ceri that she has kept close to two friends from school, Anna and Beth. They too are young people with a giving spirit who ensure that Ceri has another view of the world beyond her family, and a sense of normality and space. "They are really important to me. I can tell them anything and they are always there, no matter what happens," said Ceri.

Her only regrets in life are around the limited time that she has for herself and her unfulfilled business ambitions. The nature of the care she has to receive means that she has very little time alone, time that most of us take for granted to recharge and re-energise. Her personal privacy is non-existent, with the most basic of human functions requiring assistance.

Her business ambitions are very much directed by the state and this is a massive dilemma. She desperately wants to be financially independent and run businesses, as well as More Mascots Please, which would give her the feeling of some control. However, the game rules that society set for her and her disabilities are such that she has to either receive financial aid or not. She cannot make that monetary leap of faith, as she is often so ill that the system could not cope with her having a constantly changing situation. She has to be in or out of the system and, for her material survival, she has to be in. So, her game plan has to centre around making the very best of what she has available and playing by their rules. These rules in themselves are ever changing, with her rewards being found in the way that she can make others happy, which sits at her very core anyway.

The dignity and values that Ceri and her family display are truly humbling. Dave, Denise and Rhianna have dedicated so much of themselves to ensuring that Ceri can reach out beyond her home and touch so many people's lives for the better. Ceri has refused to allow her disabilities to prevent her from achieving her potential in so many areas, and it is only the restrictions of the state machine that has stopped her from being an entrepreneur of a large business.

Ceri Davies as a human being is a real success, a genuine survivor and one of the rare diamonds that we have within our midst. She has battled the odds playing the toughest of life's games in the most altruistic way possible.

Postscript. This profile of Ceri was written in late 2019. In October 2020, Ceri was awarded a BEM in the Queen's Birthday Honours. A truly wonderful recognition from a very grateful nation for the amazing work that she has done to improve the lives of so many people.

The Karl Denning story

Karl Denning, volunteer, disability rights campaigner and community man

I first wrote about Karl on LinkedIn and subsequently nominated him for Dudley's Volunteer of the Year in 2016, which he won. I sat in genuine awe of him then, feeling unworthy to be in his presence. As I found myself sitting with him, talking and sharing a beer, some three years later, nothing had changed. It was as though I had been transported back in time and still had the same emotions running through me as I did then, when our friendship was new and raw.

Karl Denning

We agreed to meet at lunchtime on a bitterly cold September day, and Karl was stood outside the Courthouse pub in the centre of Dudley waiting for me. He is always on time and annoyingly is never late. The Courthouse is a proper old-fashioned "Black Country boozer" that specialises in real ale. The only food it sells are cold cobs, crisps and other light snacks. It has stood the test of time in a town centre that has taken a massive economic hit with the recent moves to online and out-of-town shopping.

Besides his white walking cane, you wouldn't know that Karl is blind. He knows every crack in the pavement, the angle of every kerbstone, and the location of every doorway. Oh, and everyone knows him as well, and no one seems to be conscious of his disability either. He is not known for his blindness; he is just known to all as Karl.

Karl has been a friend since the first day we met in 2015, but I never really knew his story before the accident that so cruelly robbed him of his sight until now.

Karl was born in 1970 in Wednesbury, an industrial hub between Wolverhampton and Birmingham, right in the heart of the industrial Midlands. The youngest of five children, he grew up in a loving, close-knit family-orientated environment. Karl's dad worked in a factory as a toolmaker and his mom owned cleaning and catering businesses, ending up with a wool shop, which is how they came to move to Dudley. Karl talks about his parents and siblings with genuine affection, and it is clear that, together with his grandparents and uncle, they set a standard for him and were his main role models in life. All continually and consistently stressed the need for education for every one of the children. "You get a good education and you will get a good job," and "Education is never wasted. Those who say otherwise are just old and bitter." These phrases from the people he respected are clearly imprinted in Karl's brain, and all of the family seem to have taken to heart these mantras, as they all now have achieved something of note in their respective fields in life.

Karl has always had a love of reading, inspired again by his family. His grandmother was surrounded by books and he remembers as a child her telling him, "If you read a book, you can be transported to somewhere else in the world or the universe. It fires your imagination, it can lift you up, it can calm you down and you will always have entertainment." It was never the same for her when she lost her sight, and the family tried to help by introducing her to talking books. "The voices of the characters that came through just weren't as she would imagine them to be," Karl said, and, by a strange quirk of fate, Karl now understands this feeling more than ever.

The influence and example of his parents gave Karl a deep-seated loathing of injustice. His early memories centre around going to football matches at West Bromwich Albion. The "Baggies", as they are known, had three Black footballers in the 1970s: Cyrille Regis, Brendan Batson and Laurie Cunningham. This was unheard of for the era, with multicultural integration still in its infancy in the UK. The players were nicknamed "the Three Degrees", after the girl pop group from the USA, and played a style of football that was fast and exciting and had tremendous flair. They were different, talented, athletic, and also in a minority of footballers, as they were black. They took horrific abuse from some so-called football supporters because of the colour of their skin, and this has stayed with Karl, as it has with me, as I support the club too and attended many of the same games that are notorious to this day. It was not unusual to see bananas thrown onto the pitch, and to witness vile chanting and monkey gestures aimed at these players. These were the 1970s and the country was divided in many ways by race, bigotry and hate.

Karl describes how his father was a union man and made a point of sitting with the non-white people at lunch and breaktimes to try to set an example to his colleagues by breaking down the racial and cultural barriers. He was not always popular with his other workmates but was true to himself. These are qualities that Karl, to this day, stands by and demonstrates. "The colour of your skin should never be a barrier on any front," said Karl, repeating the words of his father.

Karl always wanted to be an electrician. He liked the risk that went with working with something that was potentially dangerous, and it gave him the chance to be creative. He controlled his game and had a plan – never imagining he would do anything else. At sixteen he was taken on as an apprentice. He had great influences at school and teachers who he felt inspired him, but in his heart he wanted to leave. His advice to his younger self now would be to stay in school and gain as many qualifications as possible. He realises that the early years would have been that much easier with these exams passed, rather than doing a job full time and taking on the learning as well. This is not true for every role, but clearly very true for Karl.

Karl went on to become a very successful electrical engineer, travelling all over the UK, working on big projects for large multinational companies, and also for the public sector. He was a subject expert and a go-to man. Raising a young family with Nikki, his wife, he also enjoyed being involved in the local community, but was often too busy at work to become as immersed as he wanted.

Always one to help anyone in need, whilst doing a favour for a friend one day Karl accidentally slipped with a screwdriver and punched himself in the forehead. Many people have near misses whilst doing DIY, but for a professional like Karl this really was unusual. What then ensued was the stuff of nightmares. Karl had inadvertently given himself an injury similar to that experienced by some bare-knuckle boxers. In a matter of seconds, he had lost his sight. Surgeons battled for him for many hours but all to no avail and, twelve hours after his accident, Karl realised that he would be blind and never see again. The ultimate game changer, and one that you can never prepare for.

The following months must have been simply hell and, while Karl doesn't dwell on these times, I know that he didn't just shrug his shoulders and get on with it.

He talks now about the accident creating the next phase of his life, and also about how he needed to firstly mourn the loss of his sight. "If you mourn constantly, though, then you get nothing done. Yes, I've lost something major, but look at what I have gained." From anyone else these words would be difficult to believe, and this is the third time now that I have heard Karl talk this way about his accident. Each time I feel a sense of sadness and emotion, and I struggle to understand just how you can gain so much from such an unlucky accident. But that is a measure of the man, and just what makes him the role model he is to me and to many others. He means every word of what he says and the sincerity and belief ooze out of him.

"Look, Andy, at my family. I've gone from not being around them to being able to spend so much time with my wonderful wife and children." And there it is in that one sentence, the foundation of family that Karl has always known, feeding him with a renewed energy and a zest for life at a time when many would struggle to cope with such a profound and massive change. He talks lovingly and protectively about them. His youngest daughter, at age ten, is more capable than most sighted guides for blind people. She has never known Karl any different, having been a small baby when he lost his sight. So for her to give a running commentary of what is happening around them, when walking with her dad, is absolutely normal for her.

There is also another member of the family who plays a crucial role in Karl's life, and that is his guide dog, Quasia. Although, at the time I write this, she is now nearing retirement from the day job, Karl has a massive gratitude and loyalty to her. "She is part of the family too and that is where she will remain for the rest of her life," said Karl.

Since finishing work a little over ten years ago, Karl has become a central pillar of the Dudley voluntary and charity communities. He has evolved into someone who is vital to the workings of many organisations and groups that seek to improve the lives of others. Here is a list of some of the things that he is actively involved with:

- His passion for supporting education means that he sits as an active member of the admissions and appeals panels for the local education authority.
- He assists as a community liaison and advisor to environmental and public health across Dudley Borough.
- Healthwatch Dudley prepare reports on community needs, and again require "on the ground" support. Karl has recently helped to prepare their in-depth community recommendation paper.
- He is an urban gardener and raises chickens too. He helps to establish growing areas across Dudley Town Centre for people to learn about the all-round health benefits to them of gardening.
- He goes to schools with Quasia to talk about his disability, helping others to understand just what it's like

to be blind and how to cope with adversity.

- He is a baker, making cakes and bread, as well as being an excellent cook. His soup is amazing, as I found out when working alongside him for the inaugural "Dudley Soup" community event.
- He is a carpenter, helping to create things and advise others on what to do, particularly with the development of a community cafe and project in Dudley Town Centre.
- He is an active member of the Campaign for Real Ale (CAMRA) and knows his beer, brewing some himself. He can be persuaded to indulge as well, but only if pressed hard. Well, not too hard.
- He is a campaigner for the Labour Party, and is often out in the community supporting local MPs and councillors.
- He is a great active supporter of Dudley Voluntary Service and is passionate about making our community a better and more inclusive place for all.
- He is a guide dog activist and campaigner for rights for blind people.
- He is committed to Dudley and the Black Country, including the history and heritage of the area, working with groups and organisations promoting this. Dudley Remembrance is the latest of these, as part of the drive to ensure that we never forget the sacrifices made in wars and conflicts to protect our freedom.

"You can take the person out of the Black Country, but you can't take the Black Country out of the person," he says with immense pride, passion and a huge grin.

Added to that, he is a devoted father and husband, and will never pass anyone by who knows him without having a chat.

His mobile phone, which is his lifeline at times, constantly beeps as text messages and the latest social media alerts come in. The app on his phone replays all of these to him with a speed of delivery that I cannot understand or follow. Karl absorbs every single word and then quickly replies where required, never once losing his train of thought or focus on me. It is remarkable to witness.

When he speaks he makes so much sense. His vision is 20/20 and stronger than ever – he just can't see the physical world around him.

He says that the advice he would most like to give to people who may read this is "To never give up and to keep going." He also says the maxim "Work to live and not live to work" is one that he would put into practice more if he had his time over again.

The accident has given Karl a different outlook on his life and the world. His game has changed beyond comprehension, and also for those around him. He is very much of the opinion, though, that if you can change the life of one person for the better, you have made a success of your own life. Again, with great humility, he then reflects further on those who have made him who he is. I get the feeling that he is now more focussed than ever on what is truly important to him. As a result, he is now controlling his game and creating a better game for everyone else. He is changing lives, aspirations and communities. He is also creating a legacy for those that follow.

People like Karl choose to place themselves at the heart of our communities and to make a difference for others. To put something back and to give to society, at a time when many would say this was their time to take, is one of the truest forms of generosity that there is.

When I see Karl walking with Quasia and his family I don't see a blind man or someone with a disability. While a part of me will always feel sorry for him, I see a man with vision much better than mine will ever be, as he can see what really matters to the world and to our communities and how to facilitate change. His personal daily challenges are massive, but his ability to cope, adapt, reconcile and then move forward with boundless energy leaves me awestruck. He is one of my real heroes, a true role model and someone I will always be fiercely proud to call a friend.

The Frankie Graham story

Frankie Graham, social entrepreneur and gambling treatment consultant

The strange thing about Frankie being a role model of mine is that I have only met him face to face on three occasions. We have spoken and exchanged numerous emails and text messages, but have not interacted for significant periods of time in the way that I have with the other people that I feature in this section.

Frankie Graham

Within the first five minutes of meeting Frankie in London several years ago, he had gained my interest and respect. He was presenting to myself, and a number of other people about social enterprises and not-for-profit businesses. This included telling his own story of gambling addiction. I have heard thousands of people speak over the years on a variety of subjects, and have been inspired and moved by some. I have also found myself very ambivalent and almost cynical at times towards others. What was so powerful about Frankie's delivery was not only his humility but also his honesty. The start of his presentation was not along the lines of, "This is what a social enterprise and not-for-profit business is and what it does", as I think everyone expected. In fact, the first words that he used were that he had done things that he may never resolve with himself and had hurt people that he loved. There was a tension in the air as he spoke; we were all silent, almost holding our breath as we waited for the next sentence, which he delivered slowly and with heartfelt feeling. It was like hearing the start of a compelling story that was being narrated to you. We got to the point of discovering what the businesses were after about twenty minutes. The way Frankie told his story made us understand why many of those who set up these enterprises, which intrinsically are forces for good in our communities, actually do so, and it is often for very personal reasons.

Covid-19 totally scuppered our plans to meet face to face in London, so instead we had to make do with the magic of the internet. This actually proved to be a more private way of meeting as, with no other people present, Frankie really did not hold back in the way that he may have in a cafe or a public space. The emotion was raw and he was able to tell me all about his life, with significantly more information than I expected. Also, he was in his flat in central London, under the first lockdown, and I sense that the pressure of not being able to be outside for a considerable length of time had worn down even more of his personal defences.

Frankie has lived all of his life in London and was born in the early 1970s. His mother, Beverley, to whom he is extremely close, was a descendant of a one-time wealthy Indian family who came to the UK as a result of the Indian partition of 1947. His father came from a different background and his family were market traders. "All Cockneys and wide boys," Frankie added.

Home life in Islington was not easy. Money was tight, and his father was at times violent towards Frankie, his younger sister Angela, and most of all to his mom. He regularly refers back to this violence and abuse during our conversation. The effects of witnessing this at first hand have clearly had a significant impact on his emotional development.

His parents' marriage, unsurprisingly, didn't last and they split up when Frankie was still in junior school. For several years, afterwards, his father did periodically reappear in his life, usually at weekends. He remembers the trips to betting shops with his dad, who, despite having Frankie with him, never changed his routines. To a young, impressionable child, desperate to be part of his father's life, Frankie developed a fascination with the atmosphere and culture that surrounded these smoke-filled, male-dominated environments that were behind frosted glass. They were an unseen world by many and, just by being there, gave him a form of kudos too. I also suspect it saw the formation of an image he had to cultivate for himself. It was an example being set by an adult on a very impressionable child.

His father also encouraged self-defence. North London in the 1970s was not an easy place to grow up for any child and, for a child of mixed-race parentage, it must have presented some considerable personal danger. "You must know how to look after yourself" was the phraseology delivered to him. Negotiation and discussion were never a part of any conflict resolution in those days in that area. Fighting for self-preservation and personal peer group standing became a natural part of Frankie's way of life.

As a child he excelled at sport, in particular football, and also enjoyed the academic side of school life too. He was a quick learner and gained good grades. A career in law or marketing was certainly within his grasp, always as well as the potential for something within sport.

The impression made on him from the betting shops, though, now carried on into the playground. Around the time that he was eleven years old, he made gambling an addition to the popular playground activities at breaktimes. Games of chance like odds and evens, penny against the wall, and several others, saw money exchange hands among these children. Sometimes school was missed for the chance to continue gambling.

The conflict for Frankie, in his mind, was also around his religion. He was raised as a Catholic and says that he has the profound sense of guilt and religious duty so often associated with the faith. He was encouraged by his God-fearing grandmother to attend church and become an altar boy. He speaks fondly of her and of her pride at his commitment to his religion. It gave him a sense of service and a sense of duty. It also exposed him to death, and he was often requested to be one of the altar boys at funerals. Images of grieving people – at some of the lowest points of their lives, clearly affected him, and he therefore sought further escape from the world around him.

The gambling continued, as did a new-found consciousness of his image as he developed into his teenage years. Designer clothing became essential out-of-school wear, and contact lenses replaced the thick lens glasses that Frankie described as "like looking through the bottom of milk bottles".

This lifestyle of choice didn't come cheaply and could not be funded by Beverley, who worked in a large department store. His father certainly didn't contribute, so Frankie had to be self-sufficient if he wanted to live this way. He decided to take on a series of part-time jobs.

His life within and outside school was very full on. Yet, despite the distractions, Frankie still managed strong grades in his GCSEs. It was 1987 and life was seemingly good for him. His beloved Arsenal were beginning to dominate English football again, he had money in his pocket, qualifications behind him, smart clothes on his back, college beckoned for A levels and his social life was continuing to be extremely lively. He had some close friends and trips to betting shops, sometimes with them but often alone, were becoming a daily occurrence. His gambling escalated further and was now heading out of control.

During the late 1980s the acid house and rave scene really exploded to life in the cities of the UK, and London was at the centre of this. The subculture of music, fashion, drugs and a hedonistic lifestyle fascinated him, and he threw himself fully into it. He still went to college, but another life funded by his various jobs quickly evolved. Everything was done to the extreme, never in moderation. He created a reputation that he had to live up to, and a persona that took over who he was. He lived in a bubble of excess – the gambling had completely taken over his life. He was betting to extinction, which meant that he would gamble until he had absolutely nothing left.

His A level grades were a great disappointment but something had to give. Unsurprisingly, he felt that these were a price worth paying at the time. He took a year out from studying and had a year of even more excess.

His mom became really worried about his behaviour and lifestyle. She asked him a lot of questions until eventually he confessed to being out of control, living a life that involved the very extreme of available vices, whilst having this addiction to gambling.

With her insistence and support, he agreed to go to a Gamblers Anonymous meeting. He actually went just to please her. He simply couldn't relate to the people that were there. It was still unreal, as people were talking about losing their houses, jobs and families, and he could not see that this could be him in the near future. He confesses now that he only went to a number of the sessions because he was nagged to go. It was the price to continue with his life as he wanted. He was not ready to embrace change, and crucially he did not want to change either.

Beverley tried really hard to get him into a better way of living, and helped him to get a job. He talks about her with a genuine affection and softness, and clearly the guilt of the impact that this had on his mom is only just under the surface at this point. I sensed it would break through into a greater wave of emotion and, as we progressed the conversation further, it did. And, when the dam of emotion broke, it was almost unstoppable.

Another year passed and, trying to find direction, he started a degree in print management. It just was not for him. The subject and the learning he found boring and there, filling the void, was the ever-present, exciting crutch of gambling. As a consequence the hold it had over him escalated even further.

Within a year he moved to study for a degree in product

development within fashion. Looking back, he still can't believe that he secured his place, as he did zero preparation for the interview and, in his words, he "blagged it". The studying fitted with his interests in subcultures and, again, the fashion, the music, the behaviours of people and what motivates them were all under his spotlight. It almost gave a justification for his continued out-of-control life as he was experiencing it first hand – and what better way to study than with "practical field assignments"?

Many of the people he studied alongside were from wealthy backgrounds. He struggled to relate to them and they, similarly, struggled to understand who he was. Gambling was a clear release, as those who he mixed with during his time of intense betting activity didn't judge him, in the same way that he felt others probably did.

With some serious hard work, he gained his degree, and this alone is a major achievement bearing in mind the jobs he was having to do to fund his lifestyle.

And here is where the Frankie Graham story could easily have had an uncomplicated and unfulfilled conclusion. He had secured a permanent role with a large department store and lasted there for ten years doing a job that he loved, working closely with people who required advice on goods that the store sold. He describes it as being akin to *Are You Being Served?*, a sitcom from the 1970s and 1980s, based in the same kind of setting, with quirky and unusual characters working there. He had a steady girlfriend and was, on the surface, calming down. However, in reality he was still gambling, drinking and back on drugs. This was also replicated in the social side of his job.

Now into his late twenties, he knew he wasn't happy, but he didn't have the capacity or the inner desire to change. He describes himself as weak and vulnerable – a Jekyll and Hyde type of character who people liked but Frankie himself loathed. He said he was living a lie, as he wasn't being true to himself.

His relationship with his girlfriend ended, and this was at

the point where his life went totally out of control. The years of hedonism were now catching up. Drug overdoses saw him hospitalised twice, almost dying both times. Criminal behaviour became a way of life in order to fund his gambling and drug addictions. He says this was his weakest time. He also became hooked on fixed odds betting terminals, which, in betting shops, were anything up to £100 per spin. With three spins a minute possible, it was also a very expensive addiction. He justified all of his behaviour to himself, and now understands that this is what addicts do. He knew that what he was doing was wrong. He knew the harm it was doing to himself and to others, but, no matter what, he always put a positive spin on his actions.

At this point in our discussion, his emotion suddenly became very visible and, it was as though Frankie was reliving this by actually replaying the moments in his head as though they were happening now. His pain was palpable, and he was clearly even more distressed as he reflected on how upsetting it was for those who loved him to see how he was ruining his life.

He also, surprisingly, talked about his dad and the scars that the domestic violence had left, including his low self-esteem. He mentioned that he doesn't know whether his dad is alive or not. He said he once saw him at a bus stop near to Angel Tube station as he went past on a bus. "Our eyes locked for a second." I was unsure whether Frankie was aware of the impact that phrase had on me, as the listener, but it was clear that the lack of his father in his life was more relevant in his own subconscious, as he expanded more about the difficult relationship that they had.

Frankie's life became a self-fulfilling prophecy. The gambling and drug taking went beyond excess, the crime to fund it also became uncontrollable, and so began the final downward spiral to a place where it would have to end in one way or another.

And end it did in one of the harshest of ways for him and his family. One day in 2006 he was unexpectedly summoned to the personnel department and presented with evidence of gross misconduct at work. He confessed straight away. He said

"I'm so, so sorry", but he knew that those words of contrition would never be enough, as the offences were serious. He would be taken to the police station, arrested and charged. He would lose his job, his livelihood, possibly his liberty and, worst of all, his dignity, together with the respect of those he loved.

This was all compounded by the fact that his mom, who had got him the job in the first place, worked at the store too and had done so all of her working life. Everyone knew that they were mother and son, and the shame that he knew this brought on her was, again, too much to bear, as he told this part of the story. "Mom is a reserved character. I cannot begin to imagine how she felt."

As he talked, he again apologised several times. At first, I thought it was to me, but I soon realised that it was to the people that he had wronged, most of all Beverley, his mom. It was as though he was now in the confessional box from his Catholic upbringing, confessing his sins and seeking absolution from me. "I was a good Catholic boy, and now being charged in a police station with criminal offences. The shame."

This was the defining moment that changed his life. If he had not been caught he said he would have taken one too many risks and would have ended up in a much worse position – with more crimes to his name, more damage and wreckage of human life left along the way, including his own. He would have served a significant prison sentence, or he would have died. Fortunately, the spiral ended at this point, his life was recoverable and he decided there and then to bring a full stop to that part of his existence.

He promised to his family that he would not live that way anymore. They had lost all of their trust in him, though, and he was met with a stunned and shocked silence as he continued to preach a message of repentance and rebirth. It would take years to win them over, with deeds and actions that were consistent, honest and overflowing with good intentions.

The court imposed a suspended sentence, which meant

that prison was narrowly avoided, but any subsequent form of criminal activity on his part would see him incarcerated for a considerable length of time. He also had a curfew imposed. He decided that he would go to court by himself and face up to what he had done. The hurt for his family was simply too great and he worried how it would impact his mother if a custodial sentence were given.

Things then began to change rapidly for Frankie, and for the better. He discovered a new-found motivation that was the most freeing part of this time. "I was now a blank canvas and could be anything that I wanted to be with the right people helping me." This was a pivotal moment for him.

He started volunteering, and highlighted that this was the beginning of the positive change in him, and the most powerful part of his recovery. It was an act of giving himself unconditionally to help others that changed his psychology. He had lost all of the baggage of gambling, drugs, crime and toxic friends that were dragging him down. He knew that he had to change, pure and simple, or otherwise he wouldn't survive.

The Holy Cross Trust at Kings Cross was, and still is, a drop-in centre for people who are seemingly socially excluded and seeking a place to find friendship, fellowship and help. The people who visit seek someone to talk to and, out of all the chaos that surrounded Frankie's life, he finally found himself and a deep sense of empathy. He could talk to people openly and on their level, with real understanding of the issues and challenges that they were facing. He had experience, time to give and a burning desire to help.

He decided that, as he was this new clean, blank canvas, counselling and helping others with practical support would be the ideal career for him. Phoenix-like, out of the ashes of the bad would emerge a person doing good for others.

By this time it was 2007, and Frankie became a support worker for the trust. One of the people who helped him along the way was Bob, who became a role model for Frankie. Bob was a service manager for the organisation and took Frankie under his wing. He understood the challenges for a former addict with a criminal record, and believed in the proposition that Frankie presented. He knew just how to help someone in recovery, how to begin the long road back to self-respect and how to start gaining trust from others. My favourite quote from our conversation was when Frankie said about Bob, "When you don't even trust yourself, to suddenly have someone who does have trust in you, like Bob did with me, is very empowering. You never give up as an addict until you are ready, and fully self-empowered."

In 2008 he began to work with the YMCA, focussing on helping young offenders, particularly with their mental health and homelessness. He began to build youth and community programmes to help to address these issues head on, recognising the seriousness of gang postcode crime well before it hit the national headlines.

Frankie encouraged the youngsters he was working with to find the best part of who they were, tapping into their creativeness around food, urban gardening and art and design, among many others. The link with Portobello Road Market proved especially important for Frankie as it gave a commercial outlet to showcase their talents.

All the while, Frankie was conscious that more of the challenges he was seeing youngsters face in society was as a result of gambling, with the use of fixed odds terminals in betting shops and online sites prevalent. They were turning to crime to fund their habit. There was an ingrained "get rich quick" culture, no matter what the cost. It all sounded too familiar, and he started to think deeply about how he could help even more.

Frankie understood from his work that, to a teenager, counselling is not considered a "cool" activity to be associated with. His strength was in dealing with outreach, and that was how the idea of his social enterprise, Betknowmore, came into being. He would establish community support hubs as a referral point, rather than specific individual one on one counselling, and what could be seen as attempts at "reprogramming".

Frankie was very clear when he said, drawing on every ounce of his life experience, that "People's motivation and capacity to change is strengthened when they can see the benefits."

Therefore, in 2013, Betknowmore (https://www. betknowmoreuk.org) was born with a clear vision, a holistic approach, and a desire to make people more aware of the devastating effects of gambling addiction. It is a non-negotiable for Frankie that this message must be delivered without judgement, always with empathy. Education is key, together with support for those with the addiction and the people surrounding them, to help them to better understand just what they are facing.

Betknowmore was the first business ever set up for this purpose in the UK. It has broken new ground ever since, continuing to help and pioneer new thinking into the dangers gambling addiction brings to individuals, their families, friends and society as a whole. Frankie understands, at first hand, just how gambling addiction starts. He has become a "go-to expert" across the betting industry, as it seeks to resolve how those of its customers with a problem can actually be helped by them directly.

Gaining funding has proved challenging, particularly having been told at the outset that gambling does not tick any boxes for direct financial support. However, with a focus on the ripple effect on other issues such as crime, family breakdowns, abuse, self-harm, cross-addiction and many others, there has been an increasing desire by authorities, and those with the monies available, to help fund the work.

In 2019, Betknowmore's "Don't gamble with health" campaign won a public health award, thereby gaining considerable recognition for gambling addiction as an illness in its own right. There is much further to go but this is truly revolutionary. There has also been a National Lottery award and many other accolades too.

Frankie sees Betknowmore as a trusted gatekeeper to work alongside other vulnerable groups and organisations, and is constantly curious about how he can keep developing programmes to facilitate change. This is some attempt at redemption after the chaotic and hedonistic life he led.

He reflected, as we drew to a conclusion, about his mom, who had been seriously ill with Coronavirus. "I have a great relationship with her now and we are very close. She's very tough, you know."

He then choked up again as he revealed that, since he had established Betknowmore, he had achieved his proudest moment as he finally knew that he had regained the trust, belief and respect from her. He appeared on the *Victoria Derbyshire* show on BBC TV, a live daytime chat show that featured many current issues of the day. Betknowmore and Frankie were selected to talk about the dangers of gambling addiction. He was accompanied by Stephen, a former gambler. With Frankie's help and support, Stephen said for the very first time, "I am an ex-gambler." None of his friends or family knew that he had this problem, so this was a big moment for him, and on national television too. Straight after the filming ended, Frankie got a call from his mom, who had been watching, and she simply said, "Well done." With those words, and in that moment, he knew that the trust and belief in him was back. She believed he would do it. He is finally walking the long path to redemption but no longer doing it alone. Now he has his greatest friend and most cherished supporter, his mom, Beverley, walking alongside him and cheering him on.

The quick wins and the ladders The traps and the snakes

These life stories and biographies were kindly and generously shared with me by these four remarkable people. To try to condense them into a series of bullet points and short sentences would significantly downplay the impact that they have. Take your time, read each one fully and extract what you wish to help your own game and the games of those you love.

Steve and Jayne Waltho

Ceri and Denise Davies

Karl Denning with members of his family.
Karl is third from the left on the back row

Frankie Graham and his mom, Beverley

Leadership

The task of the leader is to get his people
from where they are to where they have not
been.

Henry Kissinger

I take a very simplistic view of leadership. I believe that the greatest leaders are very often born. It is a gift, the same as anyone who has a given talent that comes naturally to them. Yes, it can be developed and made to be even better, and, yes, leaders can even be created by others; but the ability to drive themselves, and those around them to unimaginable heights of achievement has, I believe, to be inbuilt in some way. True leaders also have the ability to inspire confidence without saying anything. You know they are strong, full of character, in charge and integrity simply oozes out of their frame and being. You walk into a room and instantly you know whose gig it is and you can tell from whether the heads are up or down whether the team is being led in the right way.

I had the privilege to work with some incredible leaders and, without exception, they enabled me to be the very best version of myself. They allowed me to play my game to my strengths, and adapted their styles to make this possible. They also made sure that I played within the team and understood my responsibilities fully to myself and my colleagues. They never undermined me or my confidence, and knew exactly how to motivate me, understanding exactly what my own inner drivers were. They were equally unafraid to deliver a hard message and sometimes, for me, that was difficult to take. However, the team was always greater than any one individual, themselves included.

Everyone is different, and what each of these great leaders demonstrated to me was an ability to get every colleague within the team to play to their strengths, whilst contributing fully to the team as a unit, thus making it stronger. It is something akin to a chain with all of its links intact. A break in the chain sees it weakening, and a leader needs to be constantly aware of the potential for the chain to reach a tension where the pressure is too great. All of the great leaders that I have witnessed were alive to any one moment in time of what exactly the breaking strain was, and where the pressure points were, so that the chain never broke. Or, if it did break, then they were alert to it breaking and fixed it very quickly.

As a leader you are playing your own game, the game of your company/business/organisation or whatever in life that you are doing, and also the game of your employees/charges and team. You carry an enormous responsibility, and how you act and react at any one given moment can have a massive impact on everyone around you, and their dependants too. For every person that you see who you are responsible for, there are at least four people, on average, who sit behind them as family members. That is some level of responsibility to bear and, therefore, many games will be impacted by your actions. Never forget this and never take it for granted. Embrace the responsibility and the privilege too, leaving your own ego aside, as with this power you can be an amazing force for good.

Great leaders will always have a strategy and know their winning formula, which is often as simple as to define, set goals, plan and act for every objective. They reduce the complexity, breaking everything down into simple, easy component parts. They will be several moves ahead in the game, but will only take you with them to the next step once they know that you are totally clear, comfortable, fully skilled and empowered to go.

From my observations across many organisations, the participation and leadership roles that I have held (particularly later in my career), this "route map" that I have summarised below has consistently delivered sustainable and lasting results:

- Make it clear from the very outset what everyone's role is. In other words, does every team member know specifically what is needed and by when?
- Has everyone signed up to the plan that you have submitted to them, and are they comfortable, fully skilled and prepared to do the tasks that are being asked of them?
- Ensure that there is a mutual respect for the way that you and they will approach the task both individually and collectively. An atmosphere of support must exist, with no "finger pointing" or blame culture being allowed to take hold if things do start to go wrong.
- Do not overcomplicate the detail. Keep it as simple as you can. There should be no excessive PowerPoint slides, spreadsheets, flow charts or presentations. They are a distraction and can cause confusion.
- Who is accountable at what stages for the task and do they know what success looks like at any particular point in time?
- Is there a team mentality with no "terrorists" who will sabotage and break this chain?
- Encourage regular two-way communication without any apportioning of blame. Questions must be allowed to be asked and any feedback must be appropriate, transparent and constructive.

- Celebrate every milestone and success point along the way. Know what that reward looks like in advance, again with everyone's agreement that they are happy with the potential outcome (e.g. don't sign everyone up for a skydiving experience if some are so scared of heights that their confidence will be undermined).

- Make sure that there are regular breaks and prescribed downtimes. No one person or team can be flat out all of the time. The leader must be the first to let go, encouraging every person to do this at their time too. It keeps everything fresh and energised.

- Everyone should be able to play another role if needed. In other words, there must be a recovery plan should one person, including the leader, fall or be absent in some way. It is a good idea to do a "dry run" together with other disaster anticipation plans.

- Lead by example. Involve and include everyone, and always walk your talk. Have a good memory for what is important to your team as a group and individuals. Do what you say you will and exceed that by twenty per cent. Everyone else will follow too if all of the other component parts are right.

- Surround yourself with people more talented than you and have a robust recruitment policy.

- Even if you can, never be tempted to do their jobs for them. It breaks the chain of trust and undermines them and their confidence. Empower them, trust them and give them all of the tools that they need to do the job.

- Finally, always try to be humble, inspirational, know a little about a lot, be an instant coach, and remember that no two individuals in your team are ever the same. Manage people as themselves and not just to fit a specific set of measurements, or in your own image. Always remember that the buck for overall responsibility stops with you. That is the ultimate price of leadership.

After many years of being in teams and leadership roles, I have concluded that this formula will give you every chance for you and the people with you, to reach the heights of personal and collective achievement that you may seek. You have to stick to it, though, know it inside out and make it seem and feel like it is natural, which is a skill that comes with experience.

I never got it right all of the time, and was never a naturally born leader. I sought out the positions of responsibility myself, believing that I was. I made many mistakes along the way, and also worked for some truly dreadful leaders in their own right. When I was allowed to be me, and to run my teams in a way similar to what I have described, it came right and felt really good. I know now, though, reflecting back, that my strengths were always more as team player than they ever were being a leader.

The final piece of advice that I would give here is to be aware of the values that you and your team stand for. These are game defining and must be the foundation for the behaviours and actions you will follow. Knowing where the boundary line is between acceptable and unacceptable behaviours will mean that everyone knows the rules that you will play to, and that the integrity of the team, and of yourself, is not available for negotiation. Sometimes this may mean that you sacrifice a short-term win, or position in the game, but the longer-term benefits will always outweigh any of those.

Here are just a few ideas for values statements to help develop a culture that a leader can facilitate that places integrity at its heart. Note here that everyone on your team has to agree with these. If they are yours alone, and you impose them without consultation, agreement and collaboration, then they are owned exclusively by you, and that makes them a very heavy burden to bear. Make them a collaboratively created and mutually owned contract, and the sky really is the limit.

The team and its members will:

- Demonstrate a commitment to excellence and achievement.
- Act in a trustworthy, ethical and honest manner in everything proposed and attempted.
- Give full transparency, ensuring feedback lines are available and easy to navigate both upward and downward.
- Always act with humility and empathy.
- Create leadership in every role.
- Be the standard that others aspire to imitate.
- Be fully respectful of everyone in and outside of the team.
- Seek continuous improvement and development, both personally and collectively.
- Show extreme competency in every role and develop a passion for every task.
- Remove as much "red tape" and potential for confusion as is possible.
- Be inspirational with a curiosity as to how to make themselves even better.
- Be innovative and restless in the quest for success.
- Be visionary and always look to the future.
- Be aware of their commitment to their surrounding communities and environment.

A leadership case study: Eugene (aka Gene) Kranz

On 20 July 1969, with a television audience of over 600 million people, Neil Armstrong was the first human being to walk on the surface of the moon. He did so with the help of thousands of people who made manned space flight a possibility for the United States through the Apollo programme. He fulfilled a commitment made by his president, John Fitzgerald Kennedy, in a speech, some eight years earlier, that they "would deliver a man to the moon and return him safely back to earth".

The leadership of Kennedy and his vision when he said

"We choose to go to the moon in this decade and do the other things, not because they are easy, but because they are hard" is legendary. I can only dream of what the world would have been like for me and my generation had he, and his brother Robert, not been so heinously slain during that decade.

The leader I wish to talk about, though, who exemplifies all of the qualities and skills that I have shared in this chapter is a man called Eugene (aka Gene) Kranz. Many of you may not know of him, but some of you will. He was one of the flight controllers on several of the Apollo missions, and was the man who led the landing team at Mission Control in Houston during that remarkable summer at the end of the 1960s. He was also the principal flight controller on Apollo 13 when the third mission to the moon went badly wrong and the astronauts had to be saved from what seemed like certain death in outer space.

Gene Kranz was thirty-three years old in the summer of 1969, leading a team of engineers, astronauts, mathematicians, computer experts, scientists and a whole variety of people who I would describe as "boffins". Their average age was just twenty-six. Reflect on that and think about the responsibility that he had in that moment. There were billions of dollars invested and thousands of people involved across many industries making the trip to the moon possible. Millions of man hours were spent working for several years on these missions. At thirty-three years old, Kranz had the lives of three astronauts in his hands, and required his team of experts in Mission Control (most of whom were barely older than university graduates) to work with him to make this centuries old dream a reality.

The success of the Apollo 11 moon landing was also born out of tragedy, and Kranz's acknowledgement of the failure of Apollo 1 a little over two years earlier, when three astronauts died in a terrible fire in the space capsule on the launchpad. His acceptance that he and the team had failed, that he had failed personally, and their whole approach, ethos and values were flawed was a major turning point in the programme. He delivered a speech to the team, almost immediately after the tragedy, in which he brought them together, admitting his shortcomings, their collective mistakes and giving everyone accountability and empowerment. In this he redefined the whole culture of NASA, which he felt had been far too cavalier up to that point.

He said that from that moment on they would be "tough and competent". Tough would mean that they were forever accountable and would never compromise on their standards. Competent meant that they would have the knowledge and skills needed, and would never take anything or anyone for granted. They would be relentless and ruthless to attain the standards needed. He sent the teams away and had them write these words on all planning boards and in all briefing rooms, never to be erased. Tough and Competent. This was to be the way that they honoured and forever remembered their fallen friends and colleagues. Kranz later said, "Spaceflight will never tolerate carelessness, incapacity, and neglect."

This was true leadership, and why Kranz is such a giant for me in this aspect. He acted with humility and integrity, whilst recognising his own failings and those of his team. He accepted responsibility and accountability and set the vision, the pace and the standard. Yes, he got things wrong, but by stepping back and then redefining what was needed he was then able to ensure everyone pressed on to the goal that they all were seeking, and had signed up to, without ever again compromising on their values. He was always fully conscious of what was happening and the effect that his direction created around him.

In the final hour before the astronauts of Apollo 11 were about to land, they encountered a short period of radio silence on the dark side of the moon. This was a natural pause where everyone could draw breath ready for the final push to the lunar surface. The room was smoke-filled, and everyone seemed to survive on cigarettes and strong coffee with little sleep in-between their shifts. It was also a great time for a comfort and relaxation break for all at Mission Control. Kranz, though, held the floor. He told them that what they were about to do no man had ever done before and that there were only three possible outcomes, which were either a moon walk, an aborted landing or a complete loss of the crew. He said to the people gathered that, no matter what happened, they had walked into the room as a team and they would walk out as a team with everyone knowing that they had played their part to the very best of their ability. It focussed everyone, and made them realise that this was not the time for a break but the time to be even more alert as to what could happen and how to make it a complete success. He also absolved them of any blame, meaning that they would make the difficult decisions together knowing that every single one of them had each other's backs.

Many films and documentaries have been made that feature Kranz and his roles at NASA. *Apollo 13*, for example, has Ed Harris playing Kranz and is widely acknowledged as one of the most accurate on-screen portrayals of the man. His composure and ability to get the team to "work the problem", when chaos reigned around him following the in-flight explosion, is one of the great scenes of leadership on screen. Everyone is shouting, trying to understand what their monitors and displays are telling them. There is utter confusion and Kranz rises above all of this, calming people down and getting them to think, assess and then come back with the answers. People say it could be a disaster and he says that "it will be our finest hour". People say it is impossible and he says that this is what they had to do to make it work and "we won't lose the astronauts on my watch". It really is inspirational and truly puts into practice all of the component parts that I have described above for leadership.

I first heard of Kranz when I was privileged to listen to a member of the team who was at Mission Control during this time talk at a conference that I attended in the late 1990s. I am ashamed that I do not remember his name as the significance of his importance never really hit me then. He talked about the values, the culture and, at length, his friend Gene Kranz. He also recalled a famous anecdote of just how strong the team and its values had become at NASA. This part has stayed with me forever.

The story or legend that he recounted was that a US senator was on a visit to NASA and asked someone he met along the way what they did. "I help to put men on the moon, sir," the man proudly said. "Well done and thank you," said the senator. They walked away and he asked his guide exactly what the man did to put men on the moon. "He's one of our janitors" was the reply. The senator was taken aback and started to laugh in a slightly dismissive and disparaging way. "He is really important to us, sir, as, without him and the other janitors here keeping this place clinically clean, we run the risk of disease, infection, dust and other foreign bodies getting into our systems that could cause us a major problem or catastrophe. It is a big responsibility, and without him we wouldn't be able to put men on the moon." The senator laughed no more. He understood that the team was greater than the sum of the individual parts and these values were embedded into the very DNA of NASA. Their mission was clear and they were all fully committed and signed up to it.

Kranz knew that leadership was a privilege and he never took it for granted. He was aware of the personal sacrifices he was asking of his people, and the dangers involved in the whole programme. He led by example and in full consciousness of what was happening. His team followed him willingly into battle and he went on to lead many others, becoming director of mission operations before retiring in 1994. Even now, listening to podcasts, radio and television interviews, these one-time young men who were with him in the 1960s and are now old, frail pensioners, still tear up and cry at just how Kranz inspired and led them to achieve what was a first for mankind. Kranz's and NASA's legacy is around us now with much of the high-tech world that we are privileged to occupy.

It is my belief that his words of "Tough and Competent", known to all at NASA as the "Kranz Dictum", with their underlying messages, should be presented to everyone who ever aspires to leadership in any walk of life.

The quick wins and the ladders

- Knowing that the team is greater than any individual, including you as its leader.
- Being consciously aware of every member and their current mindset.
- Knowing that for every team member there are four others, on average, who are dependent on them.
- Reducing the complexity of team tasks by using define, set goals, plan and act.
- Surrounding yourself with people more talented than you.
- Setting clear non-compromising values that everyone agrees and signs up to.
- Studying the great leaders and taking what you can from their theories and actions.
- Presenting "tough and competent" as standards to operate by.

The traps and the snakes

- Assuming everyone will respect you just because you are the leader.
- Failing to plan and not establishing a values-based culture with full team consensus.
- Allowing unacceptable behaviour from yourself and others by turning a blind eye.
- Not learning from mistakes.
- Failing to question what you are being asked to achieve yourself.

42

It's ok to be happy

It's the game of life. Do I win or do I lose?
One day they're gonna shut the game down.
I gotta have as much fun and go around the
board as many times as I can before it's my
turn to leave.

Tupac Shakur

Inspired by those I love and care about, I am writing this chapter more as a plea to you, the reader, to allow yourself to be happy. Every day we go through a raft of emotions, and these often dictate the way that we play the game, and our ongoing games, at any given point. It is perfectly normal to be happy and also to be sad, and having these emotions is part of the natural flow of life for us as human beings. However, I am going to talk here about why happiness is such a good thing.

Like taking a boat ride down a calm, lazy river on a warm, sunny day, every now and then, you find some peaceful, slow-flowing water where you can take in the scenery and just enjoy the tranquillity of the time. You will feel happy just to be alive... and then, for some reason, reality kicks in, you realise you are alive and an alarm goes off in your head that tells you, "No, no, no. This is unacceptable. You cannot be happy; you don't deserve it!" or words to that effect. The moment is lost, and your game, which needs this injection of joy, becomes a grind again.

I may exaggerate – some people may never get this feeling, but I am encountering more and more younger people in particular, who are struggling with the concept of happiness. Some of it is driven by the flow of available information. It seems that we are now bombarded at every possible opportunity with adverts, soundbites, lifestyle programmes, suggestions and well-intentioned advice, all trying to convince us that we are missing out in some form or another. There seems to be fast tracks to everything supposedly good. Also we are made to feel guilty for feeling happy because as there are so many problems in the world, how can anyone possibly be happy with this knowledge? What this means is that you are playing your game by other people's rules, and these people are actively controlling who you are, who you identify as and, more importantly, your own well-being, with strategically targeted marketed dilemmas for you.

Advertising, for example, has always tried to put one product ahead of another. The various confectionery companies have all used methods over the years to seduce us to buy their product. They convince us that by eating their particular brand of, say, chocolate we will feel like we are in some tropical fantasy land, or having the greatest time of our lives. It is their game, their rules and we play willingly by purchasing more and more. There is no harm in that, though, as it helps our own happiness and very often advertising, too, can become a force for good for us.

Where we are now, though, is that the adverts, programmes, films and social media that hit us are all becoming directional messages in their own right, telling us that their output is often the route to happiness. Reality TV programmes seem to tick every box on this list and, rightly so, there has been much concern raised recently about the life consequences for participants of these shows. I personally think that there should be more examination regarding the impact on the audience too. Your game is under serious threat if you buy into the concept that you can fast track your way to happiness via instant fame. You may have some short-term success, and some quick wins along the way, but the longer-term impact can be devastating, as you may not be fully prepared for what you will face. Some do get lucky, or have the inner strength coupled with amazingly protective people around them, and my sincerest good luck to them all if that is the case. In the main, though, it is a feeding frenzy among those who seek to exploit others whilst they can and build them up to then knock them down. It is a concern that I have for everyone of any age, as it can take you on a path in your game that is weighed against you, and the personal risks are enormous. The snakes are everywhere here.

This whole subject of happiness can become overly complex, and the quest that we seem to be on to find it for ourselves often achieves the exact opposite. As I have said, in the opening to this book, any concerns that you have about the mental health of yourself, or others, should always be raised with a suitably qualified professional – and, again, that is ok. It is a strength to seek out help, although some do judge it as a weakness. I am being very clear here that it is a strength. If you can find happiness with help and support (clue again: most of us need others in our lives to do this, no matter what you are told) to unlock that good juice that can flow through your brain and body, helping the seeds of pleasure to germinate and flourish, then you will become even stronger, confident and more powerful.

This part of our lives is critical to our own well-being, and also to determine how we play our long-term game. It is one that many of us seemingly ignore as the day-to-day need to perform our required tasks, never forgetting fulfilling our parts in other people's games, more often than not takes precedence.

There are many ways to find happiness, and it is something that has to be individual to you. Trying to piggyback on someone else's happiness may not work for you, which is why I am counselling you so strongly not to follow the crowd. You could find that the exact opposite happens, in that trying to find your happiness via someone else's route actually makes you sad and you become lower than when you started. What makes one person happy doesn't always work for others. It is different strokes for different folks. Just find what makes you happy, and keep trying different things.

I have already covered previously about making your job or your cause your hobby. I will continue to promote the message that you will also always need something else besides this in your life to make you as happy and effective as you can be. The working part of our lives, though, whether it be studying, vocational or paid employment, is critical to our own well-being and how we play our long-term game. Turning that activity into something that could be pleasurable is one that many of us choose to ignore. We become wrapped up with the need to perform the required tasks and deliver the output and for most that always takes the centre stage ahead of the personal pleasure that the job can bring.

Over recent years, the phrase "happy place" has appeared in our day-to-day speak, and it does make you think of where your happy place or happy places are. It may be somewhere that you can retreat to as a place of safety, a place of security and a place where you can just escape to be by yourself – often called a bolthole. It could be somewhere that you hold in your mind and helps jump-start the happiest of thoughts and emotions that bring you inner warmth and peace. Mine is where I went as a child, for two weeks, during the summer holidays to stay with my auntie and uncle by the seaside in North Wales. I am instantly transported back to the mid-1970s and become ten years old again in my head – safe, warm and free to be me.

Happy places are important to your game, as they help to give you another form of a time out, or at least a feeling of inner well-being. Know where they are, the purpose that they serve in your game, how best to utilise them and when you need them. Something may happen that means you need to be in that place in your head, and at speed. Do not hesitate to go there if it is at all possible, never forgetting the positive impact this can have on you, and all of those who depend on you as part of their games too.

Sometimes the happy and euphoric mood that you are in can be hypnotic and give you such a rush that you lose touch with reality for a while (daydreaming, living in the moment or zoning out for too long, for example) and act impetuously. Be conscious of this as it can prove to be very expensive on all levels for your game, with your finances and your emotions sometimes being the biggest losers here. Everything could be at stake, and in seeking out a state of happiness you could cause your whole game to collapse. Enjoy the moment, but always keep your hand on your personal brake to slow and stop and always know your limits and where they lie in every aspect. To fully grasp this, please reread Frankie Graham's story as a note of caution here.

Happiness can also be linked closely to expectation. You can expect certain things to happen in a certain way, at a certain time with a certain outcome. When they don't, you can be disappointed. You may have experienced the Christmas present that promised so much when you saw the box wrapped up in bright shiny paper with a bow, and yet it proved to be a massive disappointment when it was hastily opened. You still have to smile and show great pleasure, whilst inwardly thinking, "This wasn't what I really wanted." Even worse, you may not have had a present at all. If you expect nothing, then you will never be disappointed, and therefore your happiness will never be at risk. These are easy words to say and much harder to put into action, but, if you can keep your expectations under control and in check, then your emotions will not be battered, and you won't be riding an emotional roller coaster.

So my advice is to say that being happy is ok. It's ok to give yourself permission to be happy. It is not a crime and certainly not a sin. It is a wonderful emotion and one that is designed to help us to find a state of positivity so that we are more energised. Our physical and mental health are positively impacted by a state of happiness and euphoria. Pat yourself on the back every time that you feel this, or have put an action into your life to positively change your mindset. It is good for your game, is good for those around you, and brings with it an almost infectious state of well-being.

The quick wins and the ladders

- Knowing it is ok to be happy and that it is personal to you.
- Utilising all available support to find and seek out your happiness.
- Knowing your own "happy places".
- Being aware of how your happiness can have a positive effect on others.
- Expecting nothing wherever possible so that you will never being disappointed as a result.

The traps and the snakes

- Not giving yourself permission to be happy.
- Using other people's versions of happiness exclusively as a blueprint for your own.
- Impulsive attempts at quick-fix happiness.

43

That Sunday evening feeling

Sunday evenings often feel like the weekend
is over before it's even begun.

Catherine McCormack

From a young age, many of us will recognise that feeling of dread and the queasiness that usually accompanies it, when what are often called "the Sunday evening blues" hit. Sunday evening was often my lowest point of the week, and this will resonate with many who are on the Monday to Friday, 9am to 5pm treadmill. You will have had the high of the Friday evening when you know the weekend is here, and you have almost sixty hours' respite, if you are lucky, from the pressure of school, college, work or whatever you choose to do in life. Saturday is a day when you can have some time to do what you want or need to do, which occasionally can be the absolute joy of doing nothing. You can find solace in the protection of your bed, holding you prisoner for a weekend morning lie-in, and then emerge to do things that are totally different from your weekly routine. People with young families or other commitments may also long for those times, but the chance to do something different and to be accountable only to you is what I am driving at here.

As Saturday turns into Sunday, the clock gathers pace, the

minutes roll by seemingly faster than sixty-second bursts, and, before you know it, it is early Sunday evening and the coming week is already in your sights. The black cloud of doom descends over some of us, and our energy levels and mood change. We suddenly start to think about the tasks that lie ahead for the week, the pressures, the deadlines, the meetings, the reports, the responsibilities, and so many other things that overtake our feelings of positivity.

This isn't the case for everyone and I appreciate, as I found sometimes, that being at work or in an environment of high energy and high achievement can itself become a type of addictive drug.

To start with, in this chapter, I am going to focus on improving your game and the way in which you can help to overcome the "Sunday night blues".

It begins before the Friday evening, or as you enter a period of downtime from the job or task that you are doing. By now you will be aware of how much I stress the importance of planning, and making sure that the start of your downtime is as smooth as it can be. This is vital if you are going to make this time as effective as possible for you. Try not to plan every minute, but find the happiness and the rewards that you wish to set, and have them lined up in your mind, so that you know what treats lie ahead. It may just be something as simple as being at home with your feet up doing nothing, but make it feel special and a reward just for you. Your brain will kick in again with positive energy.

Once you finish work or your task, at the end of your working period or week, then finish. I appreciate there may be some "homework to do", so get that done as quickly and effectively as you can. It has to be a golden rule, otherwise the tasks that have the greatest measurability and material reward will always trump the softer personal ones. The downtime period that you have available to relax and recover is tight and very time limited, so the minutes become precious and must be treated with that level of importance. This is like recharging your phone. The principle and the concept are very similar. You have to create downtime and regroup. For those who work from home, this is far more challenging but somewhere you have to close the door on your work and re-enter home life.

In the modern day it is very difficult to be unavailable, and I do appreciate that there are times when you have to be present, on call or on duty. However, work emails and phones, wherever and whenever possible, have to be set to off. Out-of-office and voicemails have to be switched on, and please avoid the great temptation to have a peek. You will see or hear something that you know needs your attention, or will be teased just enough to save a few minutes by responding there and then. Like all addictions, it only takes one small fix that you tell yourself "it doesn't matter", and before you know it you are back "mainlining" the work to your brain and flooding your system with more tension and adrenaline that can be, in this instance, very destructive.

If at all possible, make Sunday evenings special. You will know what to do to create the right atmosphere for you but, whether it is at home or elsewhere, make sure that you have something else to focus on besides watching the clock move ominously round.

For those of you who are addicted to work or a cause, and feel that your line reports/colleagues/fellow collaborators must also share your 24/7 devotion, take a look at yourselves and feel as sorry for you as I do in this moment. I have been there and it becomes a very lonely place. You may feel all powerful, strong and controlling, with a great record of achievement behind you, but I am telling you straight that what may work for you is not the same for your team. Sending emails at 5am, 11pm and at weekends, and then asking for an immediate response from the recipient without prior agreement (and by prior agreement, I mean that this is exclusively a one-off) makes you nothing more than a "terrorist" to them, their games and their lives.

You are wrecking the games of so many people, as this steals quality time and positive energy from them, their families and their dependants. It is not macho and is actually dangerous for everyone, showing that you have a short-term take on life. You create burnout in others, and this can lead to lost productivity, engagement, illness (both physical and mental) and, in some extreme cases that I have heard of, fatal consequences.

To illustrate this, let me explain how hooked into work I was. My week ahead started somewhere approaching 5pm on a Sunday evening, as the cloud of the coming week suddenly appeared on the horizon of my thoughts. It was like a pre-programmed alert on a radar that enemy aircraft were approaching. My body would physically stiffen and the tension suddenly increased as I became very alert and on guard. My reactions became quicker and my fuse became very short. My personality could change in an instant. Within a few minutes, what was usually a light, carefree, happy house had quickly changed into one where everyone knew they had to be careful around me. Unsurprisingly, everyone else in the household had then started to think about their week ahead, and the cloud was suddenly over us all. I had unwittingly sucked everyone else into my own vortex of dread and stress.

I would then start to work out what was going to happen for the coming days: planning meetings and action plans in my mind, goal setting as to where I wanted to be by close of play on Monday, Tuesday, etc. I even went as far as working out what my recovery plan would be if A didn't happen, and how would I handle B, C and D. By the time I went to bed I was exhausted, and had probably put in at least half a dozen hours of unseen and unpaid work already. I resisted having a pad by the side of the bed, but I may as well have, as sometimes I would retreat to another room and write things down, draft emails and even send some. Amazingly, I often had replies back within minutes, as so many of my colleagues and clients were going through similar routines. I slept terribly and would get up at 5.30am feeling absolutely shattered. Note also that the "fuel" that I was using to keep me going was a combination of sugar, biscuits, junk food, caffeine, alcohol (evenings only) and adrenaline. There was always a temptation to start smoking again, but I stopped as my doctor had told me several years ago that I wouldn't see my children become adults if I continued with that habit. This fear always prevented me lighting up, but on more than one occasion I went and bought a packet of fags just to get the rush that I might have a nicotine fix, only to then throw them away. This was a form of masochism and self-torture.

The Monday morning shower was when my planning really started in earnest. Timed goals were set for the day. I was in the zone, arriving at work by 7am at the latest and running on even more caffeine, sugar and adrenaline.

I would get back home only when the job was done and, while I was aware of the clock for appointments and goals, I never seemed to be aware of a "home time". If I was, then I would say to myself, "Well, there's no point in hitting the road now as its rush hour, so I'll let the traffic go first." I never once took my job for granted, and always remembered what I was told so regularly in the late '90s and the first decade of this century and that is, "You are only as good as your last week." This was tripped out to me by some of the very worst leaders and executives that I ever encountered. Phrases bandied about like confetti at a wedding included "The week of delivery", "The year of delivery" and, most ironically of all, "There will never be a time more important than this to you and to us". I think this fear pushed me on and justified my actions of abuse of my time to me. Thankfully, though, I never tried to take short cuts to keep the pressure at bay. Some did, though, and I can understand to an extent why they chose to. They ended up paying the heaviest of prices and their game was ruined. They lost their position, livelihood and integrity – all sacrificed just to relieve the stress of those moments in time.

And then, before I knew it, Friday had rolled round and the whole process began again.

Looking back now, I realise just how much I missed, including school events for the kids and family time, where the pleasure derived is just from being together. I feel blessed that I, and we, have survived as a family unit, but it must have been very challenging for my wife to hold it all together without ever once criticising me, accepting that the way that I was wired was necessary for so many reasons. Our game was often played at a breakneck speed, and it was mostly me that set the pace and the agenda. It was flawed, and so was I, and Sunday evenings became just the start of yet another week of high intensity and personal challenge.

Make the Sunday evenings in your life special wherever you can. Time marches on so quickly that we will dismiss them as just another part of our existence and get into a habit of missing their significance. This is a time to re-energise your game and not to be in play if you can at all avoid it. Be conscious in knowing the significance of these golden hours as they can be either an invisible ladder or a camouflaged snake.

The quick wins and the ladders

- Knowing that your downtime is very precious and treating it as such.
- Switching off the phone and not responding to, or creating, emails.
- Setting the example for everyone else by being unavailable when you are supposed to be.
- Making Sunday evenings special.
- Not missing the moments that matter, such as family time.

The traps and the snakes

- Constantly working and having no differentiation between home and work.

- Inflicting your desire to work on others in their downtime.
- Not creating any downtime for yourself or others around you.
- Allowing the Sunday evening blues to dominate.

44

Rewards, treats and enjoying yourself. What's the point otherwise?

> In the game of life, before you get anything
> out, you must put something in!
>
> Zig Zaglar

One thing that you must do regularly is to reward yourself for the progress that you make, celebrating your positive moves as you advance forward and climb the ladders. It may be that you take a moment to simply say "well done" to yourself, and that works occasionally. And, like all of the animal species on the planet, we do respond to treats and rewards.

Starting as children (and, kids, if you are reading this, there are some good tips here to manipulate your game for you), think how adults reward good behaviour and good work. It is often with some form of a treat such as sweets, money, meals out, cinema, day trips, etc. Rewards are a means of giving a positive response for a job well done. It leads to more freedom in the shorter, medium and longer terms. Good habits can be formed, including continued education, learning, a work ethic and discipline. And with that everyone wins as you choose the right path for your game. You also find that the better that you play, the better the reward, so play the games hard. Needless to say, anything that is seen as a reward for inappropriate behaviour and doesn't feel right should always be checked with an independent person as to whether it is legitimate. This questioning is critical, particularly in the young, as it helps to instil true values and beliefs.

Schools themselves use awards schemes to promote achievement, and rightly so in my opinion, as it further encourages and teaches, which is after all their principal function.

Performance is about every aspect of your life, meeting and exceeding your own standards, and then rewarding yourself accordingly too. Rewarding adequacy or even a lack of achievement is simply not right, and you are deceiving yourself and cheating your game, as you will lower your standards and those around you will lower their personal bar too.

One phrase that I was told and that sticks with me is "The price of independence is performance", and I have referenced this earlier. This may seem an authoritarian form of statement, and for some in management it can be used as a "carrot and stick" approach. I like to look at it more as a contract with yourself. If you perform well, then you will naturally gain more autonomy over your life and over your game. There is a balance here too, though, and finding the correct levels of input by you versus your values and quality of life will always be the true measure of your success.

Offering a reward-based culture can be equally destructive. There are occasions when parents give children large monetary rewards for, say, the scoring of goals at junior football matches. This is a team sport and yet the individual here is being rewarded for their own success. No monetary rewards seem to be given to the children who, perhaps, saved a goal being conceded or created the opportunities for the others to put the ball in the net. And then you go to where it got really nasty, and I have witnessed children on the same team arguing over why they should have taken a penalty as they would have materially gained from scoring it. Then, just when you thought it couldn't get worse, there have been well documented scenes when parents argue amongst themselves about their children and who deserved the reward more. Teamwork is destroyed, terrible examples set and the game of life for everyone has taken a turn for the worst, as this is what is passed down to the next generation. No one ever wins in this scenario.

I saw similar examples in the workplace, and this led to people trying to "short circuit" the systems, placing their own game and everyone else's at risk. Rules are there to protect people, and if you break them you have to accept the consequences. Often these also impact the innocent. My former industry (financial) is littered with examples where a "results at all costs" culture caused pain and misery to millions. Barings Bank, PPI and the financial crash of 2008 are just some examples of industrial, cultural, and corporate failure to manage the reward versus the risk.

Rewards have to be right and appropriate with the correct balance achieved, ensuring the level of risk is offset. People will stretch themselves to extraordinary feats of achievement just because of the challenge itself, but for some they see a reward as being so necessary to them that they will do anything to get it. That is the line where the contract with yourself must never be compromised.

There is no point in constantly keeping going unless you do take some time to say thank you to yourself, and to those around you for the work that you have done. My closest friend, and a key inspiration and collaborator for this book, always ensures that there is something on the family calendar, for everyone in the house to look forward to by way of recognition for everything that they do individually and collectively. He knows that they all work hard, strive for their very best and make a difference to the lives of others. Their treats can be something like a family meal, a cinema trip, a day set aside just to be together, a holiday, etc. It doesn't have to cost anything besides everyone creating the time, and sticking to it. As he so regularly says, "Time together is priceless as we write our book of memories." In his game, survival is key and part of surviving is to create memorable moments for everyone in the household as everyone will have contributed. There is no better way, in my opinion, than to reward effort and contribution than by adding positively to your own memory bank.

The quick wins and the ladders

- Giving yourself and those around you rewards and treats for a job well done.
- Rewarding the whole team, not just individuals.
- Performance gives you independence.
- Having something in the diary or on the calendar to look forward to.

The traps and the snakes

- Having an inappropriate rewards-based culture.
- Rewarding underachievement.
- Rewarding individual team members for their performance without acknowledging other team members too.

45

Learn to love yourself, faults and all

Love yourself first and everything else falls
into line. You really have to love yourself to
get anything done in this world.

Lucille Ball

I once heard the phrase said in a pub by a man holding court
with his friends, "If I ever had the chance to fall in love with
myself again, I absolutely would." It was said in a really arrogant
way designed to clearly show that he was the most confident of
the group. This was a show of strength, cementing his position
in his group as the big silverback gorilla and leader. I have to
admit, though, that it made me smile and it is a phrase that I
have used since, although in a slightly self-deprecating way,
usually followed by a wry smile and a wink to show that I do not
take myself that seriously.

However, if you are playing your game effectively, have
a good working knowledge of yourself and want to survive,
you have to be more than just a friend to yourself. You have to
unconditionally love yourself, and that includes loving all of the
faults that you see and perceive in yourself as well.

Several people that I have mentored, covering a wide variety
of ages, have one thing very much in common. They present the

greatest threat to their own game and as a result they will be the only one who defeats themselves. They struggle to embrace who they are and to fully understand the abilities that they possess. They are, in effect, their only competition. Helping people to overcome this barrier has been one of my greatest challenges as a mentor.

It is very difficult when you have low self-esteem, have low self-confidence and, in many cases, are constantly comparing and benchmarking yourself to others who you see as being more worthy or better than you. It is a form of "imposter syndrome".

Well, here is the news. Everyone, no matter how confident they appear to be, has self-doubts. Some just hide it, ignore it, and do not listen to that negative inner voice that can be overpowering at times for others. There is no need to be arrogant, big-headed, or self-absorbed to love yourself. You can appreciate what you have and what you give, without ever admitting it to anyone. Just be true to yourself.

Compliments received often come unexpectedly, and they can take you by surprise. They make you feel good about yourself, and you feel that rush of energy through your system. Please never follow this up by saying, "Yes, but what about…" and then going into negative commentary. It is easier for us to talk about our own shortcomings and other people will then happily pile in, adding weight to that point of view, without any thought of the later effects. Part of being a best friend to you, and loving yourself unconditionally, is that, when someone says you've done well or they like something about you, then you must accept it and say thank you. Keep the focus on the positives about you, and consciously do that. Expand the discussion further into these areas. It is no bad thing to massage your ego and also to have others do it too from time to time.

One technique that you may wish to try, if you are struggling with this, is to list the ten things that you like about yourself. Keep it available, and, when you feel down, reread it and carry it as a reminder of just how much you appreciate and love yourself.

Add to the list when someone says something good, no matter how small. It is part of you playing an inner game where you are silencing your own doubting voice.

It is also good to give back, too, as sometimes people give you a compliment wanting one in return, and that's ok. Just make sure that what you say is genuine, and, if you need to use this technique yourself, then do it. However, keep your expectations low, as, if you give a compliment to get one back, the other person may not read the signals correctly and you could easily end up disappointed.

Every now and then, ask someone who you like and trust, who is in your inner circle, for some positive words about you. It can be something as bland as asking them what they think about your appearance. You can be as direct as you want, or even disguise it by talking about something that you have done, which prompts a more detailed discussion. Make sure that you steer the conversation so that you don't go too deep, as that can sometimes bring out a development or negative area. Also make sure that, if you ask for a compliment, you know that you will get one.

When updating and writing your CV (which you should do every few months), you can reflect on your achievements and celebrate the successes, no matter how small you think they may seem to be. It may be that surviving this period of time has been your greatest achievement and, as you already know from my definition, survival in the game is your greatest success factor in itself.

The quick wins and the ladders

- Unconditionally loving yourself.
- Being true to yourself.
- Welcoming compliments, keeping the subsequent discussions to your positive traits and qualities.
- Giving genuine compliments yourself.

- Keeping a list of what you like about yourself and what you do well, thereby keeping your CV live.

The traps and the snakes

- Being your only competition.
- Constantly benchmarking and comparing yourself to others.
- Turning compliments around to focus on your negative points.
- Being arrogant and self-absorbed.
- Not giving back to others.

46

Using the right fuel

You need the right fuel for the body.

Caroline Wozniacki

I have talked about getting serotonin, and other "good brain juices" as I prefer to call them, moving through your system for effective gameplay. Like a car engine, you need to ensure your body has the right combination of fuel, otherwise it will not work or function correctly. With a car, if you put in the wrong type of fuel and fail to service it correctly, you will find that the machine breaks down regularly, becomes unreliable and eventually stops working altogether.

There are no shortcuts here when it comes to the human body. We need plenty of fluids and food for it to work. Too much of one or the other, without a correct balance, can have a harmful effect. People consume caffeine and sugar to give themselves energy and to relieve stress. The same applies to chocolate, convenience foods and alcohol. You may well say that your game needs these as treats to reward yourself, and I say amen to that, but please use them in moderation.

I am not a dietary expert, and those who know me well will also point out that this chapter could be seen with some aspects of the advice as a form of "do as I say, not as I do". If you need any specific help, have any concerns, or just want to try a different path then always consult a qualified professional in the first instance. Common sense and experience, though, lead me to suggest the following:

Say no to drugs and only use medication when advised to do so by a qualified professional. Always take advice. This must be non-negotiable and an irrevocable contract that you make with yourself.

Alcohol. The temptation is always to say that "one won't hurt". Sometimes this is true and, again, I am no saint in this area. Being sensible, avoiding binge drinking, sticking to advised limits, knowing your own limitations, and not starting the weekend wine on a Thursday or even earlier are good rules to follow. Monday evening is definitely not the start of the weekend, and certainly not the end of it either. Good lengthy breaks are important as this also allows your body to recover.

Tobacco. Very simple. It is proven to reduce your life expectancy and to give you very serious illnesses, and is not good for those around you either, who you force to passive smoke. It could kill you earlier than you would expect, and often in a slow and painful way. These are the words of my doctor when I had to stop.

Sunlight. Important that you get this as vitamin D is one of the essential nutrients for your body to function correctly. However, be aware of your exposure to the sun, and always use the correct factor sun cream and apply it at regular intervals.

Exercise. Make time to do this and for at least half an hour a day. A brisk walk as a minimum, and even better if you can do it without the stress of anything "toxic" filling your mind. Getting off the train or bus one stop earlier, or making the walk to your destination slightly longer, will help.

Diet. Eat well with a good intake of fish, fruit and vegetables. Drink lots of water too. Listen to your body and know what happens to your system when you eat certain foods. There is so much advice out there but beware of self-advising without seeking out that qualified professional first. Never forgetting, though, that the odd treat here and there is also necessary.

Sleep. Maintaining a consistent and regulated sleep pattern is the way that your body recharges and reenergises. You must rest and have complete downtime, as I have already advocated. It is not always possible, I know, and there will be times when you simply cannot get the rest or sleep that you require. Closing your eyes and just listening to a relaxation app or soft calming music, or taking yourself away to a better place in your mind, is a good practice to adopt. Prepare for this, know your routine and when to kick the self-talk in. Don't get into the panic mode of continuing to clock-watch through the night. If in doubt, get the rescue movie out.

The quick wins and the ladders

- Being aware of your lifestyle and making good choices for diet, exercise and sleep.

The traps and the snakes

- Failing to look after yourself properly, with a poor diet, little exercise and poor-quality sleep.

47

Resilience and bouncebackability, including Sam and Nathan's story

Human beings have enormous resilience.

Muhammad Yunus

There will be times in your life when you feel that the world is against you. Sometimes you can control it and other times you simply cannot stop the forces that are at work. The biggest challenge that you face here is how you cope both physically and mentally. You could encounter an illness or a tragedy and, to a large degree, these are almost always unavoidable. There could be a family bereavement, the loss of a close friend or the end of a relationship. You could simply just be in the wrong place at the wrong time. The list of "what could bes" or "might bes" is endless, and, if we spend our lives constantly worrying about the worst-case scenarios or "what ifs", then we will miss so many of the sweetest moments that life delivers to us. We will fail to enjoy our gameplay as much as we should for fear of what might follow.

Never forget, though, that even at the most testing of times it is your game, and you have the main say in how it is played. And playing the game to the very best of your ability for you, when you are under the most emotional and physical stress, is vital preparation should things take a turn for the worst. Having resilience and an ability to bounce back are critical awareness skills to develop at the earliest age possible. I learned this specifically from Ceri Davies, Karl Denning and Frankie Graham, who you will have read about previously.

Part of my message in this chapter is to help you to understand the need to plan ahead and know exactly what you would do in certain circumstances. Have the difficult conversations with those you care for and who care about you, regarding illness, death and tragedy. You will never cover all of the possibilities, and there are some scenarios that you may not wish to contemplate for the sake of your own mental well-being. However, some are one-off conversations that never need to happen again and can even be written into documents such as wills, letters of wishes and powers of attorney. Have the conversations, though, as the worst time to have them is when a crisis hits, and then hard decisions have to be made that are often irreversible. They are made under extreme emotional pressure, and making big decisions under pressure can be life-changing and life-defining, not just for you but for many others. They should be treated with respect and given the appropriate time for consideration by everyone concerned. That is why it is important that you are ready in advance and then you will stand a better chance of making every decision correctly.

It is essential also that you know about your family's health history, too, and that you have the various regular medical examinations that may be needed. It is all part of giving you a shot at adding longevity to your game for your benefit and for everyone else around you.

Having resilience and the ability to bounce back, or "bouncebackability" as I call it, are essential parts of this whole process. Two good friends of mine have recently been seriously tested in this way and I spoke to them at length to gain a closer insight into what happened to them.

I have mentored a woman I'll call Sam since her early teens.

She is now in her mid-twenties with a degree behind her and has a great job in a field that she loves. Four years ago she married a man I'll call Nathan, who is the same age and has his own growing business. I am really proud that they have made some great choices in life, have a lovely first home and are not only developing professional careers themselves but also have a great personal relationship. They are first and foremost very close friends too. They describe the fit of their personalities as "yin and yang" and, from my observations and knowledge of them, I would agree entirely with that.

Just over two years into their marriage, Sam suddenly felt ill. She had been having headaches and migraines for a while but hadn't been too concerned about them. She put it down to the stress of their wedding, buying and renovating their new house and starting a new job. But this time it had got much worse. As a precaution, Sam sensibly went to see her GP and within a few hours was in hospital having been diagnosed with a very aggressive brain tumour. It instantly turned their world upside down. They both agree that the quick diagnosis that day saved Sam's life.

The need for surgery was immediate and there was no guarantee of a good outcome for Sam. They pledged to be positive and to have total faith in the consultants and specialists. I struggle to imagine the difficulty of the conversations that they must have had together. They suddenly went from talking about the foreign holiday that they were going on later that week, through to the dangers of the operation (the success of which was not guaranteed) and even life beyond.

As they talk about this time in their lives, they do so as a joint entity. There is no separation between them and this speaks volumes about just why, when the challenges suddenly hit, they, as a young couple, were able to cope so well. Their communication with each other and friendship shone through. They were both tuned into each other's frequencies.

However, as soon as their families were told, they were in

different stages of shock. As I covered when discussing change, moving from chaos and confusion into acceptance as quickly as possible is critical to your and everyone else's well-being. Nathan says that the managing of the family was a real challenge for him. They have a large, loving and close set of relatives who all rallied round and wanted to be there to offer their personal hands-on support. Everyone meant well, but their emotions were all at varying levels. I think, for Nathan, the "crowd control" element, whilst difficult to maintain, was also a welcome distraction at times. He had to deliver an atmosphere of positivity among them while dealing with the many enquiries, requests for information and potential advice that was being offered about Sam's condition. He was able to help them to understand more of where they were at, while at the same time not ignoring his need to protect and look after himself and Sam too.

Nathan and Sam moved through the process of change, from the horror of the diagnosis through to acceptance, almost instantly. They knew each other so well and, while not having had all of the "what if" conversations that I have described earlier in this chapter, they were confident enough in each other that, whatever the outcome, they would remain positive and united and take everything that came at them one step at a time. They talked constantly, never avoiding the discussions about Sam's tumour, which many would. This was an unwritten contract that they made between themselves and, for them, it was a non-negotiable. This meant that they kept their expectations in check and trusted each other totally. They also switched off to their own emotions in front of as many people as they could, again to help achieve the appropriate levels of calm. Nathan does admit, though, that some things did set him off. A combination of anger and also raw fear did grip him at times, and this is totally understandable. Coming home alone late at night from the hospital, he just had to let go. He had left the house two days earlier for what he thought was a routine doctor's appointment for his wife. Now, returning to a cold, dark house with Sam's life in danger, the emotion overwhelmed him. Sitting in the hall were their packed suitcases as a representation of just what might have been. As he walked into the kitchen, he saw the unfrozen salmon that they had planned to cook together. This was the catalyst that bought on the natural release of tears that he needed to let go of and, as he recalled that night to me, the raw pain that he felt was very apparent and clearly still sat only just below the surface. It was vital, though, that he had that release.

What he did really well at this time was to make sure that he had trusted and good practical people around him to talk to, and he picked up the phone regularly to a lot of them. He also stuck to the agreement that he had with Sam – not to allow himself to dwell too much on the possible scenarios or outcomes either, and that they would take one day at a time at this juncture.

Both were fully conscious of every decision that they made, from Sam's operation through to the long and painful process of recovery and adjustment. They knew the game they were playing at every turn and, more importantly, how they were going to play what came at them, keeping flexibility ensuring every new emotion and feeling was always under close watch. There had to be times to let it out, but that would be of their choosing and in their own way, privately and together.

Sam says that when she looks back it was the little things that really mattered to her. She was in hospital for several weeks, and Nathan came and had breakfast with her every day. The hospital allowed this, which was essential for Sam. The journey from their home wasn't an easy one in city-centre rush hour traffic, but still he came. Some days she wasn't quite up to it, but he was always there, fitting his work around the visits. Breakfast became one of the handholds on the cliff face of sanity for her. She knew that he was in tune with her emotionally should she ever struggle, and his presence every day gave her complete reassurance. They could talk, share and keep each other going. I could tell from the break in her voice as she talked just how important this became as an essential component part of her recovery in those early stages. Talking with those you love and trust is a critical part of recovery in their eyes.

They read each other very well and, as they spoke, it was as though the other one had the script in front of them knowing what was going to be said. For two people who have faced so much, are still in their twenties and have been together for only a few years, the telepathy between them is remarkable. It speaks volumes for the genuine love, respect and affection that they have for each other and they value and appreciate so much of what they have. Their combined resilience and ability to bounce back from an event that would break some, all the time being fully conscious and in the moment, make them genuine role models for me of coping with the unexpected.

Sam's recovery has occasionally been very slow and frustrating for her, as she is usually such an active person. She is having to get used to doing some things differently, but many things are now starting to return to normal for them.

What is patently obvious from our conversation is their optimism going forward, and the fact that, now, there are no more difficult conversations between them. They are facing their futures together, ensuring that they maximise their time, without being pressured to fill every moment with activities. They just like and appreciate being together. They are not planning ahead too much into the future and are trying to take one day at a time. This is their committed game strategy from now on. They respect the chance they have been given, knowing their limitations and appreciating just how precious their life together actually is.

I am sure that many people reading this will know others like Sam or Nathan in their lives or communities, who have stared adversity in the face in one guise or another. Not everyone can talk about these times, and many have very difficult outcomes. Where possible, I do believe that talking is a vital form of therapy in itself and there are many organisations that exist for this purpose. When one of these brave people emerges to share their experiences, listen well as their stories are extremely personal and can often be harrowing. They are not easy to absorb but by listening you will better understand just what enabled them to come through the very toughest of times. If you can get to the heart of their experiences, you will find some incredible learning that you can take on should a crisis of sorts ever come your way. You will be prepared and ready, and that is half of the battle.

Some of the very best survivors at the game of life are those who know deep down exactly what survival is, what it means specifically to them, to those they love, what it is worth and who they can count on. As the wife of a friend of mine who sadly left us recently after a short painful illness, said in her letter to me, "We are all devastated and our lives will never be the same, but life goes on and I'm sure in time we will become accustomed to him not being here. In the meantime we have a trunk load of happy memories to sustain us." These are the words of resilience, bouncebackability and sheer raw courage in the face of genuine adversity. Like with Sam, Nathan and so many others who are survivors, they tell me in the clearest way possible why survival must also be seen as winning.

The quick wins and the ladders

- Having the difficult, honest conversations now with your family and those who matter about health and the "what ifs" that life can present.
- Knowing the process of change and why you react in the way that you do when difficulty hits.
- Being conscious, taking your time and not making big decisions under emotional pressure.
- Talking, knowing that there are many people and organisations, besides your trusted inner circle, who are there to help if you are ever faced with a crisis.
- Ensuring the legal documentation, such as wills, are in place.

- Facing the challenges head on and not burying your head in the sand.
- Making sure that you have an outlet for your own emotions.
- Learning from the life experiences of others.
- Savouring the memories and keeping them alive in your life.

The traps and the snakes

- Not having conversations and avoiding talking about the "what ifs" of life.
- Drifting and allowing circumstances to control you.
- Ignoring any health issues for too long.
- Allowing too many people to have their say and taking over your life.
- Being constantly negative and always looking for the worst of outcomes.
- Making instant decisions whilst under emotional stress.

48

Energy terrorists, toxic friends, the psycho boss and a few time thieves

Never tolerate a toxic person in your organisation.

Peter Diamandis

If you've got this far in, and have read the book in chapter order, then your game plan will be almost there. You will have formed, or adapted, your plans and will be aware of how to play your game so much better for you. No matter what stage of the game you are at, you will be working out exactly how to be the very best version of yourself that you can be.

What you have to prepare for now are some other unexpected game changers that can appear from time to time, and can become a snake on your board that you slide down. You know the one? It's when you get to box ninety-four out of one hundred, you roll the die and your move takes you to the square where a lurking snake takes you back to position number twenty-eight, or even lower. It happens, folks, and the good news is that this book is helping you load as much of that die as possible in your favour so that it rolls more of how you want it to.

Some of the snakes that seek to subvert your progress hide under the subtitles of this chapter, and there are many more of them to look out for.

In every family, school, place of work, or even where you may volunteer, there seems be at least one of these, and you allow them into your world and your game at your peril. They are everywhere and are invariably really nice people, too, on the surface. You find that others often say really nice things about them. They have an air of vulnerability and bring out the caring side of some. For others, they want to give them direction and help by pumping some of their own excess energy into them. Nearly always people call them "a good friend", but remember that friendship is always a two-way contract.

I am being very harsh here but these people will mostly take, take, take, while sucking every ounce of energy from you, giving you very little back. You will find that they turn to you more and more with a magnetic-like attraction, asking for your advice, for reassurance, to tell you what they have done, where they are going, where they have been, what their next plans are, who else is helping them (warning: there is guilt trip alert to get you to give them more). It is a long list, and what do they give back to you? Sometimes a very hurried, "Oh, I am sorry. I haven't asked about you. We must catch up again soon, then." And so it has begun, that ever-decreasing circle, where you are consumed into their world, into their game, feeding their desire for acclaim and applause, increasing their energy levels, and rapidly draining yours, whilst negatively affecting your mood and your all-round feeling of well-being. They can even pass their own insecurities on to you, potentially opening up your own demons. This is why I call them energy terrorists. Be nice to them and they can be great friends, but you must make sure that, whatever energy they take from you, you take as much back from them by being very assertive and clear. You will then find out just how much of a friend they really are.

"Toxic friends"

Toxic friends can also be energy terrorists, but their real power lies in their ability to totally dominate your game, to get you to change it and to play it how they want you to. Ultimately it is about their control of you. They are power freaks, power junkies and toxic to every aspect of your game. They will begin by being a good friend, and will give considerable ground to make you feel included and part of their growing circle. They will encourage you, and will go out of their way to support you at times through any of your difficulties. They are incredibly emotionally aware, picking up on every one of your vulnerabilities and fears. You reach a point where you trust them with your deepest secrets and fears and then they begin to exert their control. They have you and, if unchecked or unchallenged by others, will begin to take over your life, your behaviour and your decisions. They love nothing better than taking you on a guilt trip, whereby their needs overpower yours. You exist, in essence, for them. They are not friends. They are the enemy within playing their game with a very conscious strategy.

Also be very aware of new people who come into your life via them who may seek to get close quickly. Look at who they really are and who their followers seem to be. Do they have vulnerabilities themselves and seem dependent on others? Are they making some bad choices with aspects of their life, encouraged and cheered on by their group? Try to understand what their game is, and observe closely how they are playing it.

"The psycho boss"

The psycho boss (PB) can also be a form of psychopathic leader in your life that you are reporting to in some way, or directs your path. This person represents the ultimate challenge for those serious game players and is someone who can bring you more mental pain and anguish than anyone else in your life if you let them. For many of us who want a normal existence, avoid these people at all costs. I appreciate that is very difficult to do sometimes, but my advice is clear: avoid or brace for impact.

I have seen several across various organisations in my life and genuinely believe that all of them have the potential for mass murder. I do not use the word psychopath lightly, but I do believe that there are some people out there who are hell-bent on power and become power crazy. When they get to the top of their personal ivory tower, they will do everything to protect it, sacrificing anyone who prevents them from consolidating their position in the game, and blocking their ambitions of progressing further, by whatever means whether they be fair or foul.

If you never work for one or never come across one in your life, then congratulations. Your game has been easier than others' in this respect, and you can direct your energies into the areas of your life that are important to you, and to those that you love and care for.

There is no doubt about it: these people have the capability and capacity to ruin your game, pure and simple. They will break you, your family and friends if they can, unless you swear absolute undying loyalty to them, their ambitions, their practices and their ways. They will gladly take you along with them if you make this pledge, and allow you to have a free ride for as long as you are adding value to them. Forget your own values, beliefs, integrity and longer-term game plans, as your direction of travel becomes theirs. It may suit you to turn a blind eye to the occasional misdemeanour, or bad practice, but you will have to live with yourself and the longer-term consequences of what you then do.

For your game, the PB is likely to be initially identified as someone who will begin to micromanage you. That means everything, and I mean everything that you do is reported in to them and their central hub. A colleague once referred to this practice as akin to "weighing the pig". What you do with micromanagement is worry more about whether the pig is putting on any weight every few minutes than making it happy, feeding it correctly and letting it grow naturally.

Under this form of regime there is no latitude for creativity, variation or spontaneity. You do things in an ordered, robotic time-driven way and are managed to their plan. Oh, and forget any illness you may have or issues that develop as those are unacceptable to them. It creates a problem and one thing PBs hate is problems.

The PB will also have people reporting about you to them via a network that they create, and will then use that information, tactically at times, to undermine you. The game means that you rarely have any victories in the short term, and have to take the pain. My advice again is that you treat this like a tornado that you cannot outrun. You make everything watertight and do exactly as you are directed to, unless it is against your values and beliefs. If and when you can get away from them, then do so. Run, or ride out the storm but protect yourself. Keep copious and detailed notes, or a diary, as you never know when you may need evidence against them. I must emphasise just how important this can prove to be. A PB believes they are invincible and untouchable, so your record keeping must be better than theirs as their arrogance means that they are inherently lazy with tasks like this.

At the very worst for me, one of the PBs exhibited all of the traits, and more, that I describe. My personality changed, my confidence and self-worth were shattered, and I was literally reduced to a medicated quivering wreck. He caused me several years of lost position in my game, and almost my sanity. I will always bear the scars, but I emerged stronger and wiser as a result. So when eventually I came across another potential holder of this title, I was much better placed to deal with the situation. I now view myself as a survivor, not a victim.

Hold onto this famous quote if you are ever unfortunately in the eye of this particular storm: "Revenge is always a dish best served cold." What this proverbial phrase is saying to you is that you will get to see the person who has wronged you fall and fail one day, as they always do, although you may have to wait a while to see or hear of it.

If you are reading this and recognise yourself as a PB, then change your ways now. I can assure you that unless you do so you are being judged daily, loathed and only making your successes short-term wins. Without change, your game and your legacy are already lost. You are a bully and a coward, worthy of no other titles than these.

In keeping with this theme, another quote that I have always carried with me is, "Keep your friends close but your enemies closer". These are words taken from a scene in *The Godfather: Part 2*, where Michael Corleone, a Mafia godfather and head of one of the largest criminal families in the USA, is reflecting on advice given to him by his father. Just another scene from a movie? No. This is life advice being given to each and every one of us for our own game strategy. It is given by a character who, we should keep in mind, can be seen as very much on the wrong side of the law, with values and beliefs that can never be condoned. In effect it is a PB telling us how to manage a PB.

It is my strongest wish that you read this and say to yourself, "I have no enemies, therefore this section does not apply to me." If that is the case, then I am delighted for you. You have played and are playing an exceptional game, being totally true to yourself and your values, very much against the way of the *Godfather* character. Be aware, though, that enemies come in all shapes, sizes and personalities. They may actually not be "enemies" in the rawest sense of the word, but people who can cause chaos, confusion and frustration to you, to your life and to your game. Keep them close, as that way you will have knowledge and with that some personal control too.

"Time thieves"

One of the most precious things that you have within your game is the ability to create time for you. However, be very aware that there are some people who wish to steal this most valuable of assets from you, whether it be consciously or subconsciously. Being ever alert to these often well-meaning thieves is essential.

They appear from out of nowhere with the "Can I just have a minute of your time?" or "Can I have a word?" This is where it starts, and it goes on from there to "Before you go, can I just ask…" through to "I'll call you later and we can discuss this more fully". There are many other examples that I can give, but let's just say that anyone who asks for a minute of your time, or for a word, wants considerably more than that. And they also want to offload onto you, increasing your physical and mental workload.

To repeat a phrase from a previous chapter, be courteous with people and ruthless with time. Always manage the expectations of the other person, and be very clear on exactly how much time of yours that they have. It is, after all, your time.

There are some who take your time to offload all of their own problems onto you, without offering something similar in return. They not only take your time but also leave you with no energy and compassion to give to yourself or others, who probably need it more. There are, as you will detect, crossovers with the other characters I have described in this chapter. Be very polite, but break that conversation as soon as it starts, unless you are in a position to give the gift of your time and attention, knowing the full consequences for you and your game.

A person I once encountered had an old-fashioned, large sand-filled egg timer on his desk that when turned upside down drained from top to bottom over a four-minute period. When I first met him he shook my hand, offered me a seat and said, "My time is very precious, Andrew, and I only give it to those who I consider are worthy. You have four minutes to impress me, starting from now." He then turned over the egg timer and looked directly across his large, dark oak desk at me. I am delighted to say that three-quarters of an hour later I left his office. The pressure, though, as that egg timer was turned and those words were spoken to me was very intense and one that I have never forgotten.

That is an extreme example, but I and everyone else that he met knew where they stood with him. Meetings that were scheduled for forty-five minutes took exactly that and no longer, as I discovered when we met again. Our discussion ended after 44 minutes and 20 seconds, according to his digital clock, which was an ever-present feature on his desk next to the egg timer.

Being aware of time thieves means that you are also aware of how to steal other people's time, if you are so minded, to benefit your game. Only the sneaky would do that, as it is not necessarily playing the game true to your own beliefs, if you play it benevolently. Therefore, if you plan to steal someone else's time, tell them what you are doing, apologise and also ask if it's ok for you to do this. It is always wise to make an offer of another date and time as well. That way you invariably will get what you seek. Most people, if you approach it in this way, with a smile, will usually acquiesce. If they don't, you know that they probably aren't the person that you needed anyway.

Finally reflect on this. You have the capacity to be a time thief to yourself. Never put off what you can do today or can do now, as for sure it will still be there needing to be done in one minute, one hour, one day, etc. Face the task square on, use a time planner or a calendar and figuratively kick the backside off it, knowing that you know that you can use your time in the way that you want as your reward. Sometimes that means doing absolutely nothing and very well deserved it will be too.

You will recognise all of the characters that I have described, no matter what age you are, either in full or at the very least you will have seen some of these traits of those who you engage with. Consciously being aware of who is around you, what they want, what they need and how you will "manage" them is another means of playing your game as effectively for you as you possibly can.

The quick wins and the ladders

- Knowing who the takers of your time and energy are.
- Never compromising your values.
- Being ruthless with time and courteous with people.
- Refusing to be railroaded by others.
- Knowing how to deal effectively with all of those who are potential threats to your game.
- Strategically dealing with the psycho boss as described above.

The traps and the snakes

- Stealing other people's time and energy without gaining their permission.
- Actively and knowingly seeking to control the lives of others for your own self-gratification and benefit.
- Turning a blind eye to, or supporting, bad behaviour from another person.

49

The end of your game is nigh

I believe every human has a finite number of heartbeats. I don't intend to waste any of mine.

Neil Armstrong

So when does the game end and when do you, or when can you, stop playing? I am sorry to have to inform you that you don't stop rolling the dice until you finally expel your last breath on this planet. And even then you are still in play for years to come as your legacy, both tangible and intangible, is assessed and pored over by those who knew you. In some cases, you are also tried without a jury whilst being measured and weighed by those who didn't know you. For those in the public eye, judgement can be never-ending.

I am firmly of the view that, if you survived the game for long enough to leave a positive lasting contribution to the world, then not only have you survived but you will have gone as close to winning as any mere mortal can. The real gold for you is if you can say that you achieved all of this without bringing harm or hurt to another person. As a consequence you will have avoided many of the snakes that are there and you will have climbed most of the ladders too. The world is a better place for you having been in it. People will remember you for the change that you have facilitated, for the good that you have fostered and for the resulting legacy that you have left behind; your mission will be complete.

If you can start or even restart your game with this ambition in mind, then you actually have given yourself a chance at playing the game for you. You will have set your strategy with a clearly defined goal. No matter what stage of your game you are at, if you wish to seek change, then you can be the change yourself and for others too. You cannot always put right all of the wrongs along the way, or change some of your actions or their consequences that have gone before, but, by seeking out change, you have made a contract for making amends. If possible, leave no baggage behind as you go, and, most importantly of all, leave nothing left unsaid with those you love.

Many people reach a point in their lives when they become aware of their own mortality, where they ask questions of themselves about what the point or purpose of it all was. It is a defining period, where you reflect, learn, and all too often focus on the negatives. My belief is that we should do this form of introspection on a regular basis and in a positive way too, and not leave it until we are closing in on our latter years. Our self-assessment, critique and celebration should be done as we progress, as only then can we truly change or adjust our longer-term course if we need to.

The biggest and best part of your legacy then comes down to how the generations that follow take your lead on the course that you have set. If they can pick up the baton that you pass to them and run at pace with the right values, beliefs, ambitions and abilities, taking others with them, then you can sit back and say that your work here is as good as done. They will also come to understand and know where more of the snakes to avoid are lurking and, more importantly, they will also know where the ladders that they can climb exist.

50

A few final words and a favour to ask

Life is a game. All you have to do is know
how to play it.

Unknown

And that is it. You have now reached the end of this book, and I sincerely wish you bon voyage and good luck on your journey through the game of life, no matter what point of it you are currently playing at. I hope that you have found some good advice within these chapters and over the coming days, months and years will be able to become the very best version of you that you can be. If that is the case for just one person who reads this and feels that they have a good game plan to survive, then my purpose in writing for you has been fulfilled.

The favour I ask of you all is that you go online and leave a review with Troubador, Amazon or any other platform that you may find this book. You can also contact me via my website, andrewjmullaney.co.uk. Every review will help me to understand the reach and effectiveness of my words and also how you may have benefitted too. You never know; it may spur me on to write another book.

Finally, make conscious gameplay a way of life as it will serve you well, and mean that not only will you survive but you will also have some great, enjoyable victories along the way.

And always remember that, if someone by chance ever asks you, "Didn't anyone ever tell you?" you can jump in as quick as a flash and say, "Yes, I know... it's all a game."

References

Books and websites used in my research

The following books and websites were used to assist with my research:

Fowler, F.G and Fowler, H.W. (Eds) (1987) *The Oxford Handy Dictionary*. Chancellor Press.

Partridge, Eric. (1965) *Usage and Abusage*. Book Club Associates.

Dutch, R.A. (Ed.) (1978) *Roget's Thesaurus*. Penguin Books.

D'Adamo, P.J. with Whitney, C. (2017) *Eat Right 4 Your Type*. Arrow Books.

https://www.collinsdictionary.com

http://www.quotationspage.com

https://www.greatest-quotations.com

https://www.brainyquote.com

https://www.keepinspiring.me

https://wisdomquotes.com

https://www.bizbible.co.uk

https://www.ekrfoundation.org

http://www.history.co.uk

https://wehackthemoon.com

https://www.nasa.gov

https://www.imdb.com

https://www.betknowmoreuk.org

https://croomewalledgardens.com

Podcast used for research

13 Minutes to the Moon, from BBC World Service, was a source that helped with the leadership chapter and specifically the profile of Gene Kranz.

The following films and television programmes referred to

The Truman Show. Produced by Scott Rudin Productions. Distributed by Paramount Pictures (1998). 35mm. 108 minutes.

The Godfather Trilogy. Produced by Francis Ford Coppola, Alfran Productions (1), American Zeotrope (3). Distributed by Paramount Pictures (1972, 1974 and 1990). 35mm. Total Run time 583 minutes.

Frost/Nixon. Produced by Universal Pictures, Imagine Entertainment, Working Title Films, Digital Image, Studio Canal (in association with), Relativity Media (In association with). Distributed by Universal Pictures (2008). 35mm. 122 minutes.

Pay It Forward. Produced by Warner Brothers, Bel Air Entertainment, Tapestry Films. Distributed by Warner Bros (2000). 35mm. 123 minutes.

Apollo 13. Produced by Universal Pictures, Imagine Entertainment. Distributed by Universal Pictures (1995). 35mm. 140 minutes.

Minority Report. Produced by Twentieth Century Fox, DreamWorks Pictures, Cruise/Wagner Productions, Blue Tulip Productions, Ronald Shusett/Gary Goldman, Amblin Entertainment, Digital Image Associates, Parker's/MacDonald Image Nation. Distributed by Twentieth Century Fox (2002). 35mm. 145 minutes.

Dragons' Den. Produced by BBC Manchester and Sony Pictures Television International. Distributed by BBC, BBC America and Dave.

Strictly Come Dancing. Produced and distributed by BBC.

Dancing with the Stars (USA). Produced by BBC Worldwide Productions.

The Generation Game. Produced and distributed by BBC.

Music referenced

"Reasons to Be Cheerful, Part 3." Ian Dury and the Blockheads. Released 20/7/1979. Label – Stiff Records. Songwriter(s) – Ian Dury, Chas Jankel and Davey Payne.

The Wall. Pink Floyd. Released 30/11/1979. Label – Harvest. Producer(s) – Bob Ezrin, David Gilmour, James Guthries and Roger Waters.

Useful resources

There are so many organisations and forces for good that are available online that to list all of them would be a book by itself. However, here are a few that may help you with your gameplay and could also be sources of inspiration.

Business, community groups and helpful organisations

https://www.bitc.org.uk
https://www.britishchambers.org.uk
https://www.dofe.org
https://fareshare.org.uk
https://www.fsb.org.uk
https://www.girlguiding.org.uk
https://wearencs.com
https://www.ncvo.org.uk
https://www.princes-trust.org.uk
https://www.the-sse.org
https://www.scouts.org.uk
https://www.gov.uk/find-a-community-support-group-or-organisation
https://www.gov.uk/browse/business
https://www.unltd.org.uk/index.php

Thought-provoking

https://www.ted.com/talks

Interviews, CVs, careers, etc.

https://nationalcareers.service.gov.uk/careers-advice/interview-advice
https://www.mindtools.com/pages/article

https://www.linkedin.com
https://www.franklincovey.com

I would recommend that you use various online search engines for specific questions and look at every recruitment agency that you can find for additional help and support. There is so much out there.

Mind, self-help and well-being

https://www.mind.org.uk
https://www.mentalhealth.org.uk/home
https://www.nhs.uk/conditions/stress-anxiety-depression/improve-mental-wellbeing
https://www.nhs.uk/conditions/cognitive-behavioural-therapy-cbt
https://www.psychologytoday.com/gb/basics/self-help
https://www.getselfhelp.co.uk//selfhelp.htm
https://www.counselling-directory.org.uk

There is also an excellent series of books by Dr Tim Cantopher that focus on understanding and overcoming depression, anxiety and stress.

Money and advice

https://www.moneyadviceservice.org.uk/en
https://www.moneysavingexpert.com
https://www.findyourcreditunion.co.uk/about-credit-unions
https://www.gov.uk/government/organisations/hm-revenue-customs
https://www.icaew.com/about-icaew/find-a-chartered-accountant
https://solicitors.lawsociety.org.uk
https://www.moneyadviceservice.org.uk/en/articles/choosing-a-financial-adviser
https://www.unbiased.co.uk
https://www.gov.uk/browse/education/student-finance
https://www.citizensadvice.org.uk
https://www.which.co.uk

There are again many different sources of advice available. Your local authority will also have a specific section on their web pages for this and all other aspects of your life.

Some organisations and charities that make a difference and can help you

https://www.ageuk.org.uk
https://www.alcoholics-anonymous.org.uk
https://www.barnardos.org.uk/index
https://www.betknowmoreuk.org
https://www.childline.org.uk
https://www.christianaid.org.uk
https://www.citizensadvice.org.uk
https://www.supportline.org.uk
https://www.cruse.org.uk
https://www.drinkaware.co.uk
https://www.macmillan.org.uk
https://www.nspcc.org.uk
https://www.salvationarmy.org.uk
https://www.samaritans.org
https://www.shelter.org.uk
https://www.talktofrank.com
https://www.tht.org.uk
https://www.victimsupport.org.uk

Personal links for some of the people quoted in the book and/or acknowledged

Peter Basford	https://www.bgcn.co.uk/coach/peter-basford
Matt Booton/Ellis Smith	https://www.klofinancialservices.com
David Coxsell	https://www.davidjamescoxsell.co.uk
Chris and Karen Cronin	https://croomewalledgardens.com
Ceri Davies	https://moremascotsplease.co.uk
Richard Elwell	https://ethicalinfluence.co.uk
Eileen Fielding	http://dudleycvsreview.org
Frankie Graham	https://www.betknowmoreuk.org
Adrian Grainger	https://www.griffiths-pegg.co.uk
Josie Hadley	https://www.omgonline.co.uk/about-us
Lawrence Family	https://www.lawrencecleaning.co.uk

Sarah Mullaney	https://www.shesawriter.co.uk
Daniel Owen-Parr	https://www.bgcn.co.uk/coach/daniel-owen-parr
John Reed	http://www.theoldfellah.co.uk
Tan Sandhu	http://www.henrysea.com
Chief Schubert	https://www.artstation.com/chiefyarts
Mary Whitehouse	https://linktr.ee/wordservice

Didn't anyone ever tell you? It's all a game!

Appendix 1

Dreamcatcher Worksheet

D	Date when you set this dream and a very flexible date for when it comes to fruition
R	Reason(s) why you have set this dream. This is to remind you as you progress what your motivation(s) was.
E	Environment and Energy - what do you need to commit to and change in you and the world around you to make this dream possible.
A	Activities and Actions - these link into the ones above but be specific around what you will do to make this dream come true.
M	Marker points along the road - where you wish to be at with your dream at key points in time.
S	Success - know what it'll feel like. Write down your thoughts now at the start as to how you will feel once you have achieved it and document your progress as you edge ever closer to realising the dream.

Appendix 1

Appendix 1

Useful adjectives list

Able	Comfortable	Eager	Forceful	Independent	Mature	Proactive	Shining	Unassuming
Above average	Communicative	Easy-going	Forgiving	Innovative	Measured	Proud	Shy	Uncomplaining
Adaptable	Compassionate	Ebullient	Forthright	Inspirational	Meticulous	Prudent	Sincere	Understanding
Admirable	Competent	Efficient	Frank	Inspiring	Modest	Punctual	Skilled	Unintimidated
Adventurous	Confident	Eloquent	Free-spirited	Integrity	Motivated	Quick-witted	Smart	Unique
Affable	Conscientious	Emotional	Friendly	Intellectual	Natural leader	Quiet	Sociable	Unpretentious
Agreeable	Conscious	Empathetic	Fun-loving	Intelligent	Neat	Radiant	Sophisticated	Unusual
All-rounder	Considerable	Empowered	Generous	Interesting	Non-judgemental	Rational	Spectacular	Uplifted
Altruistic	Considerate	Encouraging	Genial	Intuitive	Numerate	Ready	Splendid	Valuable
Ambitious	Considered	Endless	Genial	Inventive	Observant	Realistic	Steadfast	Versatile
Amiable	Content	Energetic	Genius	Involved	Open-hearted	Reasonable	Stellar	Vibrant
Approachable	Convivial	Enlightened	Gentle	Irresistible	Open-minded	Receptive	Stoic	Victorious
Articulate	Cooperative	Enlivened	Giving	Jolly	Optimistic	Refreshed	Straightforward	Vivacious
Artistic	Courageous	Enquiring mind	Goal-orientated	Jovial	Opulent	Rejuvenated	Strong	Warm
Aware	Courteous	Enthusiastic	Graceful	Joyful	Organised	Relaxed	Stupendous	Warm-hearted
Balanced	Creative	Ethical	Gracious	Joyous	Passionate	Reliable	Subtle	Wealthy

Bold	Credible	Excited	Gregarious	Jubilant	Patient	Remarkable	Successful	Well-mannered
Boundless	Curiosity	Exhilarated	Grounded	Keen	Perfect	Reserved	Super	Well-prepared
Brave	Curious	Experienced	Happy	Kind	Persistent	Resilient	Sustained	Well-read
Bright	Decisive	Extraordinary	Hard-working	Kind-hearted	Persuasive	Resourceful	Sympathetic	Well-represented
Bubbly	Dedicated	Exuberant	Healthy	Knowledgeable	Philosophical	Safe	Tactful	Well-rounded
Businesslike	Dependable	Fabulous	Helpful	Leader	Pioneering	Satisfied	Talented	Whole
Calm	Detailed	Fair	Holistic	Likeable	Placid	Self-accepting	Tenacious	Willing
Candid	Determined	Fair-minded	Honest	Lively	Plucky	Self-confident	Thankful	Witty
Capable	Devoted	Faithful	Humble	Logical	Polished	Self-disciplined	Thoughtful	Wonderful
Careful	Diligent	Favourable	Humorous	Loving	Polite	Self-starter	Thriving	Worthy
Cautious	Diplomatic	Fearless	Imaginative	Loyal	Positive	Sensational	Tough	Young at heart
Centred	Direct	Firm	Impartial	Magnanimous	Powerful	Sensible	Triumphant	Youthful
Charming	Discreet	Flexible	Imperturbable	Magnetic	Practical	Sensitive	Trusting	Zealous
Clever	Dynamic	Focussed	Incredible	Magnificent	Precise	Serene	Trustworthy	Zestful

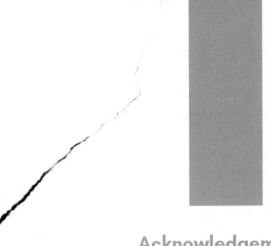

Acknowledgements

There are many people who have helped me throughout my life to become the very best version of me that I can possibly be. I am still a work in progress and I guess I will always be. I have made many mistakes over the years, but I feel that overall I have got more things right than I have got wrong. I have always played the game of life unconsciously and have only in recent years awakened to what I believe I always knew deep down. And that is that life is a game, and a series of games, and we all must play it in full consciousness to give ourselves the best possible chance of survival with some victories along the way.

I will be forever thankful to my late parents, Ann and Bill, for the start that they gave me in life and for creating a stable family home that everyone should enjoy. I have levelled some honest criticism at them in this book, but I will always be grateful that they helped me to create my foundations and values that I have been able to build on. They will always be in my heart and will forever have my love.

I will never be able to thank my wife, Catherine, and my children, Sarah and James, enough for everything that they have given to me. I am heavily in their debt and know that I will never break-even with them, but I am trying. They are my inspiration and my reason. Catherine, together with Sarah's assistance with the editing in advance of the final draft of this book, has made a massive difference to the overall output, giving me added confidence and belief that this was worth seeing through to the end. This book is dedicated to my wonderful family and rightly so.

There are so many others who have helped and supported me along the way from my childhood through to now, some of whom have also collaborated with me here and some who sadly did not make it to see the book published. To name everyone would take many pages, and apologies if you read this and feel that you should have been included, but extra special thanks from me must go to: Phil, "Adult" Sarah, Charlotte and Kieran Garrattley, and Ellie Muckle. Richard and Caroline Warby. Paul Jordan, Caroline Schubert-Jordan and Angela Jordan. Uncle Bob, Auntie Elsie and Alison. Gerald and Anne Mullaney. All of the Mullaney and Pitt families, including specifically Graham Hewitt, Steve Pitt and "Young" Ken Mullaney. Jemma Cooke. Ceri Davies and her family. Karl Denning. Frankie Graham. Steve and Jayne Waltho. Trevor and Margaret Davies. Richard Elwell. Tan and Sonam Sandhu. Stephen Dunster and all of the staff, volunteers and pupils that are in the communities within the Stour Vale Academy Trust. John Reed. Kulli Khossa. Chris and Karen Cronin. Peter Davies. Lisa Cunningham. Lord Ian Austin, Eileen Fielding and the team at Dudley Council for Voluntary Service, Adrian Grainger, the Lawrence family, Josie Hadley and everyone who opened their warm hearts to give me the opportunity to make so much of a difference during my time as a business connector (BITC) in that most rewarding and life-defining of roles. Graham and Karen Knight, Andy Moss, Andy Northcote, Steve and Jayne Wilkinson, Peter Basford, Chris Adams, Daniel Owen-Parr, Mike Richardson, Jerry and Jackie Taylor, Paula Rogers, Ellis Smith, Matt Booton, and the many wonderful colleagues who I worked with and got to know over the thirty-five years that I was with Lloyds Bank.

It would be very remiss of me not to mention James Martin

and Mary Whitehouse for their wise counsel, setting me on the right path when I was losing direction. Thank you both as without your guidance I don't think this would have happened.

I must also acknowledge Paul Matthews, Amrit Sandhu and Ian Mullaney for reading this book in advance of my submission to the publisher just to check that what I am trying to say here makes sense. Again, they have given me belief that this has the potential to make a difference.

Extra special thanks must go to Chief Schubert for creating the cover and the Dreamcatcher Worksheet, taking my thoughts and interpreting them perfectly into graphics. You are supremely talented, a good listener and very patient. Thank you.

I am delighted to have also met David Coxsell via LinkedIn. Dave was extremely brave to risk his photographic equipment to take my profile photograph in full knowledge that I have a face for radio. Thanks, Dave, for being the person that you are and for taking me on.

Dealing with Hannah, Fern, Jonathan and the team at Matador has proved them to be amongst the best in their field for me and a delight to work with. It is a scary process as a first-time author having written a manuscript that you wish to publish and Hannah and her team respect that fully. Thank you for figuratively "holding my hand" throughout this process.

Finally, in the spirit of "pay it forward, give it back", I will be donating twenty-five per cent of any personal income that may arise from *Didn't Anyone Ever Tell You? It's All a Game!* to charities and organisations associated with Ceri Davies, Steve Waltho, Karl Denning, Frankie Graham, Chris and Karen Cronin, and "Nathan and Sam", who so kindly and generously shared their detailed life stories with me and trusted me to tell them.

Andrew J. Mullaney